Carpentry and Woodwork

by Edwin W. Foster

Contents

PREFACE

There is a period in a boy's life, roughly speaking between the ages of ten and sixteen, when his interests and energy turn in the direction of making things. It may be called the creative period, and with many of us it ends nearer sixty than sixteen. At one time it will take the form of a mania for building boats; again it may be automobiles or aeroplanes.

The boy is very susceptible to suggestion. A great automobile race occurs, and for weeks the building and racing of toy automobiles goes on apace. The papers are filled with accounts of an aero meet. Immediately the boy's energy turns to the study and manufacture of aeroplanes. This abounding interest in the real things of life is perfectly normal and should be encouraged rather than discouraged; but the boy needs guidance, if this energy is to be properly directed. He needs strengthening in his weak points, otherwise he may become superficial and "scattering" in his work, and fail to stick to a thing until, overcoming all obstacles, he succeeds in doing the one thing he set out to do. He may acquire the bad habit of never finishing anything, though continually starting new schemes.

The ability of the average boy is far beyond the general estimate, but intelligent supervision is needed. The pocket knife is his natural tool, yet not one boy out of a thousand realizes its possibilities. An attempt has been made in this volume to suggest some of these, especially for boys living in the city, where a little work shop for himself, unfortunately, is too often a luxury.

The two boys here depicted form a composite picture of several thousand American boys whom it has been the pleasure of the author to guide.

The ability to design new things, and to adapt general rules to personal requirements, is to be encouraged at all times, and this idea has been exemplified in the following pages.

I

INTRODUCTORY

Two boys sat on a log whittling. Conversation had ceased and they both seemed absorbed in their work. Presently the younger one became aware of the silence and glanced at the older boy. He gave an exclamation and jumped to his feet. "Why," he cried, "you are making a knife out of wood. Isn't it a beauty! Is it a dagger?"

"No" replied the other, "it is a paper-knife for opening letters and cutting the pages of magazines. It is for father's desk, for his birthday."

"It's a dandy!" continued the youngster. "How can you make such fine things? Why can't I do that kind of work?"

"You can do it," replied Ralph, "but just now there are several reasons why you don't."

"What are they?"

"Well, in the first place you start to whittle without having any clear idea of what you are at work on. It's for all the world like setting out to walk without knowing where you are going. If you start that way, the probabilities are that you will get nowhere, and when you get back and father asks where you have been, you say, 'Oh, nowhere; just took a walk.' That's the way with your knife work. You just whittle and make a lot of chips, and when you get through you have nothing to show for your time and labour. If you want to know a secret—I never start to cut without first making a careful sketch of just what I want to make, with all the important dimensions on it.

"Another reason you don't get any results is that you don't know how to hold your knife, and still another is that you work with a dull tool. Why, that knife of yours is hardly sharp enough to cut butter."

"Will you show me how to do that kind of work?" asked the youngster humbly.

"Yes; on certain conditions."

"What are they?"

"That you will do just as I tell you."

"Will you show me how to make a paper-cutter now?"

"There you go, right off the handle! You are like a young man learning carpentry; you want to start right in to build a house instead of first learning how to use your tools. Why, it has taken me two years in the manual training school to learn how to do this work. No, indeed, if you want to learn how to do woodwork like this you must begin on something simple, learn how to handle wood, and how to keep your tools sharp."

"All right," sighed the younger boy; "I am willing to take lessons and begin at the beginning. What shall we do first?"

"The first thing to do is to throw away your folding penknife. That kind is of very little use. The steel is so poor it won't hold a cutting edge for any time at all, and the knife has a treacherous habit of closing up on your fingers. I will give you a good Swedish whittling knife like mine, and we will start by putting a good cutting edge on it."

So the boys began the first lesson. The fun they had and the things they made, their many experiences, the patience required, and the great skill developed with tools are described in the following pages. What they accomplished, any other boy may do if he will but apply himself with all his energy.

II

FIRST EXPERIMENTS—THE KNIFE AND ITS POSSIBILITIES

The older boy, after a search through his treasure chest, selected a knife with a blade about two and a half inches long.

Incidentally, the smaller boy caught a glimpse of the inside of that chest and it made his eyes bulge—but that is another story.

Fig. 1. The whittling knife

"This knife," explained Ralph, "is one I used for over a year in school and it's the most perfectly shaped tool for whittling that I have ever seen. Of course knives come in hundreds of shapes for different purposes, and later on, when you have become skilled in using this one, we will try some others, but our first motto must be 'one thing at a time.' A knife with either blade or handle too long or too short is awkward, but this one seems to fit my hand, and undoubtedly will fit yours. Try it."

Harry took it and went through the motions of whittling an imaginary stick.

"Now," said Ralph, "we will go out to the wood pile and see what we can find. White pine makes the best wood to start on, because it is usually straight grained, soft, and free from sap; but it is getting scarce and expensive, so we must be economical, as it is a very easy matter to waste lots of lumber."

After some searching, they found part of a pine board, about a foot long and an inch thick. Ralph chopped out a piece with a hatchet and deftly split it to about an inch and a half wide. His skill was a revelation to Harry, who saw that even a hatchet could be used with precision.

"Now," said Ralph, "I want you to cut this piece of rough pine to a smooth, straight piece, just an inch square."

"Oh, that's easy," replied Harry eagerly. "Just watch me."

"Take care," said Ralph. "I said an inch square; anything less than an inch will be wrong. Just imagine that this is a problem in arithmetic and you are trying to find the answer. If you succeed in making it just an inch square the answer will be correct; anything larger or smaller than the exact size will be wrong. In the first place, hold your knife so that it makes a slant or oblique angle with the wood, like this (Fig. 2)," he said, taking the wood in his left hand and the knife in his right. "That gives what we call a paring action, and is much easier (Fig. 3) than the stiff way you were holding it, at right angles with the stick."

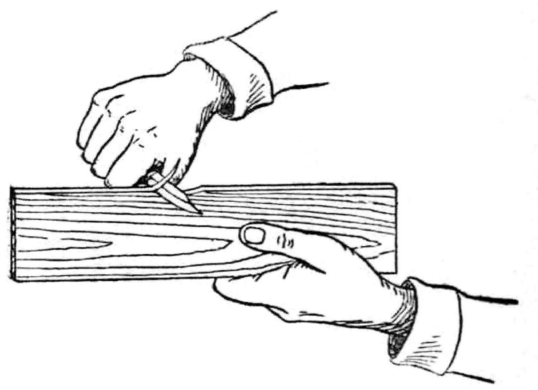

Fig. 2. Correct way to hold the knife

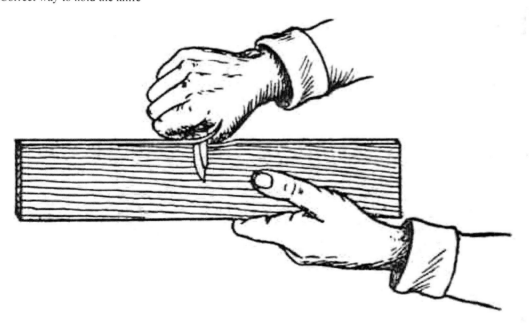

Fig. 3. Incorrect method of holding knife

7

Photograph by Helen W. Cooke
The Boy and His Jack Knife

"Now remember that the trouble with beginners is that they usually take off too much material. Make light, easy cuts and try to get one side of the wood perfectly straight first."

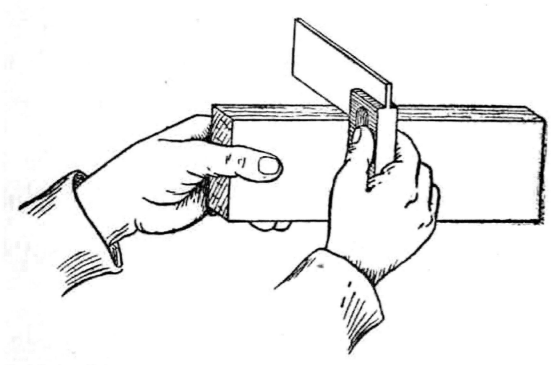

Fig. 4. Testing with the try square

This was a harder job than Harry had expected, but after much testing and sighting (Fig. 4) Ralph said it would do for the first attempt. "Now," he said, "you may consider this first side the foundation of your house. Make a pencil mark on it near one of the edges, what the woodworker would call his witness mark. It means that this side or face is finished and the edge nearest the pencil mark is to be trued up next."

This proved even a harder job than the first, because after whittling and testing until he had the second side straight and true, Ralph tested it with a square and found that the second edge was not at right angles with the first, or working face. It was finally straightened, however, to stand the try square test fairly well.

An inch was next marked off at each end on face number one, and a sharp pencil line drawn from end to end. Harry then whittled this third side down to the line, and tested again with the try square. It seemed easier to do now, and the thickness was obtained in the same way. It looked as if they never would get that piece of pine exactly square, and even when Ralph said it would do, they measured it with a rule and found it an eighth of an inch too small each way.

Harry was disgusted. "The answer is wrong after all," he exclaimed, "but I'll learn to do that if it takes me a month."

"That's the right sporting spirit," said Ralph. "Keep at it till you get it. It's the hardest thing you will ever have to do with a knife, and it's unfortunate that you have to tackle it the first thing; but it's like learning to play the piano, you must learn the notes and scales and how to use your fingers before you can play a real piece. Every time you try this, you are gaining skill and the control of your hands. After a while you will be able to do it easily and think nothing of it."

Several days later Harry brought in a piece that he had been working on and Ralph tested it carefully with rule and try square. He gave Harry a pat on the back. "Good for you, boy; you are coming along splendidly." he said. "How many of these have you tried?"

"Twenty," said Harry meekly.

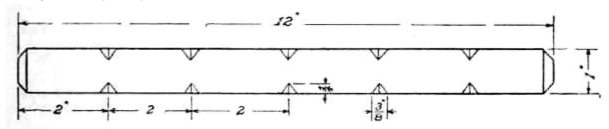

Fig. 5. The notched trophy stick

"Well, now, I'll show you how the Indians used to record their exploits. We'll put a notch on this stick for every one you've tried to make, and you can keep it as a souvenir of your first attempts at whittling." So with great care they measured off six two-inch spaces on each edge, carefully drew notches with a pencil and rule, and as carefully cut each notch to the line. (Fig. 5.)

Harry was delighted with the result.

9

They then hunted up a small screw eye, found the exact centre of the end of the stick by drawing two diagonals, fastened the screw eye in the centre and tied to it a piece of red, white and blue ribbon. A quarter-inch bevel was made around each end as a finishing touch.

This piece of white pine, with its twenty notches, hangs to-day in Harry's room, and every once in awhile he counts the notches to make sure they are all there, and recalls the trial that each one represents.

Harry was so much pleased with his notched trophy stick that he wanted to begin something else at once, and he was immediately started on a key rack.

"Too many homes," said Ralph, sagely, "have no definite place to keep keys. Those that have no tags are always a nuisance. Every key or bunch of keys should have a tag attached and should be hung on a certain hook where it can be found without searching. Now we'll make a sketch of a key rack before doing anything else, to find out just how large a piece of stick we shall need."

The drawing they produced is shown in Fig. 6 and called for a piece of wood seven inches long, an inch wide, and half an inch thick. As the key rack was to be a permanent household article, they decided on gum wood as more suitable than pine, it being easy to work and having a satisfactory appearance.

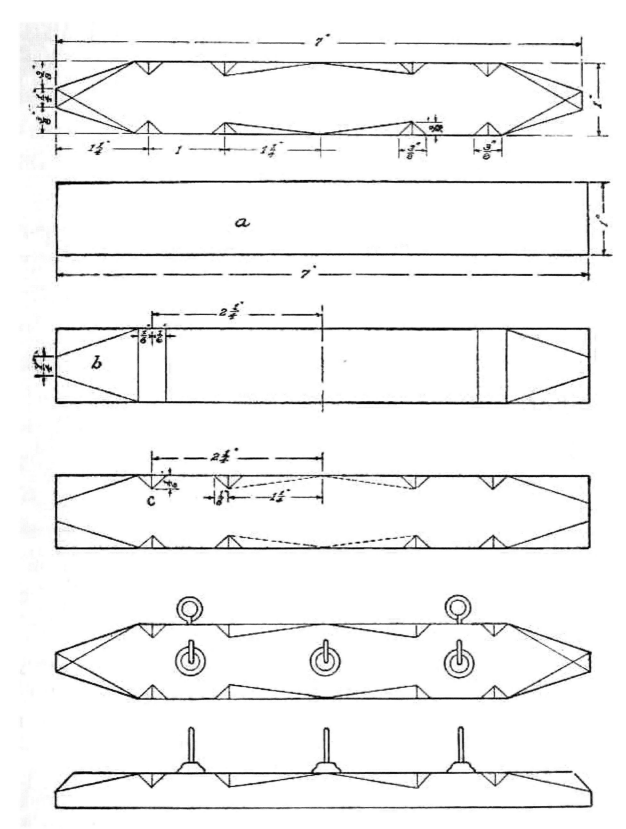

Fig. 6. The various steps in making a key rack

The different stages in the process of cutting out are shown in Fig. 6. At *a* is shown the stock squared up with the knife to the extreme outside dimensions. The ends were then whittled down to the form shown at *b* and the blank piece was ready for notching. The notches

11

were carefully drawn with a sharp hard pencil and cut as shown at *c*. The ends were bevelled by whittling to the lines, and the inner edges of the notches in the centre were whittled back to the middle of each edge. Then the knife work was finished.

Three brass screw hooks were placed in the centre of the large blank spaces, and two small screw eyes fastened into the upper edge for hanging the key rack on the wall.

Each stage of the work had been worked out so carefully that the boys hardly realized what a satisfactory result they were getting. When it was finally hung in the boys' room, of course some keys must be put on it, and as they had no tags, the making of some followed as a matter of course. A search through their small stock of woods disclosed a few little pieces of holly, the remains of fret saw work, about an eighth of an inch thick. This proved to be ideal material, and half a dozen key tags were made of the size and shape shown in Fig. 7. The holes were made with a brad awl, the tags fastened to the rings by small pieces of wire, and the names of the keys printed on the different tags with black drawing ink.

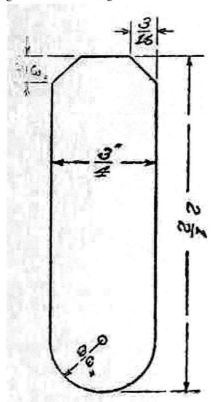

Fig. 7. The key tag

The boys, from this time on, seemed possessed with a mania for making articles to be used about the house. One thing to be manufactured without delay was a winder for their fishing lines.

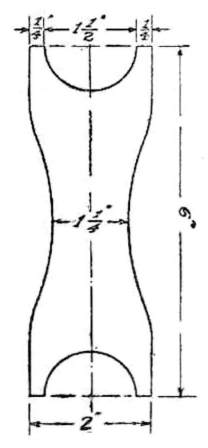

Fig. 8. Fish line winder

The form they finally decided on is shown in Fig. 8. Ralph insisted on the design being carefully drawn on a piece of thin wood, a quarter of an inch thick. Harry found whittling to curved lines somewhat harder than notching, but he produced a fairly satisfactory result. Ralph was a very exacting teacher, always having in mind his own training in school. He showed Harry how to cut out the curves at the ends without cutting his thumb (Fig. 9.) and gave him much advice about whittling away from himself, whenever possible.

When the knife work was finished, Ralph explained that where curved edges were cut it was allowable to smooth with a piece of fine sand-paper, although as a rule it was to be avoided.

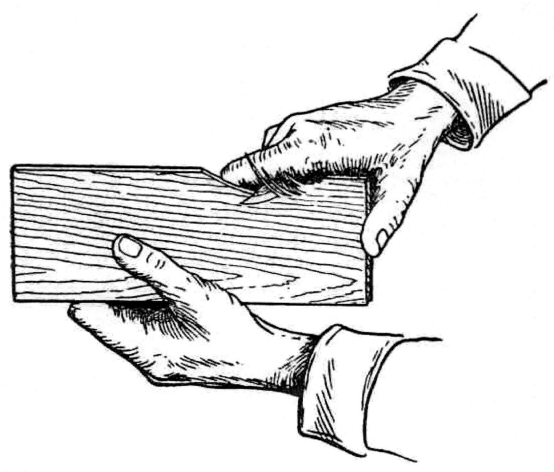

Fig. 9. Cutting concave curves

Harry wanted to know why, and Ralph explained that, generally speaking, sand-paper was the hallmark of a poor workman, one who could not do good work with his tools. Sand-paper leaves a scratched surface, for the grit becomes embedded in the wood to a certain extent, and it will immediately ruin the cutting edge of a sharp tool in case one has to be used after the sand-papering. "So," he summed up, "keep your sand-paper and knife as far apart as possible."

About this time the ladies of the household thought that a winder for worsted would come in very handy, and the boys evolved a new form, shown in Fig. 10. This was made only an eighth of an inch thick, and proved so easy of construction that each of the boys made two and "allowed" that "they ought to satisfy the sewing department for some time to come."

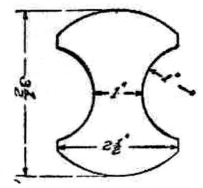

Fig. 10. The worsted winder

"Do you know," exclaimed Harry one day, "we could make lots of things for Christmas and birthday presents!"

"Why, certainly," said Ralph, "and people appreciate things that you have made yourself much more than things you buy. Anybody can go to the store and buy ready-made presents, but those you make yourself mean more."

"In what way?" said Harry.

"Why, they represent much more of your time and labour, and thought; and, by the way, if we are going to make many Christmas presents, we must start right away, because we only have a few weeks and you know how little time we have outside of school hours after getting our lessons."

The result of this talk was that the little building in the yard which they called their "shop" became a perfect beehive of industry for several weeks. With what money they had saved they purchased a supply of lumber and a few tools the use of which Ralph said he would explain later. He suggested that Harry begin by making some calendar backs, as suitable New Year's presents, because they were easy; and the more complicated articles could be made after Harry had developed a little more skill with the knife.

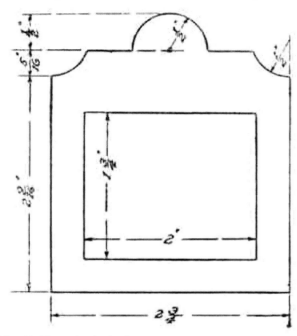

Fig. 11. First calendar back

The drawing he made is shown in Fig. 11. This called for a small calendar about two inches long, an inch and three quarters high, and a space this size was drawn on the centre of the calendar back, while the calendar was glued to the wood.

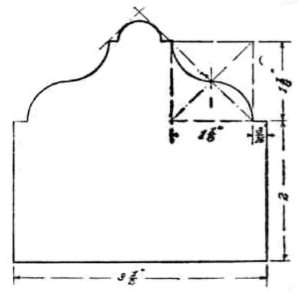

Fig. 12. Second calendar back

After two or three of these had been made, Harry decided that they were too small to suit him, and a new design somewhat larger was worked out on paper. It was a little more difficult to follow, because the outline had two reversed curves, but the boys were too busy and interested to be daunted by a trifle like that. (Fig. 12.)

Ralph suggested simple picture frames, and this brought the new problem of cutting out an opening for the picture.

15

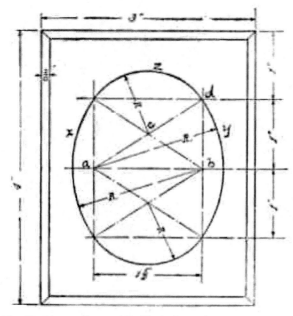

Fig. 13. Picture frame with elliptical opening

The first design they tried is shown in Fig. 13. Ralph had to show Harry how to make the ellipse with compasses by first constructing two squares or rectangles touching, and with both diagonal lines in each square. By taking for a centre the point where the squares touch, as *a* and *b*, and using the length of a diagonal line as a radius, two arcs were drawn at *x* and *y*. The ellipse was finished by taking *c* as a centre, and the distance *c d* as a radius, to draw arc *z*, and the other end was finished in the same way.

Ralph explained that this was not a perfect ellipse, but would answer for a small picture frame. The drawing was easy compared to the question of how to cut out the wood to this curved line.

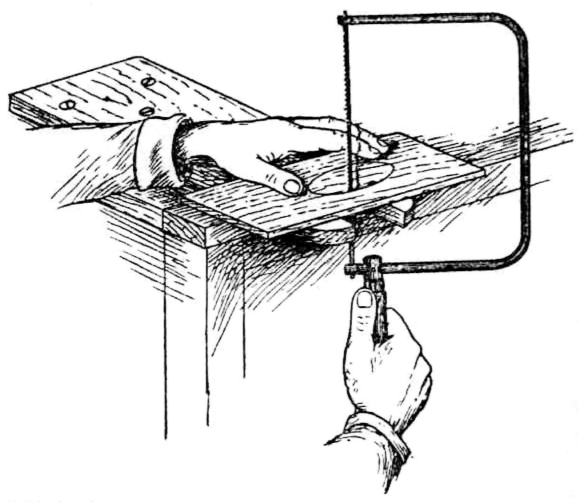

Fig. 14. Using the coping saw

One of the new tools was brought out, and Harry was introduced to the mysteries of the coping saw. (Fig. 14). A thin saw blade was produced and fastened in one end of the frame, the other end being left free. A hole was made inside of the ellipse with a brad awl, the free end of the blade passed through the opening and fastened in the frame of the saw. Resting the picture frame on the edge of a bench, the ellipse was sawed out roughly about $\frac{1}{16}$ of an inch inside of the drawing. This remaining sixteenth of an inch was then whittled to the line with a knife and finished with sand-paper. Harry found some difficulty in getting this elliptical opening smooth enough to suit him, so they tried designing for half an hour, and produced a new form (Fig. 15).

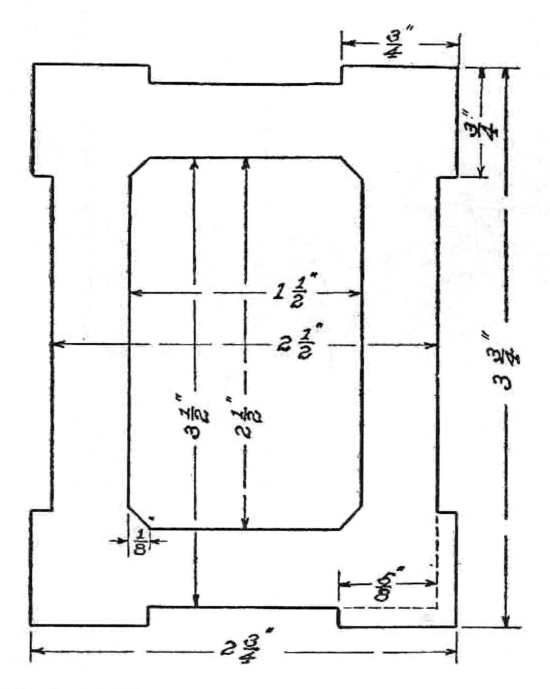

Fig. 15. Picture frame in straight lines

This was easier, as there were no curved lines, and it could be sawed close to the outside as well as the inside lines, to save time in whittling. While Harry was finishing this frame, Ralph was busy on a new design and finally passed over the drawing shown in Fig. 16.

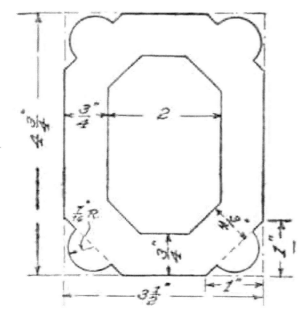

Fig. 16. Third picture frame

"Do you know there is as much fun in getting up new designs as there is in making them in wood?" said Ralph.

"Yes, but you have to know how to draw," replied the younger boy. "Can't you teach me?"

"Yes. I first make a rough sketch of my idea, and then a careful drawing of its actual size, with the drawing instruments."

"That's the part that I want to learn: how to use the instruments."

A lesson in mechanical drawing followed, and as it is a very important subject to young woodworkers, it will be given in full in the next chapter.

III

MECHANICAL DRAWING

"In taking up mechanical drawing," said Ralph, "always remember that accurate and neat work, containing all necessary dimensions, is half the battle. You will probably feel, as I did at first, that it is a waste of time, but you can always consider that when your drawing is finished the work is half done. You can judge from it the number of pieces of stock required, and their over-all dimensions This saves much time at the wood pile, and tells at a glance to just what size you must square up each piece of stock.

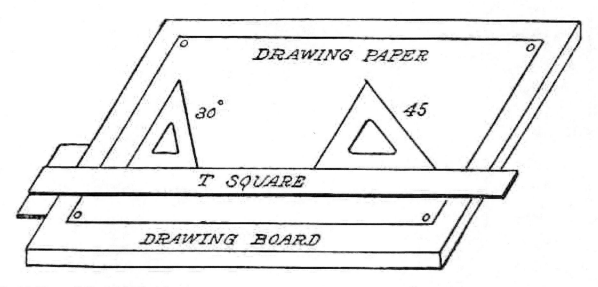

Fig. 17. The outfit for mechanical drawing

"The drawing board is an absolute necessity. It need not be perfectly square, but the surface must be flat and true, and at least one of the edges absolutely straight. (Fig. 17.) The T square must have a thin blade—about $\frac{1}{16}$ of an inch, and be made of hard wood. It should form a right angle with the head, which slides along the left-hand edge of the drawing board, and that must be the straight edge.

"The T square is used as a guide for the pencil in drawing horizontal lines, and it should always be kept on the same side of the drawing board. When drawing a vertical line, one of the wooden triangles should be placed on the T square and the line drawn along the left-hand edge of the triangle. Circles or arcs of circles are drawn with the compasses held at the extreme top."

With this introduction, the boys proceeded to fasten with four thumb-tacks a piece of drawing paper to the upper part of the drawing board.

"Why don't you put the paper in the centre?" asked Harry.

"Because, if one worked on the lower part of the drawing board, the T square head would extend below the edge of the board, and touch the table. You would have to watch it constantly. The head of the T square should always be tight against the board, for when you slide it too far down, it sometimes strikes the table without your knowing it, and you find your horizontal lines are *not* horizontal; so I always like to have the drawing paper as high up on the board as possible."

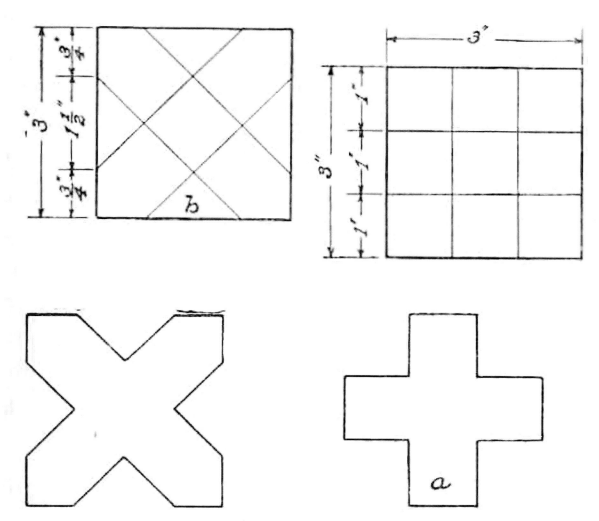

Fig. 18. Blocking out the crosses of St. Andrew and St. George

The boys agreed that while the younger was learning to make drawings, each one should represent something to be made later in wood. Drawing number one was a square, 3 inches on a side. Ralph showed how this was made with only two measurements. Drawing one horizontal and one vertical line, 3 inches were marked off on each, the other two lines drawn through these new points, and the square was finished. Ralph insisted that all lines be very light, as they could be darkened up later, if necessary, and were easy to erase in case of a mistake. (Fig. 18.)

Harry was then told to divide the upper and left-hand sides into even inches, and to draw across the square vertical and horizontal lines from the four points obtained.

Thus the large square was subdivided into nine 1-inch squares, and by darkening the lines shown in the figure at a the cross of St. George was produced.

Another 3-inch square was drawn, and marked off, as shown at b. The points were connected by oblique lines by means of the 45-degree triangle, and by darkening the lines shown at c the cross of St. Andrew was formed. After explaining that the British flag was a combination of these two figures Ralph said, "While we are drawing crosses, we may as well make a Maltese one."

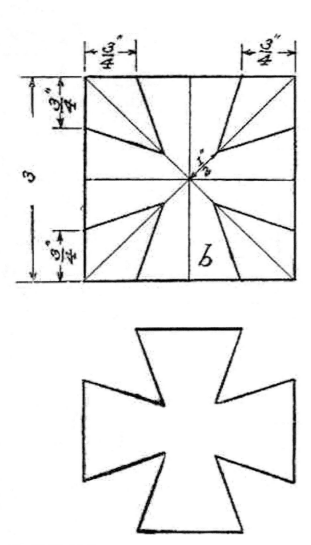

Fig. 19. The Maltese cross

Starting with a 3-inch square again, it was measured off as shown in Fig. 19. The lines were connected and darkened, as shown at *b*. "Now," said Ralph, "you can cut that out of wood, tie a ribbon on it and wear it as a medal."

"Huh," grunted Harry. "Pretty big medal—three inches across!"

"Well, make it any size, an inch or even less."

"That's not a bad idea. I'll make it out of white holly, and put a red, white, and blue bow on it."

"And print on it 'American Order of Junior Woodworkers'."

"Not a bad idea either; we can find lots of boys who would be glad to join and come here Saturdays to work in the shop."

"There would be no trouble to get candidates; the trouble would be to take care of them. They would fill the yard and overflow into the street," said Ralph.

"But why couldn't we——"

"Come now, let's do one thing at a time; you are supposed to be learning mechanical drawing. We'll leave the organization of the A. O. J. W. till another time. I'm going to show you how to use the compasses."

While they were drawing the circle, quarterfoil, heart, and oval, shown in Fig. 20, Ralph reviewed his pupil on the meaning of diameter, radius, circumference, etc. "If you want to cut hearts out of paper or wood, I would advise you to wait until St. Valentine's Day, and reserve the oval or egg until Easter.

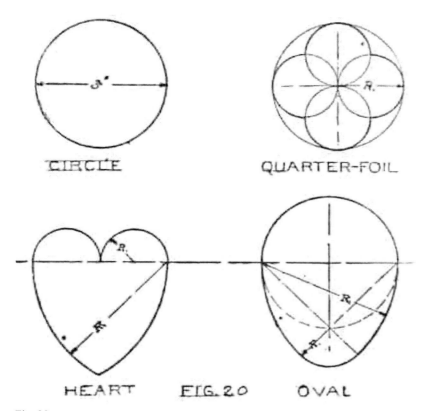

CIRCLE   QUARTER-FOIL

HEART   FIG. 20   OVAL

Fig. 20

"The circle is a wonderful figure. By marking the radius off on the circumference, with the compasses, we find that the former divides the latter into exactly six equal parts, and by connecting the points, we have a perfect hexagon. By connecting the alternate points we obtain a perfect equilateral triangle, and by connecting the remaining points we get another triangle of the same size. The two triangles form a six-pointed star. (Fig. 21.)

"Now," said Ralph, "I am going to give you a problem by dictation; all you have to do is to obey orders. First draw a circle 3½ inches in diameter."

"What's the radius?" asked Harry.

"That's for you to find out."

Harry thought a moment, divided three and a half by two, and setting his compasses at 1¾ , drew the circle.

"Now divide the circumference into three equal parts."

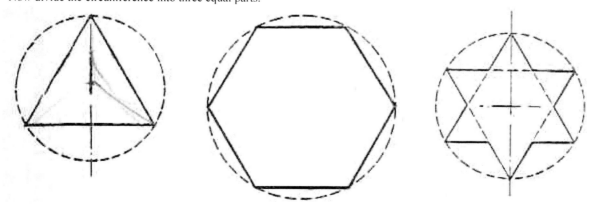

Fig. 21. Triangle, hexagon and star

The boy puzzled over this for a moment, then marked off the radius, cutting the circumference into six parts, as if for a hexagon, and erased every other point, leaving three.

"Draw radial lines from these points to the centre."

"Easy," remarked Harry, and drew a line from each point to the centre with the edge of one of his triangles.

"Find the centre of each of those lines."

23

"Easy again," said the boy, as he set his compasses at ⅞ of an inch, and from the centre of the circle cut each of the straight lines with an arc. (Fig. 22.)

"Draw a semicircle from each of these points with a radius of ⅝ of an inch."

"Easier still," quoth Harry, as he drew the semicircles. The drawing then looked like *a* (Fig. 22).

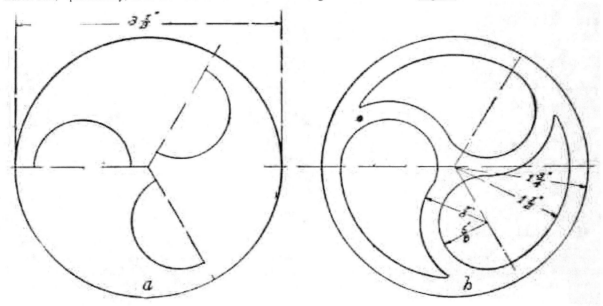

Fig. 22. Pulley design

"Now," said the teacher, "let me show you something." He made a few strokes with the compasses, and the drawing as shown at *b* was finished. "That is enough for to-day. The compasses are about the easiest of all instruments to use, provided you keep in mind that the pencil point needs to be sharpened to a chisel, or flat shape, the same as any other drawing pencil. The number of designs which may be made with it are simply endless, as you will learn later on."

IV

MECHANICAL DRAWING: Continued

The next day, as they were about to resume their study, Ralph said: "There is so much to drawing that I hardly know where to begin, or what to leave out; but in shop drawing, a picture will not do; imagine an architect trying to build a skyscraper from a picture. The shop drawing must tell the mechanic everything he needs to know about the object he is making. He cannot keep running to the office asking questions; the drawing must answer them all. That is the reason why the draughting-room is such an important part of every manufacturing plant. Drawing is the language the designer uses to tell the workmen what he wants made. It is doubly important when the designer is hundreds or thousands of miles away from the workman.

"A battle-ship can be designed in Australia and built in England, so this language of the shop has grown to be a very interesting and important art. Every one who works with tools must learn it sooner or later, the sooner the better.

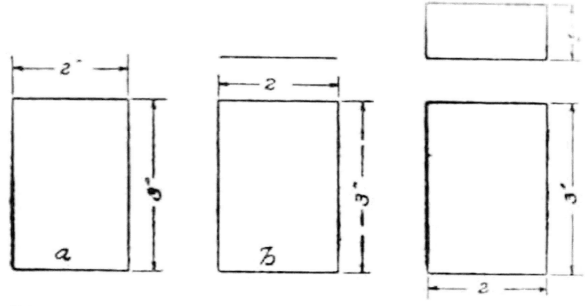

Fig. 23. Front and top views

"Usually it is necessary to represent even the simplest object by at least two views. For example, suppose I hand you this sketch a (Fig. 23), and tell you to make two out of wood. You wouldn't know what to do because no thickness is shown, but if I give you this sketch b, you would see immediately that it has practically no thickness and might be a sheet of paper. You learn that from the top view looking down on it.

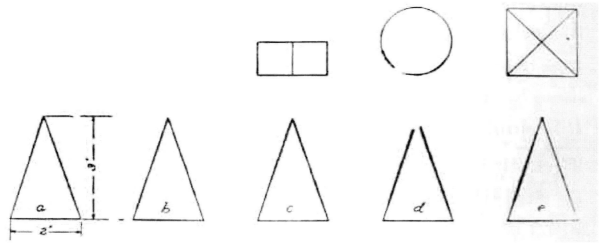

Fig. 24. Showing necessity for top view

"The first view is called the front view. Now, suppose I change the top view to this c; thickness is shown here, and if I say, make two of these out of white pine, you would know all that would be necessary to go ahead.

"Again, suppose I give you this sketch a (Fig. 24), and ask you to make two out of gum wood. You would be completely at sea, because that front view might have any one of these top views shown at b, c, d, e (Fig. 24). In other words, it might be a triangle without thickness, a wedge, cone, or pyramid.

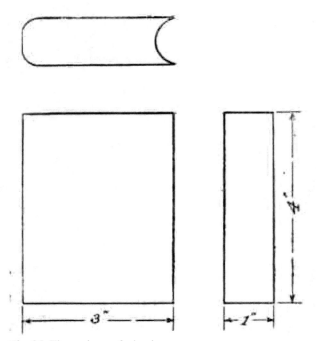

Fig. 25. Three views of a book

"So you see, two views are absolutely necessary, and very often a third, taken from the right or left side. The three views of a book would look like Fig. 25. The side view is not necessary in this case, but that is the way it would be drawn if a third were needed. You will have plenty of opportunities for practising this as we get along with our tool work, because in order to understand drawings you must be able to make them. Suppose you try your hand now, by drawing the two views of a cylinder, two inches in diameter and three inches high."

Ralph rolled a sheet of paper up until the ends met, to illustrate a cylinder, and the drawing produced by Harry looked like *a*. (Fig. 26.)

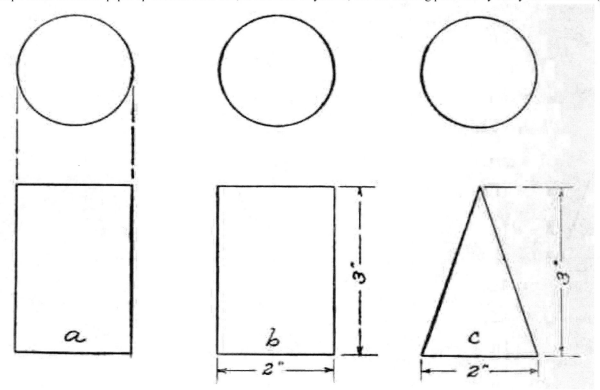

Fig. 26. Mechanical drawings of cylinder and cone

"Now," said Ralph, "no shop drawing is complete unless it shows all the necessary dimensions; so I will put them on to show you how it is done, but after this you must dimension every drawing you make."

The finished drawing of the cylinder is shown at *b*.

Harry was told to make the mechanical drawing of a cone, 2 inches in diameter, and 3 inches high. While he was working at this problem, Ralph disappeared, and when he returned Harry asked where he had been.

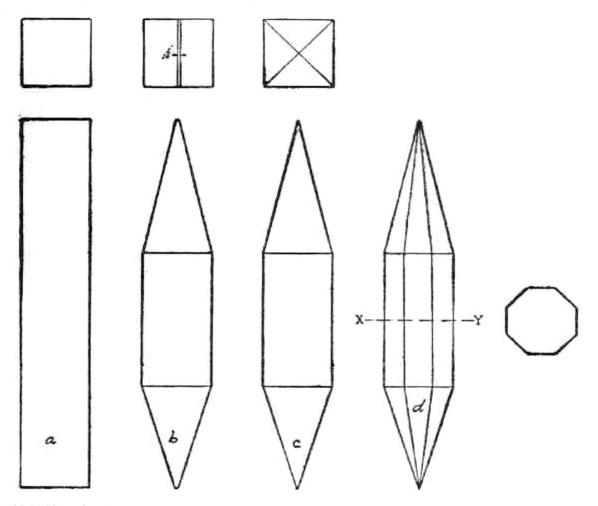

Fig. 27. Making a tip cat

"Never mind. Let me see your drawing," *c* (Fig. 26). "All right." Then he laid a little wooden object on the table.

"Why, it's a cat," said Harry.

"Yes, a tip cat, and as soon as you make a working drawing of it, you are going to manufacture one with your knife. Please notice that the tip cat is a cylinder with a cone at each end, and two views will show everything about it."

The drawing took longer to make than Harry imagined it would; or it seemed longer because he was so impatient to get to work with his knife. His finished drawing is shown at *a* (Fig. 28).

The different stages in the making of the tip cat are shown in Fig. 27.

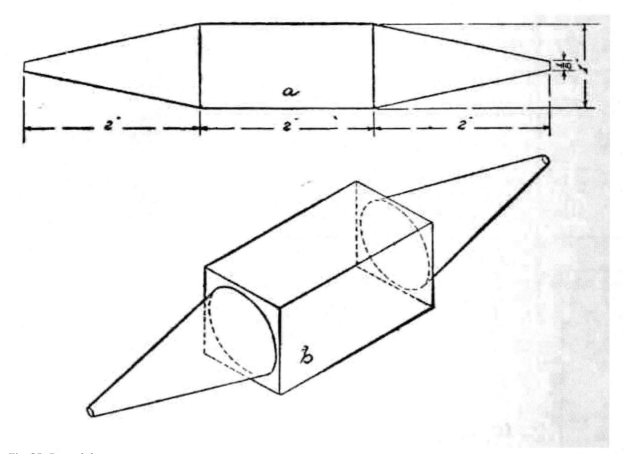

Fig. 28. Second tip cat

First came the squaring up, shown at *a*. Then the two ends were whittled down to wedges as shown at *b*, and these two ends reduced to square pyramids, as at *c*.

Lines a quarter of an inch from each edge were drawn on the four sides of the square part and continued out to the points of the pyramids, as at *d*. Cutting to this line changed the square to an octagon, and the square pyramids to octagonal ones.

The edges were again whittled off until there were no more to be seen; the cat was smoothed with sand-paper, and called finished.

Harry was delighted, but Ralph said: "That is not the best form for a tip cat, because it will roll. We will make a bat for it now, and after we have played with it awhile, we'll make a better one; just the same except that the centre part will be left square and only the ends rounded." (Fig. 28, *b*.)

The bat they made is shown in Fig. 29. Its handle was cut out with the coping saw and whittled to the lines. Ralph explained that anything to be held should be rounded, or it would be hard on the hand, so all the edges were curved with the knife and finished with sand-paper.

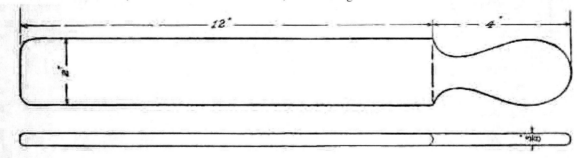

Fig. 29. Bat for tip cat

They had so much fun with the cat and bat that woodwork was forgotten for two afternoons. The third day it rained, so the boys were glad to get at work again in the shop.

Ralph suggested that, as they were doing so much drawing, it might be well to make a pencil sharpener.

The drawing they produced is shown in Fig. 30. This was easily worked out in ⅛-inch wood with a piece of sand-paper glued in the oblong space.

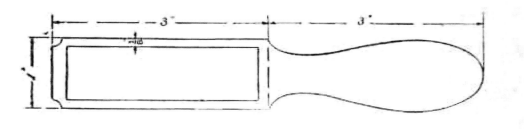

Fig. 30. Pencil sharpener

The sand-paper suggested match scratchers, and as they are useful articles, several designs were worked up for Christmas gifts. Three of these are shown in Fig. 31, but after a good deal of discussion it was decided that for scratching matches a longer space for sand-paper was necessary, and three other designs (Fig. 32) were the result of several hours' work.

Fig. 31. First match scratchers

"I'm getting tired of match scratchers," exclaimed Harry; "let's make some toys!"

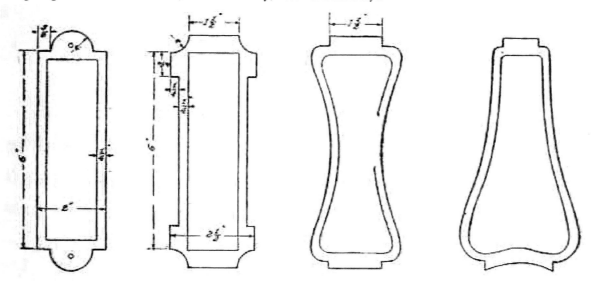

Fig. 32. Later designs in match scratchers

"Very well, we'll get ready for Santa Claus, and provide a stock of things for our numerous young cousins," replied Ralph. "This will give us a chance to use our coping saw, and I have been wanting to do that for a long time."

V

TOYS

"In making presents for little children," said Ralph, "we must always remember that the toys will be played with and receive a great deal of rough handling. So to begin with, they must be strong and of simple construction. The youngsters don't care so much for finely finished articles as older people do, and they tire very quickly of things that are so complicated that they get out of order easily. Suppose we first make some neat boxes. They can be filled with candy, and after that is gone they will be used for a long time to keep treasures in."

Fig. 33 shows the drawing of the first box the boys made. The two oblong pieces form the top and bottom. The latter was nailed on with $\frac{3}{8}$-inch brads. The two cleats were nailed to the under side of the top to hold it in place, while the sides and ends were fastened with a little glue, and one brad in the centre. This made a very serviceable box, the material being basswood $\frac{3}{16}$ of an inch thick.

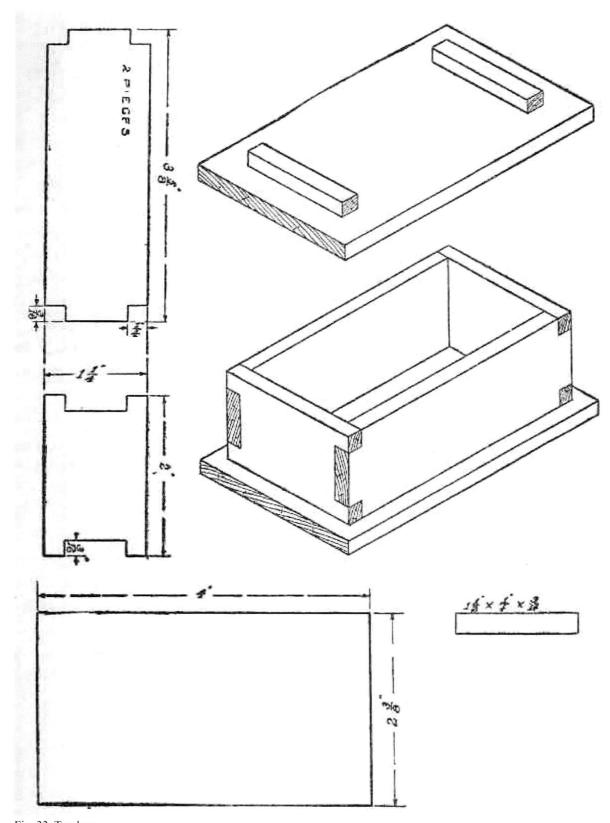

Fig. 33. Toy box

The sled shown in Fig. 34 came next, made of the same material as the box. Ralph was delighted with its strength and graceful lines. Two cleats were glued into the grooves in the sides, and the top nailed on with ⅜-inch brads.

31

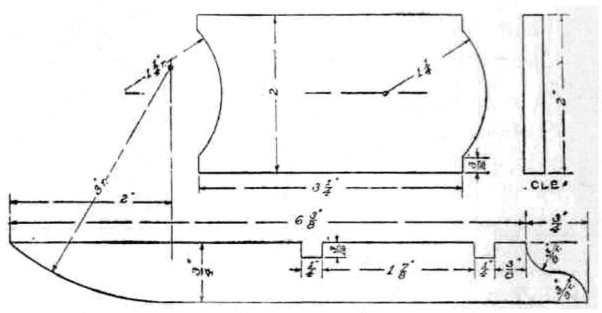

Fig. 34. The toy sled

In each case the drawing was made directly on the wood, which was sawed close to the lines with the coping saw, and finished to the lines with the knife.

The dog house (Fig. 35) brought out some new features of construction. The opening in front was cut out with the saw and finished as usual. Sides and ends were then put together with glue. The two pieces forming the roof were nailed together with ³⁄₈-inch brads, to make a right angle and were then placed in position and nailed to the front and back pieces.

Ralph explained that it was a saving of time and trouble to draw a light pencil line to mark the location of the brads. If this is not done, the brads are apt to come out in the wrong place and will then have to be withdrawn and placed again. This is a waste of time and it very often spoils the looks of the work, so that the drawing of the pencil lines really saves time in the end, and the lines can be erased.

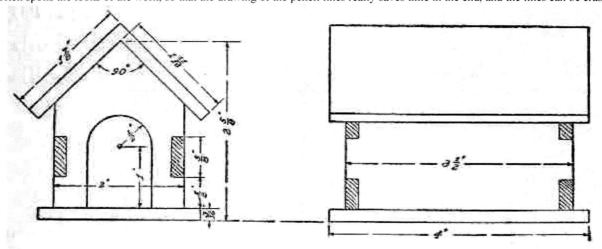

Fig. 35. The dog house

Fig. 36. Indian chief

"We can make any amount of this dolls' furniture," said Ralph. "In fact we could build a doll's house and equip it with chairs, tables, and beds, but what the youngsters really like best is something that works, something that moves, so I move—no pun intended—that we design a toy that has some life to it. We can cut it out with the coping saw and there need not be a great deal of knife work to it. Suppose we make an Indian paddling a canoe!" This was more of a problem than they had bargained for, as it was necessary to look through an encyclopædia to find pictures of canoes, Indians, tomahawks, etc. Harry traced the figure of an Indian chief, transferred it to the surface of a piece of ⅛-inch basswood, and on sawing it out found that he had a very good silhouette of an Indian, but it did not move (Fig. 36). The problem was still unsolved, and experiments along that line used up several afternoons.

Fig. 37. Indian paddlers

33

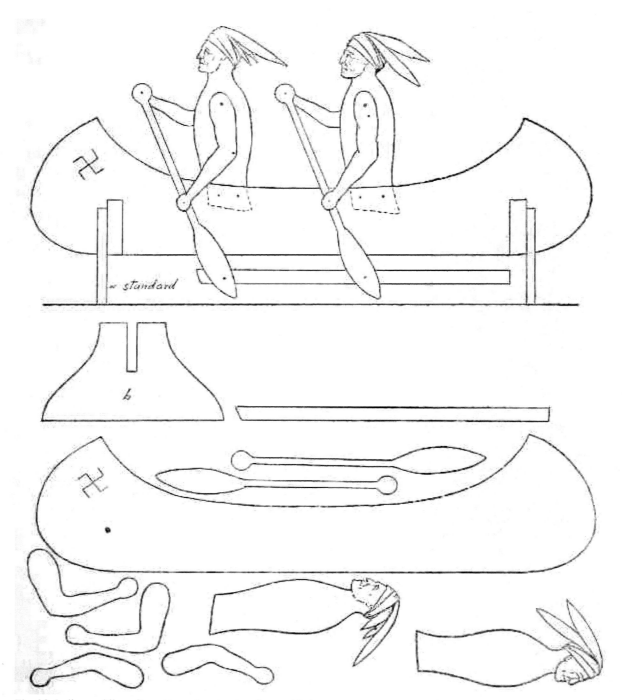

Fig. 38. Indian paddlers. Separate parts cut out and assembled

What was finally worked out is shown in Fig. 37. The arms were made separate from the body, and were fastened to both the paddles and the bodies by brads, which acted as pivots. The bodies were then fastened to the canoe in the same way, but a little glue was used as well as brads, as they were to be immovable. How to make the paddlers move in unison was a hard problem, finally solved by fastening a narrow strip of wood to the lower part of each paddle. It was found that by moving this strip back and forth the two figures moved with the precision of a machine. In each case where a pivot was required it seemed only necessary to drive in a ⅜-inch brad. (Fig. 38.)

The success of this moving toy was so great that the boys went rushing into the house to show it to the family.

Soon they came rushing back again, determined to try their skill on something else. Ralph had to remind Harry that the Indian paddlers were not yet finished, as the toy would not stand up, so the standards shown at *b* were sawed out, smoothed with the knife, and one fastened at each end, as a support, by means of brads and glue.

Fig. 39. The fencers

After much boyish arguing, it was decided next to try two swordsmen fencing. This called for some posing, and looking in books to get the correct position of a man fencing. The drawing shown in Fig. 39 was finally copied from a book on athletic sports.

The different parts of the figures are shown clearly in the illustration. It was found, by experimenting with paper figures, that by making one leg of each figure in two parts, the body, arms, and other leg could be sawed out of one piece.

The work of cutting out and assembling this combination, seemed much easier now that the boys had gotten into the swing of it, and they were so anxious to see it work that they almost spoiled it in their haste. The swords, or foils, were made of two pieces of soft iron wire.

Ralph insisted on filing these out flat near the ends to make them look realistic, and they were fastened by drilling a hole in each hand, passing the wire through and clinching it with a pair of pliers. It was much safer to drill these holes, as a brad awl sometimes splits wood that is very thin. This combination worked to perfection, and while they were trying it Harry caught a glimpse of its shadow on the table. The silhouette in black looked even more realistic than the toy itself, and it gave the boys an idea. (Fig. 40.)

These toys could be used for moving shadow pictures, and immediately their imagination began to conjure up the programme of a show.

"Our first selection, ladies and gentlemen, will be a shadow picture, entitled 'Before the Coming of the White Men'," exclaimed Harry, moving the Indian paddlers.

35

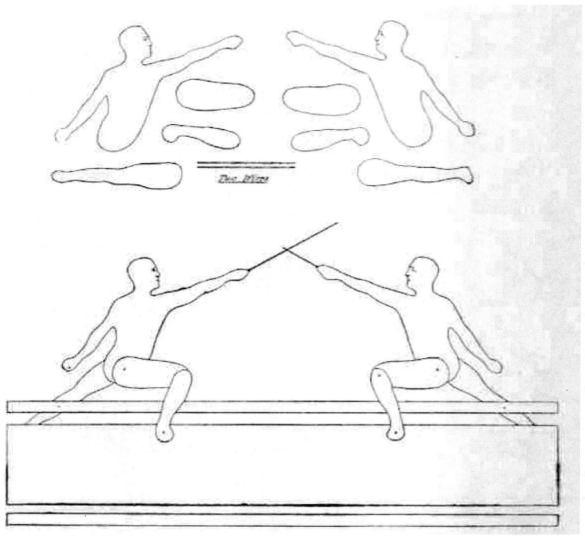

Fig. 40. The fencers. Pieces assembled

"And our next will be entitled 'The Duel'," said Ralph.

"Not a very good historical show," said Harry. "We ought to have the 'Landing of the *Mayflower*'."

"Not a bad idea, either," said Ralph. "I think we could rig up a ship in a storm. Let's try that next."

VI

MOVING TOYS

The problem of making a ship roll proved somewhat of a strain on the engineering corner of Ralph's brain, and after awhile Harry grew restless.

"Can't you give me something to do while you are designing that ocean?" he said.

Ralph, pausing a moment, replied, "Yes, try two men sawing a log."

Harry began to draw, but found that he knew very little about saws, so had to go out and look at one, measured it, and after awhile produced the sketch shown in Fig. 41. Ralph criticised it rather severely, suggesting the addition of a log and saw buck, and advised that the arms of the men and saw be cut out of one piece. The drawing shows the separated pieces, two bodies, four legs, a saw and arms in one piece, two straight pieces for the saw buck, the log, and a little triangular piece to go between log and saw buck. The object of this triangle is to leave a space between the log and saw buck for the passage of the saw back and forth, as shown in the sectional view.

The two pieces forming the buck were halved together, and the log, triangle, and buck are fastened with glue and two brads.

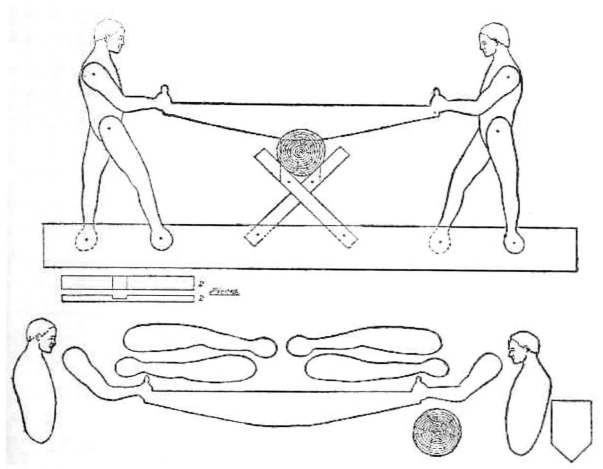

Fig. 41. The sawyers

After all the pieces had been cut out, the men were first put together by fastening both legs to the body with one ⅜-inch brad.

The feet were next fastened to the straight piece, 10 inches long, representing the ground, by one brad through each foot, the bodies standing upright, and the feet two inches apart. The arms came next, with one brad through each man's shoulder, and lastly, the saw buck, with the log already fastened rigidly to it, was nailed on the back of the ground piece with the log in front of the saw. To make this toy stand up, two standards were fastened to the ends of the ground piece, the same size as those attached to the fencers in Fig. 40.

It took Harry two hours to make this figure in wood, after he had the drawing finished. In the meantime Ralph had worked out a scheme for giving a boat a rolling motion.

"We'll be mechanical engineers by the time we finish this," he told Harry. "This piece of mechanism calls for a crank, a shaft, two bearings, and a cam, not to mention a ship, an ocean, and a few miscellaneous articles too trivial to mention."

37

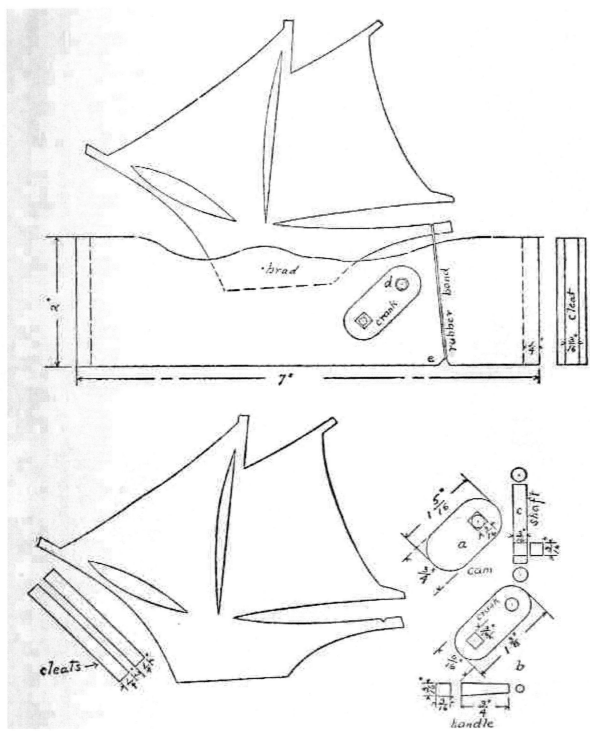

Fig. 42. Boat in storm

The various parts of "the ship in a heavy sea" are shown in Fig. 42. At *a* is the cam, at *b* the crank and handle, and at *c* the shaft. The boat was sketched free hand and cut out with the coping saw in one piece by sawing exactly on the lines. The ocean was represented by two pieces corresponding to the ground piece in the sawyers, and the wavy outline was not made until everything had been cut out and the combination was ready for assembling.

The most difficult part—the shaft—was made first, and entirely with the knife: A piece of basswood was cut exactly a quarter of an inch square, a section was marked in the centre of this $3/16$ inch wide, and notches were made on each corner. The two ends were then whittled to an octagonal shape and rounded. The square section in the centre was reduced to $1/8$ inch wide and the rounded ends sand-papered smooth.

Next, the cam was cut out, and the square hole made. This was accomplished, after spoiling one, by drilling a quarter of an inch hole in the square and cutting the opening square with the point of the knife.

The object of the square opening was to prevent the cam from slipping when in operation. The cam was then placed over the round part of the shaft and glued to the square section, over which it fitted snugly. Next came the crank. This was made the same shape as the cam, but the $\frac{1}{4}$ inch hole drilled in one end was left round, while the other was cut square as in the cam. The shaft fitted into the round hole and was glued in after the assembling. For the handle on the crank, a piece $\frac{1}{4}$ inch square was fitted into the square hole, and the rest of it whittled round and sand-papered.

Two cleats, 2 inch × $\frac{1}{4}$ × $\frac{3}{16}$ inch, were cut out with the saw and everything was ready for assembling. The two sides of the ocean were held together and the $\frac{1}{4}$-inch hole at d drilled through both pieces at once.

The two notches at e were cut after the assembling was finished. After the holes were drilled, the wavy line was sawed, and the two ends of the shaft inserted in the holes with the cam inside.

The two cleats were inserted in the ends of the ocean and fastened with brads and glue.

Next, the boat was slipped in between the two sides, with the sloping stern just touching the cam, and a $\frac{3}{8}$-inch brad was driven through the three thicknesses, sides and boat.

The crank was next slipped over the shaft and glued in position. The crank handle was inserted into the square hole and fastened with glue, and lastly a light rubber band was slipped over the notch on the stern of the boat and the two corresponding notches on the bottom of the ocean. This was to hold the boat against the cam, which gives the motion.

To make this toy more realistic, the boys got out a box of water colors, painted the body of the boat black, the ocean green, and left the basswood sails their natural color—white.

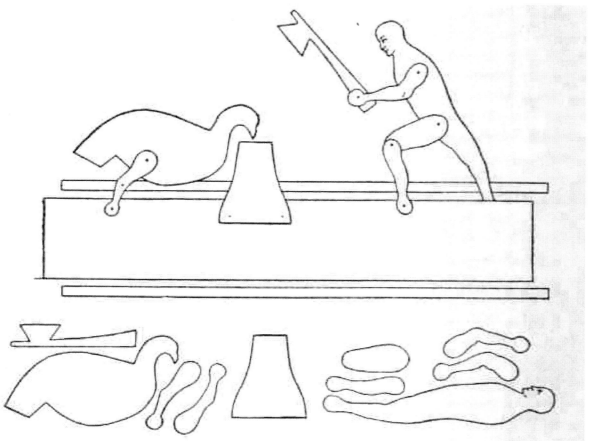

Fig. 43. Turkey and executioner

"There," said Ralph when it was finished, "the youngsters can raise a storm at any time they like by simply turning the crank. This toy ought to be very serviceable, as it can't very well get out of order and is almost unbreakable."

The subject of moving toys is almost endless, being limited only by the imagination of the designer. Thanksgiving suggested the turkey and the axe, and in the toy these boys worked out the turkey evades the axe every time.

The parts are shown in Fig. 43. The legs of the turkey are stuck rigidly to the body by brads and a little glue, and they are fastened to the ground piece by one brad, which acts as a pivot.

The axeman's body and right leg are in one piece, the left leg being in two pieces. The arms adhere rigidly to the body, and the axe to the hands, by means of brads. The operating strip is $\frac{1}{4}$ inch wide and 9 inches long.

It is fastened between the legs of the turkey, and to the rigid leg of the man, by one brad for pivot in each case.
The stump is nailed to the ground strip from the front.

VII

DESIGNING MOVING TOYS

The boys found this making of toys so fascinating that one was barely finished before another was suggested. So absorbed did they become that even meals were forgotten, and they regarded it as a hardship to be called in to supper, while to be told that it was bedtime was absolute cruelty. They found that it saved time to be systematic, and the usual method of procedure was about as follows:

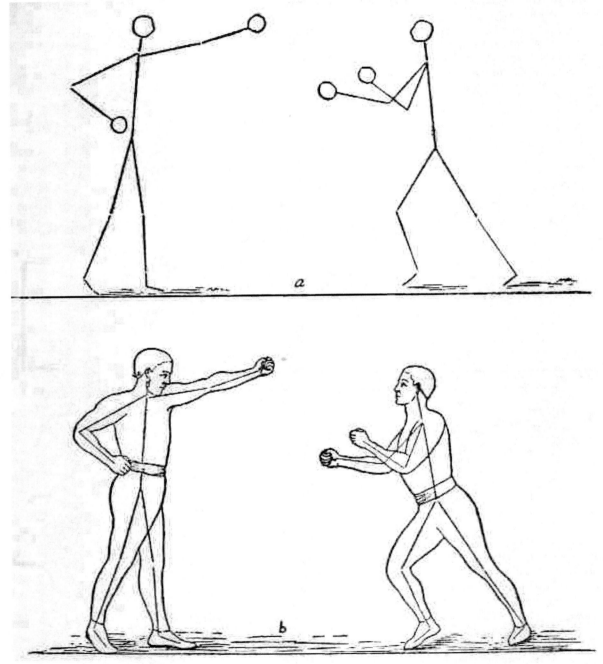

Fig. 44. The boxers

First, to decide on the practicability of the idea. Second, to sketch out a skeleton figure, as in *a* (Fig. 44), the boxers. When the proper action was secured in these skeleton figures, the bodies were sketched roughly around them as shown at *b*. Third, the movement of the figures was thought out, and separate drawings traced from the assembled drawing on tracing paper. Fourth, these separate pieces were traced on ⅛-inch basswood with the grain of the wood running the long way of the piece, wherever it was possible. Fifth, the pieces were sawed out, and the edges smoothed with knife and sand-paper. Very often, through anxiety to see how it worked, the smoothing of the edges was neglected. Sixth, the parts were put together with brads, and where the points came through they were bent over or "clinched" on the further side. Seventh, after experiments to discover the best position for it, the moving strip was fastened to the legs by ⅜-inch brads, and last of all the feet were pivoted to the ground piece in the same way.

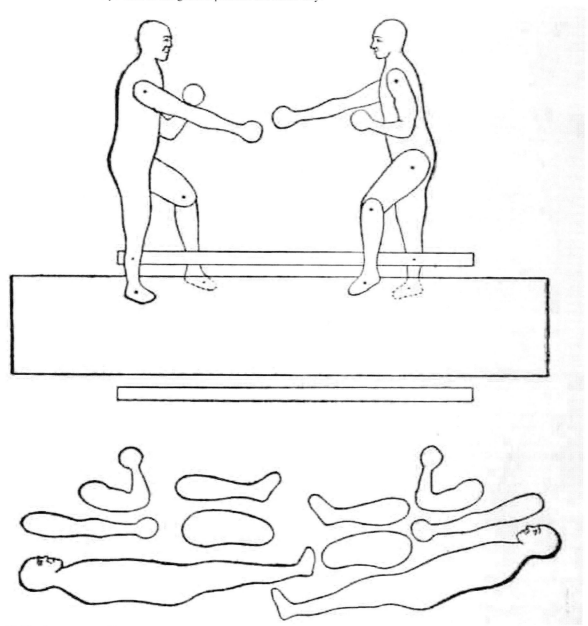

Fig. 45. The boxers assembled

The boys learned many things not to do: for example, all the finer details of the face and hands must be omitted, as they are very apt to be broken off in sawing. It was found best to make the feet nearly round or the brads would split the wood. For that reason wherever a brad has to be driven through, the arm or leg should be made larger than the proportionate size.

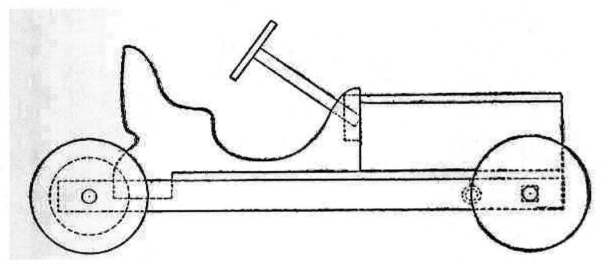

Fig. 46. The racing automobile

The most surprising feature about the figures was the fact that the shadow they cast on a white wall or sheet was more realistic than the figures themselves, and our boys never tired of exercising these toys in order to watch the shadow pictures.

Of all combinations, perhaps the design and construction of a racing automobile, that would actually go, gave them the greatest amount of amusement as well as the largest number of problems to solve. The history of trials and failures need not be given, but the machine, as finished, is shown in Fig. 46. The body and hood are comparatively simple. The principal trouble, as with larger machines, was with the motive power, and the boys finally compromised by using a rubber band. The four wheels were sawed out of $\frac{3}{16}$-inch basswood, and smoothed with sand-paper, the two driving wheels for the rear having a $\frac{1}{4}$-inch hole drilled to receive the ends of the axle. The rear axle was $\frac{1}{4}$ inch square at the centre for half an inch, and the rest of it $\frac{1}{4}$ inch in diameter, rounded with the knife and sand-paper. The total length of the axle was four inches, and the wheel base seven and one-half inches.

For the driving gear, three disks shown at a (Fig. 47) were sawed out, the two large ones, $1\frac{1}{4}$ inches in diameter, from $\frac{1}{8}$-inch basswood. The edges of these two were rounded with knife and sand-paper. The small disk, $\frac{3}{4}$ inch in diameter, was cut from $\frac{1}{4}$-inch wood or two $\frac{1}{8}$-inch pieces placed together and glued.

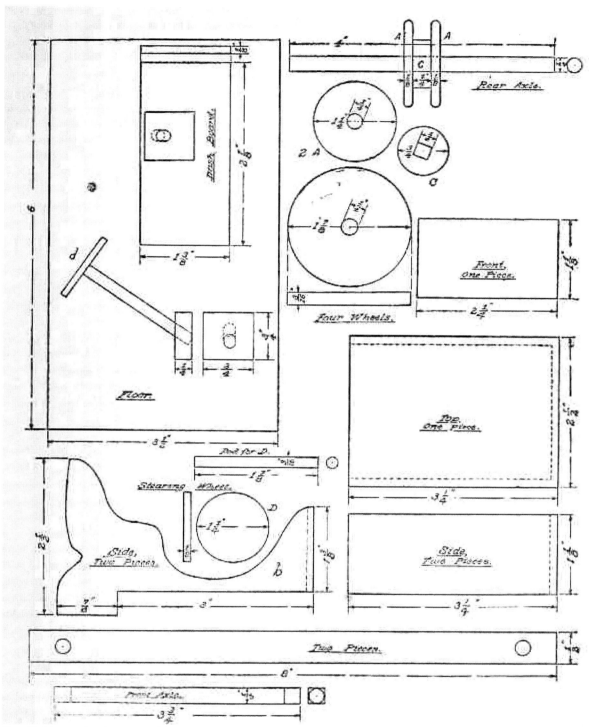

Fig. 47. Pieces of racing automobile

A square hole was cut through the centre of each of these disks with a knife, and they were then put together with glue and brads, making a very serviceable grooved pulley, which was slipped over the shaft and fitted over the square part in the centre. As it was a snug fit no glue was necessary, and the square part prevented the pulley from slipping on the shaft. The forward axle was made 3¾ inches long, ¼ of an inch square, except at the ends, where for a distance of ⁵⁄₁₆ inch it was rounded, ¼ inch in diameter. This completed the wheels, axles, and transmission pulley.

The chassis, or frame, which supports the body, consists of two pieces of ³⁄₁₆-inch basswood 8 inches long and ½ inch wide, with a ¼-inch hole drilled ¼ inch from each end. The floor of the auto, on which the body rests, is ⅛-inch basswood 6 × 3½ inches, and it binds the whole machine together, giving it strength and rigidity, but it must not be fastened in place until the structure is ready for assembling.

43

The hood is simply a box $3\frac{1}{4}$ inches long, $2\frac{1}{2}$ inches wide, and $1\frac{1}{4}$ inches high without a bottom. The top piece may be left unfastened, if desired, with two cleats on the under side to hold it in position. The hood then becomes an available place to keep small articles, tools, etc.

The body of the automobile is composed of five pieces: the two sides of the shape shown at b, the dash-board, to which they are fastened with brads, the seat, and the back. This body can be taken off and replaced by other bodies, made to represent roadsters, touring cars, limousines, etc.

A block of $\frac{1}{4}$-inch basswood $\frac{3}{4}$ inch square is fastened to the dash-board. This block has a $\frac{3}{16}$-inch hole drilled through it at an angle of forty-five degrees, and into this hole is glued the steering-gear, consisting of a basswood stick, whittled to $\frac{3}{16}$ inch diameter, with a $\frac{1}{8}$-inch wheel $1\frac{1}{4}$ inches in diameter fastened at the top, d.

The method of assembling is important. First, insert the front and rear axles through the holes or bearings in the chassis, or frame; then nail the floor to the frame with $\frac{3}{8}$-inch brads. This gives a rigid structure to work on, the front edge of the floor being even with the forward ends of the frame. Now screw into the under side of the floor, $1\frac{1}{4}$ inches from the front end, a $\frac{1}{2}$-inch screw eye or screw hook, or even a flat-head nail. This is to hold one end of the rubber band which is to supply the motive power.

The hood may now be put together and fastened even with the front of the machine by nailing it from the bottom with brads. The body is put on by nailing the two sides to the dash-board, and the dash-board to the hood. The seat and seat-back are afterward put in place with brads and the steering-gear glued in position against the dash-board.

The wheels should be put on last of all. Before placing them in position, slip two or three new rubber bands over the screw hook under the car, and tie the free end to the driving pulley so tightly that the cord will not slip on the pulley.

The front wheels are fastened to the axles by $\frac{1}{2}$-inch flat-head wire nails, and worked until they revolve freely on these pivots; the flat head holds the wheel on.

The rear wheels are the drivers, and must be fastened rigidly to the axle by glue. When the glue has hardened—this takes several hours—the machine may be sent across the room on the floor by winding the rear axle backward as much as the rubber bands will permit without breaking, and setting the machine on the floor.

The first time the boys tried it, the rubber band uncoiled so quickly that the auto shot across the room and nearly wrecked itself against the wall. This was too realistic, especially as it broke one of the forward wheels, and a new one had to be made.

When such an automobile is to be presented to little children who want to draw it around with a string, it is necessary to remove the rubber band; otherwise the rear wheels will drag.

When our boys had finished their machine, the question came up to whom it should be given for Christmas, and Harry blurted out, "I want it myself." This was the greatest of all their difficulties. When they had finished a piece of work they hated to part with it, but Ralph was older, and he knew that as Harry became interested in new things he would gradually lose interest in the old ones. So they played with this machine, made another with a roadster body, and auto races became the rage for awhile. After several afternoons of racing, they decided, just as their elders had done before them, that what their machines needed was improved motive power. The accomplishment of this would take them out of the realm of woodwork, so Ralph suggested that they stick to their motto of "one thing at a time." "And our business just now is woodwork."

VIII

THE MODEL AEROPLANE

The automobile experiment naturally suggested the aeroplane, and after much reading of magazines and animated discussions as to the relative advantages of biplanes, monoplanes, gliders, etc., the boys decided to try their skill on a biplane of their own design, a combination of the features and proportions of the Curtiss and Wright machines.

The automobile was child's play compared with the problems confronting the young aviators in designing and working out a flying machine, and, as in the former case, the question of motive power was the most difficult. We might add it has not yet been satisfactorily solved.

Fig. 48 shows the general appearance of the boys' model, which was eighteen inches long from front to back, and the planes, made of light card-board, were 14 inches long and $3\frac{1}{2}$ inches wide. The frame, braces, rudder, and tilting plane were made of $\frac{1}{8}$-inch basswood, put together with $\frac{1}{2}$-inch brads clinched wherever the points came through.

The parts composing the frame were made first, and all small details, such as rudder, propeller, tilting plane, etc., cut out later.

The separate parts are shown in the drawing. Four straight pieces like a were required to support the tilting plane in front, and two pieces each b and c for the rudder in the rear. Two pieces a, one of b and c were fastened together by means of two uprights d, forming one complete side of the machine. This was completed, and the second side made identical with it.

These two sides were then fastened parallel with each other, rigidly, by means of the two rudder posts e e and the cross pieces ff, by brads. The rudder posts bound the two sides rigidly at the rear, the cross pieces at the centre, and at the forward end the tilting plane was held in position by the brads, which also acted as pivots.

This made a remarkably light and yet strong framework. The card-board planes were not placed in position until everything else was finished, as they could be attached easily and quickly, but were very much in the way when experiments were being made on the propelling apparatus.

Of course there had to be a propeller, and the problem of making it required some practice.

Ralph introduced the subject by showing Harry how to make an old-fashioned toy, shown in the detail drawing, of two pieces, one the propeller, the other a balancing stick.

The propeller was made of a piece of $\frac{3}{8}$-inch basswood, 4 inches long and $\frac{1}{2}$ inch wide. A $\frac{3}{16}$-inch hole was first drilled at the exact centre. The two ends were then whittled down to the shape shown at k. The balancing stick was next whittled down until one end fitted tightly into the hole drilled in the propeller, and the rest of the stick then rounded until it was of uniform diameter. This stick was glued into the hole, and allowed to dry.

There was plenty of work to do while the glue was hardening, as the cross pieces g g had to be fastened to the frame to prepare for the installation of the power plant.

When the glue was dry, Ralph took the balancing stick between the palms of his hands, drew his right hand toward him with a quick motion, at the same time releasing the stick. To Harry's amazement, the whole thing flew up and struck the ceiling, and for a few minutes aeroplanes were forgotten while the two played with this interesting but ancient toy.

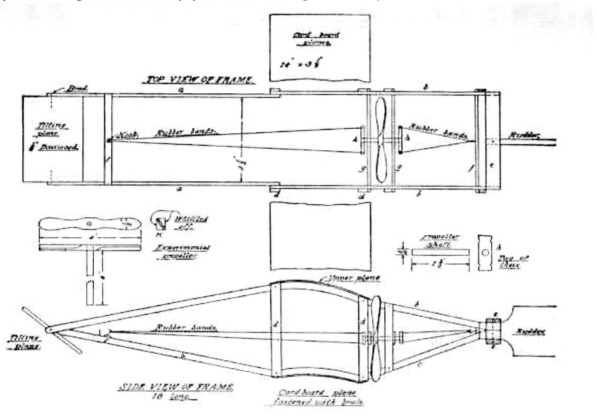

Fig. 48. The toy biplane

Ralph explained that the propeller was simply part of a screw thread, and had actually worked its way through the air just as a screw works its way into a piece of wood. Its lifting power had been shown by the way it carried the balancing stick with it up to the ceiling.

"Now," he continued, "when we place a propeller horizontal it will worm its way forward through the air in the same way and carry the aeroplane with it, for the simple reason that it is so placed in the frame it can't get out. As the free space it has to revolve in is only 3 inches, we shall have to cut the blades down to about $2\frac{3}{4}$ inches to give it clearance."

They whittled out a shaft $1\frac{1}{2}$ inches long and fastened the two notched pieces h h to it after placing the propeller in position between the two cross pieces g g which had been previously drilled with $\frac{1}{4}$-inch holes to act as bearings.

New rubber bands were then passed over the notches, stretched out to the front and rear of the frame, and tied to cross pieces.

By winding up the propeller, these bands were twisted tightly, and when the propeller was released, the bands unwound, causing it to revolve rapidly.

The rudder was now pivoted in position by brads, and the two planes fastened by the same method.

The power derived from the bands was not sufficient to propel the aeroplane fast enough to support it in the air, so it was necessary to experiment with strong thread until the centre of gravity was found. It proved to be near the centre of the planes. Small holes were made with an awl at this point, the thread passed through them and tied. By suspending the aeroplane from a chandelier it took up a horizontal position.

45

Then the forward tilting plane was elevated slightly and the propeller wound up. On being released the aeroplane slowly and majestically sailed through the air in a great circle, limited by the length of the suspending thread.

The boys never tired of this toy and all it lacked was the ability to fly in the open air, which would require a more powerful motor. This would more than double the weight of the machine, and therefore call for larger planes to support it. There you have the great problem of the aviator.

Ralph wisely suggested that as they had not yet reached the stage of designing gasolene motors they had better leave the aeroplane as it was, or it would be necessary to abandon their woodwork, which neither of them had any intention of doing.

IX

THE MONOPLANE

A very satisfactory monoplane can be made from the plans shown in Fig. 49.

The material for the frame should be quarter-inch white pine or spruce. The six long strips are 30 inches in length, and for fastening, holes should be drilled and the connection made by passing fine soft wire through them and binding fast.

The top frame, formed of four of these long strips, should be made first, with particular attention to the measurements, so that both sides shall be exactly the same size and weight.

At the rear end the two long strips may be wired together temporarily. The propeller shown in the drawing can be made at any time from a piece of white pine ⅞ inch thick and 12 inches long by 1¾ inches wide. It is a good piece of whittling work.

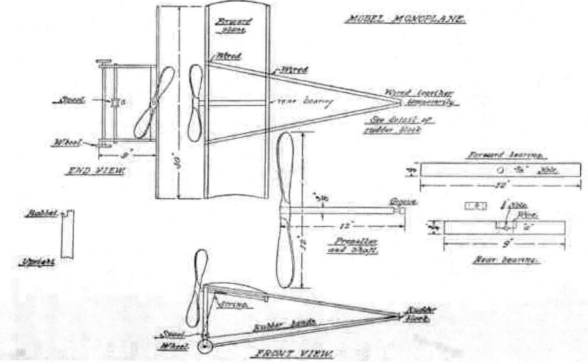

Fig. 49

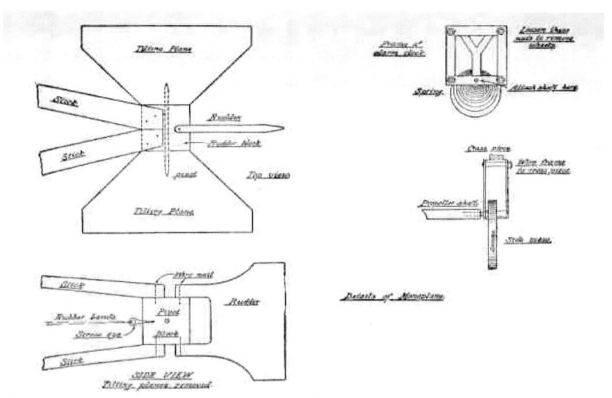

Fig. 49 (a). The toy monoplane.

The ⅜-inch hole for the shaft should be bored first, and the propeller blades reduced to a thickness of ⅛ inch at the centre of the blade, and ¹⁄₁₆ inch or less at the edges.

The shaft needs to be strong, and should be made of a piece of ⅜-inch dowel rod. Make a saw cut with back saw in the end, which is to be fastened in the propeller.

When ready to assemble, push this end into the ⅜-inch hole in the propeller, drive in a soft pine wedge with a little glue, and a rigid fastening will result.

The groove in the rear end of the shaft is to take the thrust of the propeller, and hold it in the machine. This groove may be readily cut out with the knife, and smoothed with sand-paper. Two bearings are necessary to hold the shaft in alignment. The forward one is a strip of pine ¼ by ¾ , with a ⅜-inch hole bored at the centre. This hole should be sand-papered until the shaft turns in it freely. The rear bearing is a strip ⅝ by ⅜ inch, laid out as shown at a. The quarter-inch hole must be bored first. Next, drill two small holes with a fine drill on either side of the hole for the wires which are to hold the two pieces together. Next saw on the pencil line shown, removing the small piece x. Test the bearing by placing the small grooved section of the shaft in the quarter-inch hole to see if it turns freely. When this has been accomplished, the propeller and its bearings are ready for the monoplane.

Looking at the front view, the two uprights are 9 × ¾ × ¼ inches. At the top ends they are rabbeted as shown, and wired to the top frame. At the bottom they are wired to the long strips which form the long sides of the bottom frame.

Before putting these uprights on, a ¼-inch hole should be drilled 1½ inches from the bottom of each. These are to receive the ¼-inch dowel rod which acts as the axle for the spool s. This rod should be 10 inches or more in length, so that brads or wire may be passed through the ends outside the uprights to keep the axle in place.

The small spool which acts as a pulley must be perfectly free to turn on this rod, and be kept in place by two brads driven through drilled holes on either side of it.

The front and lower parts of the frame are now ready to be assembled.

The four long strips constituting the body of the frame are all wired together at the back, temporarily. To finish the forward part, saw out a strip ⅜ × ¼ inch, and form on each end a rounded bearing, as in the automobile, for two wheels 1¾ inches in diameter. Saw the wheels out of ³⁄₁₆-inch basswood, drill a hole at each centre, place on the bearing, and fasten in place with a flat-head wire nail and a small washer next to the wheel. Sand-paper the wheels smooth, and see that they turn freely. Tack the strip, or wire it to the uprights, as low down as possible.

The rear end of the monoplane is a nice little problem. Cut out a block of pine from 1 inch to 1⅛ inches square. In the side facing the front place a screw eye for fastening the spring or rubber bands.

The rudder is shown in the drawing. Drill two holes, as shown, and drive in brads or flat-head wire nails, as large as the hole, so that the rudder may be turned by hand, but not free enough to turn with the wind.

Next drill a hole clear through the block for the axle of the tilting planes.

47

It is not necessary that the axle be at the exact centre of the cube. It should extend quite through both planes as well as the cube, and be bent around the edges, so as to make them rigid. They should be snug enough to turn by hand, but not loose enough for the wind to shift.

The four sides of the frame are now whittled down to fit the block, and wired to it.

Last comes the question of motive power.

This is *the* great problem. The writer is opposed to encouraging boys to believe that these toy aeroplanes can be made to fly great distances. The propeller would have to be made to revolve at high speed for several minutes in order to accomplish this, and the tension of rubber bands is not equal to it. The machines can be made to fly short distances only. The problem of aviation is now a question of motors, and the smallest gasolene motor, with its tank, etc., requires a fairly large aeroplane to lift it. No doubt, the problem will be solved within a short time, but it has not been done at the time of writing.

For this size of toy monoplane several large rubber bands may be tied together, fastened at the screw eye on one end and to a piece of strong linen kite cord at the other.

Pass this cord forward under the spool and up to the propeller shaft.

Drill a small hole in the shaft, draw the cord taut, and fasten it through this hole.

While the model has no planes as yet, it is wise to get the propeller working before putting them on, as the space for working is freer. Wind up the propeller until the bands have been stretched to their limit, then let go. It may be necessary to place wheels at the rear, the same as in front. On a smooth floor, the machine should be drawn forward several feet by the action of the propeller.

It is entirely practicable, on a plane of this size, to use the works of an ordinary alarm clock in place of rubber bands.

Remove the outer casing of an old clock; loosen the four brass nuts that hold the frame together, and take out all the wheels, except the axle on which the mainspring is fastened. Put the frame together again with the four nuts.

The axle for the mainspring extends outside of the frame, and is threaded to receive the handle for winding. Take this handle off. Drill a hole in the end of the propeller shaft, slightly smaller than the mainspring axle, and screw the latter into the propeller shaft.

You now have the clock-works on the end of your shaft, and it is necessary to fasten a strip of pine ½ in. by ¼ in. to the upper sticks of the frame in order to wire the works fast, as they must not be allowed to turn. By turning the propeller you wind up the clock, and as soon as you release it, as there is no escapement now to regulate the spring, it tries to unwind at once, and the propeller starts at terrific speed. Look out for your hands, as the propeller blades have no conscience.

This action, although strenuous, is short lived, but much more powerful than rubber bands. The spring of an ordinary alarm clock is powerful enough to drive a wooden two-bladed propeller 12 inches in diameter with blades two inches wide at the outside. It will draw a monoplane of this size along the floor several feet.

Having finally decided the question of power, it remains to attach the planes.

The remaining long strip is wired to the top pieces, 12 inches from the front, and the plane, made of silk, oiled paper, or very thin cardboard, attached.

In many toy aeroplanes the bands of rubber are not stretched, but twisted. The shaft in this case is a wire which, after being fastened to the propeller, passes through a glass bead and then the frame, ending in a hook to which the rubber bands are attached. There must be a perfectly clear space from front to back of the frame. The glass bead between the propeller and frame is to relieve the friction.

X

KITES

Making and experimenting with aeroplanes calls for much patience and often ends in disappointment—the lot of inventors generally. This is no reason why work should stop, as all progress is made by attempting the supposedly impossible, but it will be restful after a while to turn to the ancient and gentle art of kite making.

Incidentally, something may be learned about the effect of wind on plane surfaces that will prove helpful in aeroplane work.

The aeroplane kite shown in Fig. 50 is simple and effective. It may be given the appearance of a Blériot monoplane by modifying some of its features, as shown at *b*, the planes having a slight upward slant. The arrangement of the frames is clearly shown in the drawing. Spruce or white pine may be used, as lightness is an essential.

The method of fastening the sticks is important. It is not wise to halve them, as their strength will be reduced below the safety point, and nails are likely to split them. Bind them securely with strong linen kite cord or fine soft wire.

Kite *a* is open to criticism on account of the single stick connecting front and back. The second form is better, and the two long sticks may be correspondingly lighter without reducing the ultimate strength of the frame. The method of joining three sticks, as at the forward end, is shown in detail in Fig. 50. Wherever a butt joint occurs, join the two pieces by means of small strips of tin cut to size with a pair of tinsmith snips. Drill holes through tin and sticks, pass fine soft wire through the hole, and twist tightly with a pair of pliers.

The planes or sails may be of light, strong paper, or some light fabric, such as lawn or cheap silk. The fabric should be cut to size, allowing two inches each way for the hem. Pieces of cord are fastened to the hem, and tied to the ends of the sticks through small holes drilled for the purpose, or tied to notches cut with the knife.

The advantage of this method is that the sails, or planes, may be drawn tightly or removed without loss of time. In this way a number of fabrics can be used for experimental purposes. Paper, on the other hand, must be lapped over sticks and wires, and glued.

48

Propellers may be fastened to front, rear, or both, to create the appearance of a real aeroplane.

The restraining action of the cord holding one of these kites up against the wind brings into action the same force that supports the glider or aeroplane, and the sails, especially fabrics, assume the curve of a boat sail, when close-hauled and sailing into the wind.

The forms that are possible are infinite, and limited only by the imagination of the designer.

It is well to begin with one of the standard types, and leave experimental forms until some experience has been gained.

The Americanized Malay, Eddy, or parakite is shown in Fig. 50. The two sticks are of equal length, bound together with twine or soft wire. Distance $c\,e$ should be from 14 to 18 per cent. of the total length $c\,d$. The vertical stick remains straight, but cross stick $a\,b$ is bent back like a bow, the distance $e\,f$ being 10 per cent. of the total length of either stick, and maintained by a string from a to b. The four points $a\,c\,b\,d$ are joined by a cord drawn taut, to make sure that the sticks are at right angles.

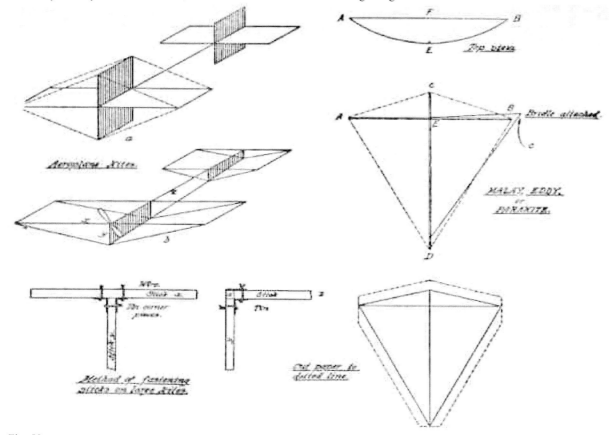

Fig. 50.

The material should be cut as shown, the amount lapped being uniform all around. This is important, as a slight difference in weight between the two sides would result in erratic flying. For Eddy kites up to three feet in height a light-weight wrapping paper will answer very well. Larger sizes require nainsook, lawn, or China silk. Like all the kites described here, this is a tailless one, and the method of fastening the bridle is shown. Make a small hole in the covering, pass a cord through, and tie it to cross the stick at its centre. Fasten the other end about half an inch from lower end of upright, and make a loop at o for attaching the line.

The kite line should be the light and strong linen twine made especially for this purpose, and sold by toy and sporting goods dealers. A ball containing 600 yards of cord, strong enough to hold any three-foot kite, will cost about fifty cents.

For larger sizes, it pays to make a reel, to save time drawing in and to avoid bad tangles. A simple form of reel is shown in Fig. 51.

The frame has a generous-sized hole bored as shown at h. Cut a small branch in the form shown, i, and use this as a stake. Drive it into the ground through h, and use it as a pivot to shift the reel as the wind changes. With this arrangement the kite cannot drag the reel, and it is possible to leave the apparatus with the kite in the air. The writer was driven to using this device after seeing his reel go tearing across the fields until stopped by a four-foot fence. The pull exerted at the reel by a train of three or four kites is sometimes sufficient to give a boy all he can do to hold it. The height to which a kite will go is illustrated by the diagram. S is the starting point, and $s\,t$ the direction of the string at the start, when but little cord has been played out. The position of the kite at various times is indicated by letters $a\,b\,c\,d\,e$, the actual path being shown by dotted line. The solid, curved lines from s to these points show the position of the cord as it is played out. This is a mathematical curve resulting from the weight of cord and kite, wind pressure on cord, and lifting power of the plane.

It will be seen that the kite finally moves along horizontally, no matter how much cord is played out. This occurs when the lifting power equals the force of gravity and wind pressure. In other words, the kite can do no more without an increase of wind.

To make it go higher, we must raise point s by tandem flying, attaching another kite and cord to the first one, as shown at x.

49

Three or four Eddy kites may be flown in this way, the lines of equal or unequal length joined at a common point to the main line; and, strange as it may seem, if they are well balanced kites they will not interfere with each other. In fact, there seems to be an electrical repulsion among the lines, so that they spread out like a broom.

This is one of the most interesting discoveries in kite flying, though badly upset in actual practice, when one member of the team becomes erratic and proceeds to make a braid of the four cords by diving under and over the others to bring about a general demoralization. For this reason, it is wise to test each kite separately, first, to discover any possible tendency to freakishness.

A weird experience may be enjoyed by leaving the tandem out after dark. Run the main line down by slipping it under your arm, and walk out until you reach the junction of the four lines, where a light-weight lantern can be attached. Let go, and see the lantern apparently drawn up into the air by noiseless, invisible hands.

Flags and other devices may be attached as indicated in the drawing; a light stick at *a b* will keep the flag from blowing up into a heap, and loops at *a* and *c* are tied in the main line to avoid sliding.

THE BOX KITE

The cellular kite is made in several forms. The rectangular box variety is perhaps the most common, and with the bridle attached is shown in Fig. 51. The standard dimensions are: length *a b* 79 inches, width *a c* 78 inches, depth of cell *c d* 32 inches, and width of cloth covering *c e* 25 inches. A very convenient size is obtained by dividing approximately by two, making length and width 40 inches each, and depth 16 inches.

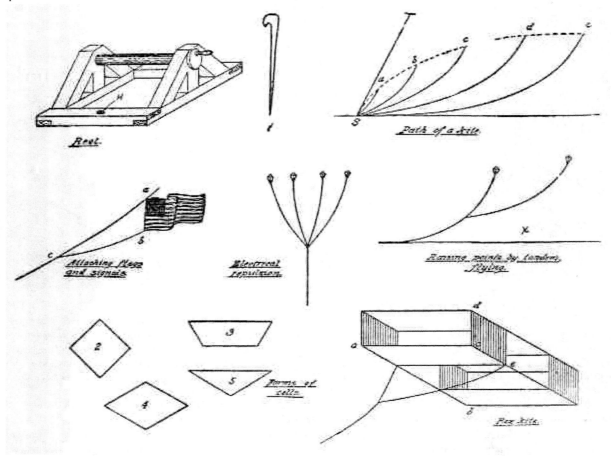

Fig. 51. Kite details

Mr. H. H. Clayton, of the Blue Hill Observatory, has patented one form of this kite known as the "Blue Hill Naval Box Kite," so the amateur must confine his use of it to experimenting. Other forms of cells which have been used are shown at 2 3 4 5. These all possess the advantage—that each plane is a lifting surface, whereas in the rectangular form the vertical planes have only a rudder action, tending to hold the kite parallel with the wind.

When launching a box kite, the assistant stands in front of and under it, while with the Malay he stands behind it and lets go at a given word. About a hundred yards of line should be run out before launching, and only a few steps backward by the boy at the string should be necessary. Running is only required when the line out is insufficient.

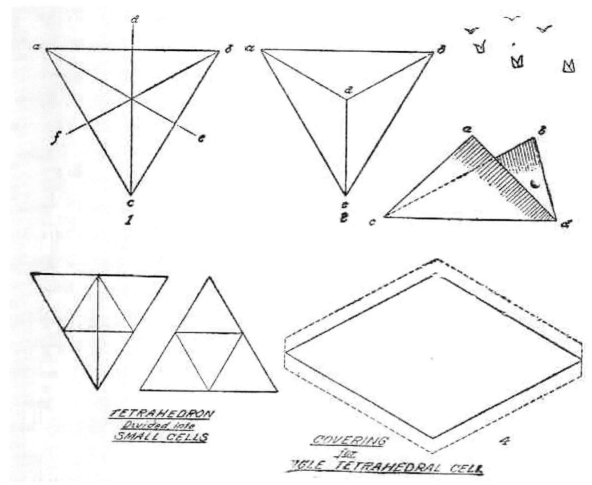

Fig. 52. The tetrahedral kite

The tetrahedral form invented by Dr. Graham Bell is unique and interesting. Based on the geometrical figure, it has a remarkable strength of frame, and possesses a surprising lifting power. The principal difficulty in the construction is in fastening the sticks, as three of them meet at every point. The frame consists of six pieces of equal length. Drill a $\frac{1}{32}$-inch hole in each end of all the pieces, about $\frac{1}{4}$ inch from the end. Place the pieces on the floor as shown at 1. Pass a piece of soft iron or brass wire through the three holes at a and bind lightly. Do the same at angles b and c. Now raise loose ends $d\,e\,f$ until they meet over the centre, as at 2. Join with wire and tighten all the joints with a pair of pliers. (Fig. 52.)

Each face of the frame is an equilateral triangle, and the covering is to be on only two sides, as shown at 3. The shape of the piece to be cut is shown at 4. This forms a single cell, and the large sizes are broken up into many small tetrahedral cells. The line may be tied at c or d.

The designing of fancy figure kites is a fascinating occupation, but unless certain fixed principles are kept in mind may end in much experimenting and many disappointments. The question of steadiness or stability seems to be summed up in the mathematical expression—"dihedral angle."

A kite having a stiff, flat surface presented to the wind will often cut up queer antics, while the same frame covered with a more flexible covering will fly beautifully. The reason is that the flexible covering will be bowed back by the wind, forming an approximate "dihedral angle."

In the triangular box and tetrahedral kites this bowing back is not so necessary, because the dihedral angle is provided in the construction.

In these kites, when a sudden gust of wind presses harder on one side than on the other, the first side is pressed back, reducing the resistance, and the other side is brought forward until both sides receive equal pressure, or the kite is in equilibrium, facing the wind; and the shifting of the breeze is constantly provided for. The bowing back of the covering of an Eddy kite takes care of sudden changes in the same way. Double Malay kites or two tetrahedral kites, fastened together, tandem fashion, will be found stable, especially if the rear one be slightly smaller than the forward one. (Fig. 53.)

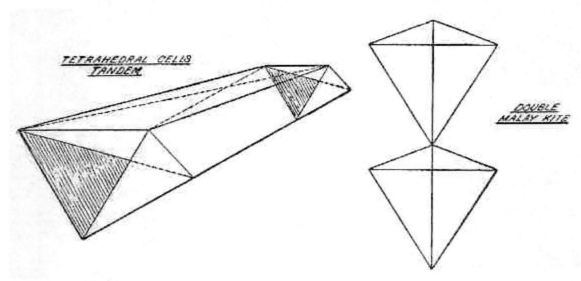

Fig. 53. Double kites

Geometrical forms like the hexagon, six-pointed star, and even the circle are used, but these generally require a tail.

A butterfly design may be used, provided the body is designed as a keel and the two wings are tilted backward to provide the required angle. In some of the Chinese kites, in the form of insects, the wings have split bamboo frames, flexible enough to bend backward and provide the necessary stability. A flexible lower end on the frame also has a good balancing effect.

XI

CHIP CARVING AND KNIFE WORK

"Making moving toys is a form of dissipation," said Ralph. "It is very fascinating and interesting, but the making of many toys will never make one an expert woodworker. The accuracy and skill required can be developed only by actual constructive work. I suggest that we take up a form of decoration which can be done with the knife.

"There are two ways of making an article in wood pleasing to the eye. One is by varying the outline, as we did in our match scratchers, and the other is by some kind of surface ornamentation. There are many ways of decorating surfaces—carving, pyrography, staining, polishing, etc., and very often several of these methods are combined.

"As we have started to learn the possibilities of knife work, I propose to teach you a form of carving which can be done with the knife alone. Very elaborate work is done with the regular carving tools. This requires a great deal of time and skill, but with the knife alone a wonderful variety of beautiful work can be done even by small boys.

"It is very important to approach it properly, so I am going to give you a few simple exercises and the elaborate designs will come along naturally.

"The work is not new, and evidently grew out of the still older art of notching. Primitive peoples probably saw in it a way to improve the appearance of their various wooden implements. Not only could the edges be notched, but the cutting could be done on flat surfaces as well."

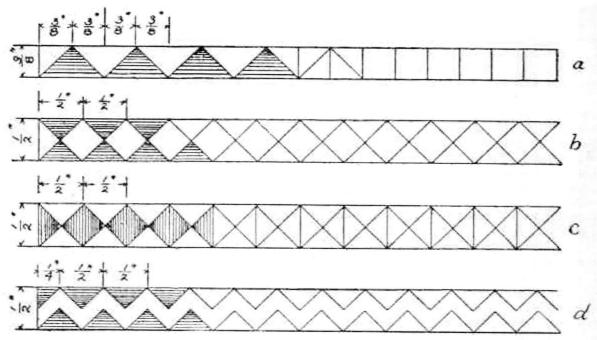

Fig. 54. First cuts in carving

Fig. 54 at *a* shows one of the earliest designs. It is simply a border of triangular cuts, and while this may be done with the whittling knife, Fig. 55 shows two knives which are better fitted to do accurate work.

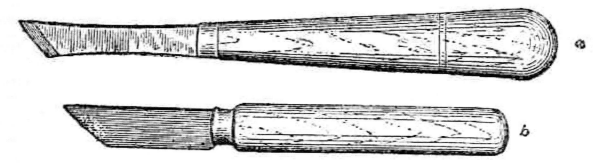

Fig. 55. Two good types of knife for carving

The positions for carving are shown in Fig. 56. Hold the knife in an upright position, with the cutting edge away from you, and the point on the apex of the triangle. Press the knife down and then away from you along one of the sides of the triangle. Place it in position again, and repeat the motion along the other side of the triangle, always directly on the line. This brings the deep part of the cut at the apex of the triangle, and it remains to take out the triangular chip. This can be done in either of the two ways shown in Fig. 56, by cutting away from you or toward you. It is well to practise both ways, as in complicated designs the direction of the grain makes it necessary to cut sometimes in one direction, sometimes in another.

The rest of this border is a repetition of the same stroke, and the more elaborate designs are simply different arrangements of triangular cuts.

In Fig 54, *b* shows two rows of these same shaped cuts, one row inverted, to produce a diamond-shaped border; *c* shows a border in which the drawing is similar to *b*, but vertical triangles are cut instead of horizontal ones, as this gives a cut across the grain of the wood instead of parallel to it, and is a trifle harder.

53

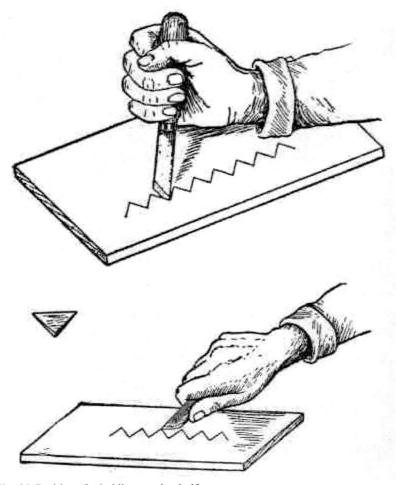

Fig. 56. Positions for holding carving knife

Our boys practised on these simple borders for awhile, using knife *a* and ¼-inch basswood. The work proved fully as fascinating to Harry as the making of toys, and it was decided that from that time onward the outlines of their woodwork should be simpler, and the decoration should be in the form of chip carving.

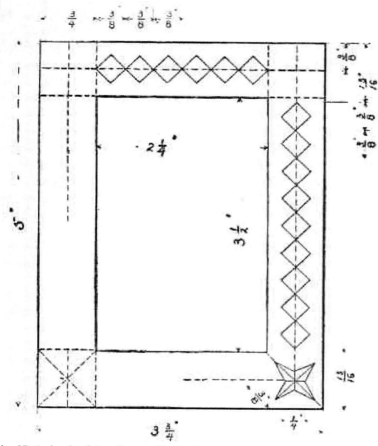

Fig. 57. A simple picture frame with carving

While Harry was practising on these simple borders Ralph made the basswood photograph frame shown in Fig. 57, and drew the carving design, as shown, with an H pencil.

To carve this was simply to repeat border *b*. This was so satisfactory that Ralph decided to try his pupil on finer work, and the design shown in Fig. 58 was tried. In each case Harry found that he was making triangular cuts, and removing triangular chips, just as in the first border, only the triangles were in different positions. Ralph suggested that they begin to decorate some of the things they had already made, and the little basswood box shown in Fig. 33 was brought out, and the design shown in Fig. 59 drawn and carved upon it.

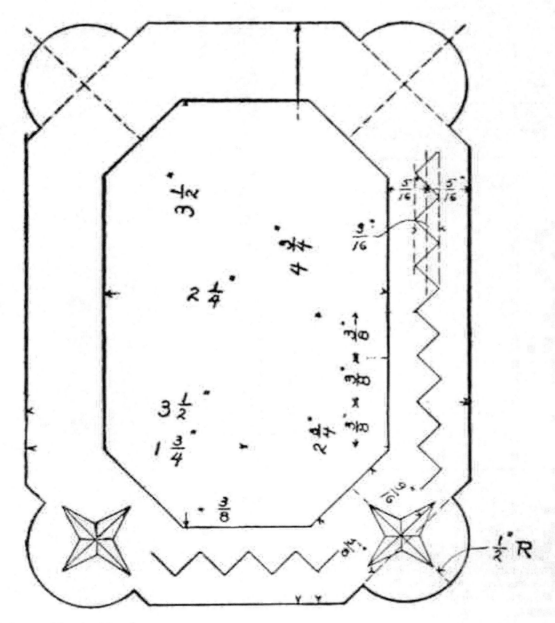

Fig. 58. A more elaborate picture frame

There followed a number of "backs," which Ralph explained could be used as thermometer backs, match scratchers, calendars, key racks, and in other ways. In each case, the design was drawn carefully on paper, and thence transferred to the surface of the wood with the same care that it had been done on paper. The designing required considerable thought.

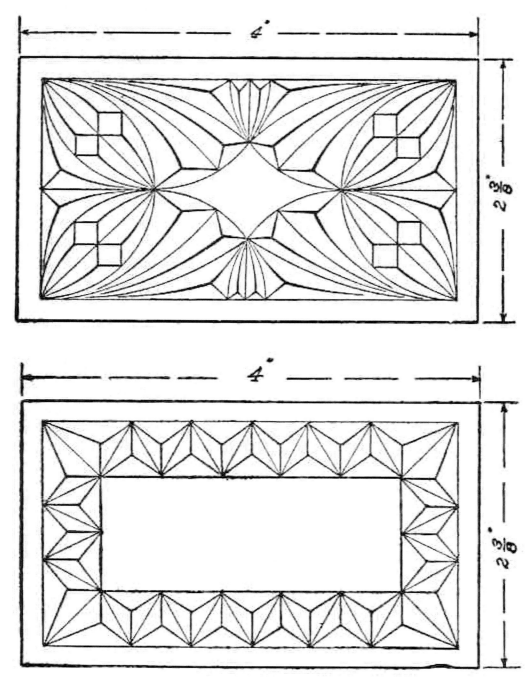

Figs. 59 and 60. Designs for box covers

Where a border continued around four sides, the corner became the most difficult and interesting part of the design, and was worked out first. (Fig. 61.)

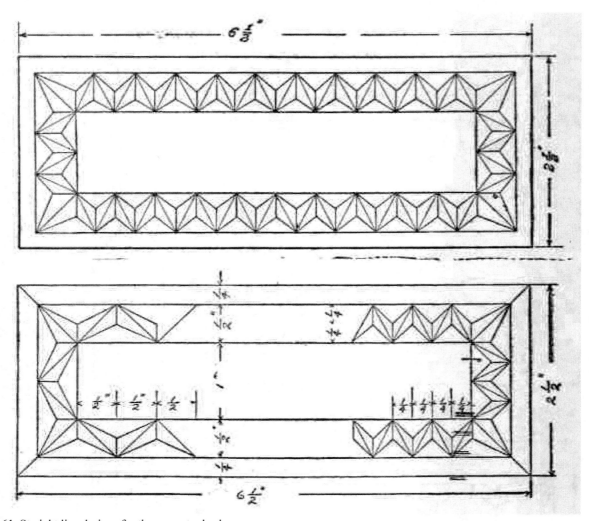

Fig. 61. Straight line designs for thermometer backs

Very soon the boys found that it was necessary to draw only half the design on paper, and in many cases a corner or quarter sufficed.

The next step was to initiate Harry into the mysteries of curved cutting, a departure from triangular cutting.

He was informed that the cuts were still three-sided, one or two of the sides being but slightly curved.

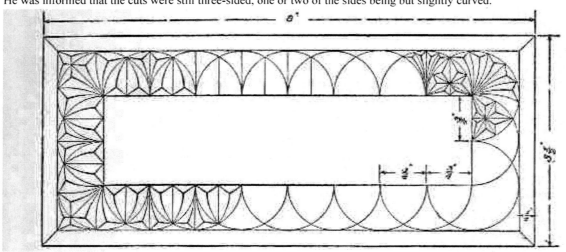

Fig. 62. Curved cuts.

Fig. 62, used as an enrichment of a "back" in ⅜-inch gum wood, was Harry's first effort in curved chip carving. The edges of the blank piece were bevelled with a plane and Ralph showed his pupil how to do this by holding the blank against a bench hook. The long sides were bevelled first, the ends last, to avoid breaking off the corners.

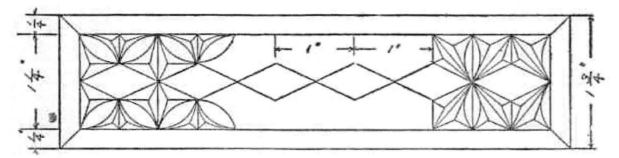

Fig. 63. Key rack

The key rack (Fig. 63) gave an opportunity to use centre pieces inside a border, diamonds of the flat surface being left uncarved for the placing of the screw hooks.

A pencil box for school followed, the various pieces being shown in Fig. 64. The two sides and ends were made in one strip 1¼ inches wide, and afterward cut to length. To secure this strip of uniform width, the shooting board shown in Fig. 65 was used, the plane being laid on its side, giving the ¼-inch piece of gum wood a perfectly square edge.

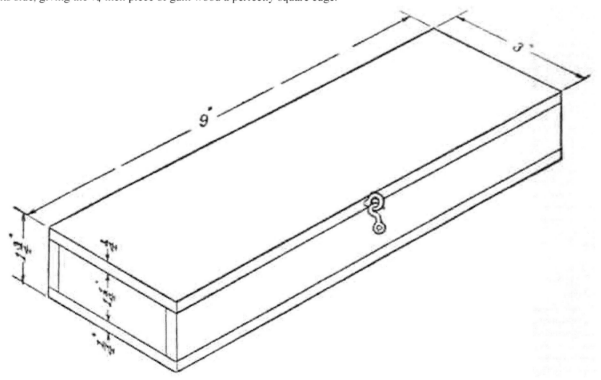

Fig. 64. The pencil box

Ralph was having his own troubles as a teacher about this time, for he wanted to reserve Harry's education in the use of bench tools until later on, when he should have exhausted the possibilities of the knife; but this method of using the plane was necessary if Harry was to produce blank forms fit for decoration.

The six pieces being squared up, a ¼-inch margin was left on all sides of the pieces to be carved—the top, front, and two ends.

This ¼-inch space was for the brads.

Fig. 65. Use of shooting board

The assembling was not done until the carving had been finished, and it consisted of fastening the long sides to the ends with ⅝-inch brads, with a little glue on the end grain of the end pieces. The bottom was put on with brads, and the top hinged to the back by two small nickel-plated hinges. A little hook and eye from the hardware store were put at the front to hold the cover on, and two small cleats were glued to the under side of the cover to keep it from warping.

The time spent on this pencil box was several hours, but the result was a box the like of which could not be bought.

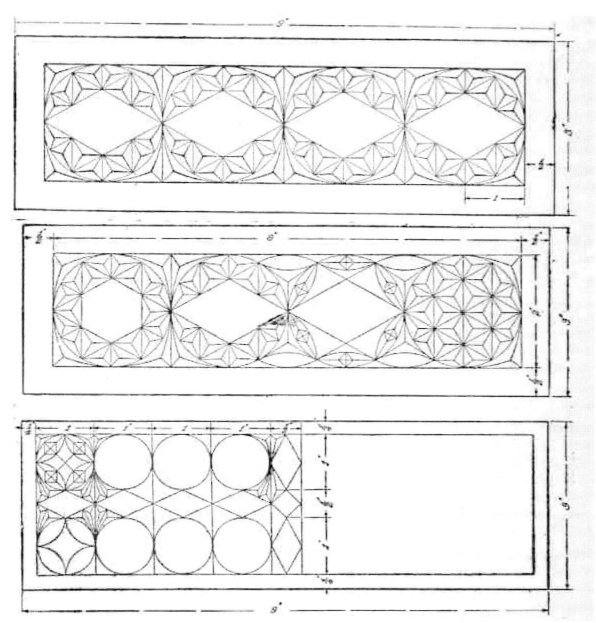

Fig. 66. Carving designs for pencil box

Pencil boxes became the rage with our boys, and although they made several of the same size, in each case the design was different. (Fig. 66.)

XII

CHIP CARVING: Continued

Among the many useful articles which can be made with the knife in thin wood, with carving as enrichment, are the numerous desk accessories, such as envelope holders, letter racks, stamp and pen boxes, pen trays, blotting pads, etc. The boys, after exhausting the subject of pencil boxes for school use, took up the design and construction of letter racks. These, they decided, should be in two compartments for answered and unanswered letters. This called for three uprights, or partitions, and a base. They decided to make them of about uniform dimensions, as shown in the blank form (Fig. 67). The problem of the outline was somewhat affected by the fact that the front was to be carved. This called for a simpler outline than would have been the case had they expected to leave the surface plain. Some of the designs they worked out are shown in Fig. 68.

61

The form marked *a* was selected as a beginning, the three partitions cut out exactly alike, and the front piece carved as shown in Fig. 69. The middle partition and back piece were left with plain surfaces.

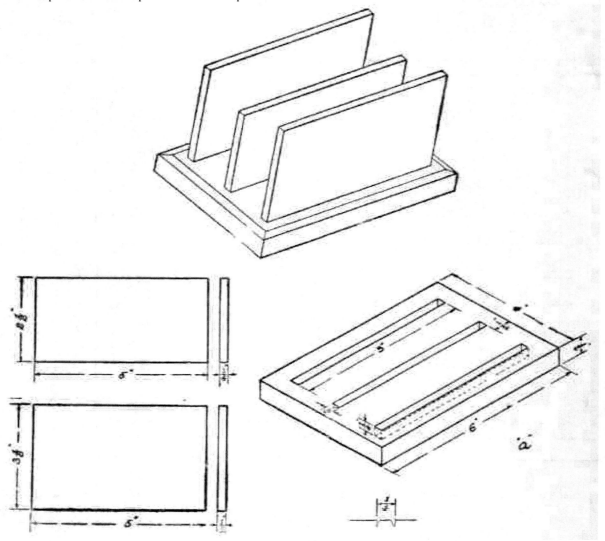

Fig. 67. Parts of letter rack

The cutting of the grooves in the base was a new problem, and Harry was allowed to try his skill with a chisel. The method used was first to make the drawing shown at *a*, Fig. 67. The long side lines of each groove were scored with the point of the knife, going over each line several times, to make the cut as deep as possible. An under cut was then made, as shown in the figure.

Fig. 68. Boys' designs for letter racks

The wood in the centre was removed with a ¼-inch chisel, and the process continued until a uniform depth of ¼ inch was reached. After all three grooves had been cut, the edges of the base were bevelled with the plane. This bevelling could have been done readily with the knife, but much time was saved by using the plane, always doing the long sides first.

In all the letter racks shown in the illustrations the construction was the same. First, the three blank partitions were made, then finished in their outlines with knife and sand-paper. The carving was always drawn carefully on the surface of the front piece. Third, came the making of the base, and last, the gluing of the partitions into the grooves. To increase the strength of a letter rack, ¾-inch brads can be driven from the bottom into the partitions, but where this is done it is safer to draw pencil lines on the bottom directly under the centre of each partition. Place the point of the brad exactly on the line before hammering.

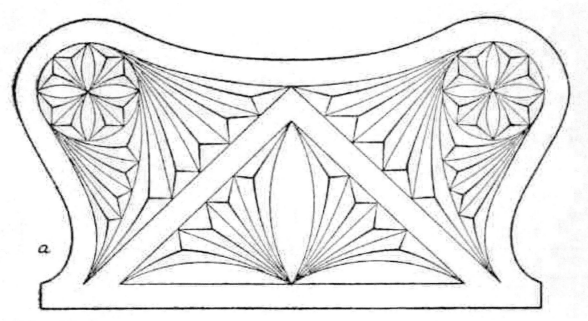

Fig. 69. Form "A"

Although the forms of the letter rack are endless, the one which our boys found most interesting was based on the ellipse. It called forth a very instructive drawing lesson. Ralph showed Harry first how the figure could be drawn by a string, with two pins to represent the foci of the ellipse. The figure has two dimensions called the major axis and minor axis. (Fig. 70).

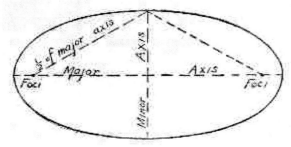

Fig. 70.

The combined length of the two lines drawn from any point on the ellipse to the two foci must always be the same and equal to the length of the major axis. This is readily seen with the two pins and string. (Fig. 71.)

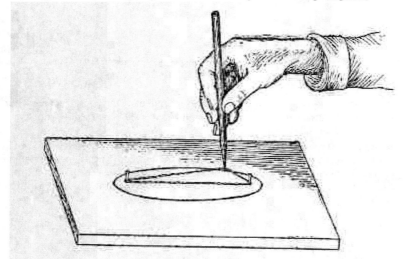

Fig. 71. Drawing the ellipse with string and pins

The pencil point as it traverses the ellipse represents any point, and the string remains the same length. Where it is required to draw an ellipse of definite size, say two by three, it becomes necessary to find the foci before the string can be used, and as it requires considerable skill to get the string the exact length, Ralph showed the boy another way, called the trammel method. (Fig. 72.)

Suppose the problem is to construct an ellipse 6 inches × 2½ inches. First draw the two lines *a b* and *c d* at right angles, intersecting at the exact centre. Take a straight piece of paper, lay it along *a b* with one end at *a*. Make a dot on the edge of the paper where the lines cross, and mark it *x*. Next, lay the same strip of paper along *c d*, with the original end at *c*, and again mark a point where the lines cross. Mark this point *y*. At any position of this strip of paper when the points *x* and *y* touch the two axes *a b* and *c d*, the end of the paper strip will be on the ellipse. By shifting this paper trammel and keeping the two points on the axes a series of points may be made at the end of the paper. Connecting this by a pencil line will complete the ellipse. This is a very simple method and a very accurate one.

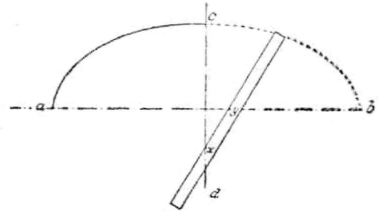

Fig. 72. The trammel method

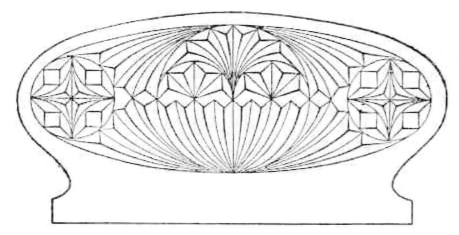

Fig. 73. The ellipse used in carving designs

Our boys drew this figure, 6 × 2½ inches, with a trammel and then worked out the design from it shown in Fig. 73. It made a very satisfactory form for the letter rack, and gave an elliptical space for carving, a new problem in chip carving design.

Fig. 74.

Two more of these elliptical designs are shown in Fig. 74.

Another feature of this rack was a change in the middle partition; the form is shown at Fig. 75. The making of the base and gluing into the grooves were similar to the earlier designs.

The next design was characterized by an outline composed largely of straight lines.

The middle partition was lower than the front and back pieces, as shown in Fig. 75.

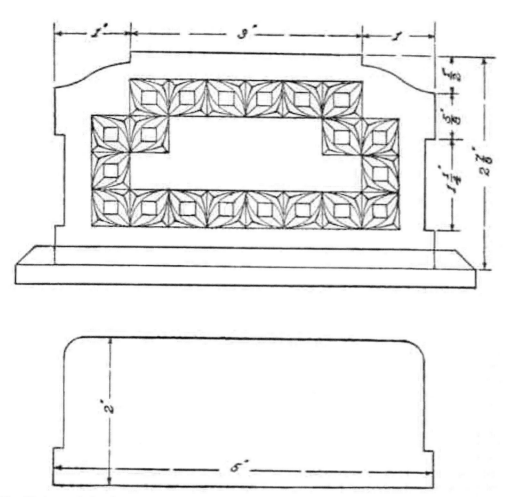

Fig. 75. A neat design for a letter rack

The boys found a great deal of pleasure in working out a decorative scheme for the carving. Having discovered how easy it is to carve the long flowing curves, they introduced them wherever possible. The general shape of the carved section must of course conform to the outline of the wood, but while filling in these flowing curves they soon learned to sketch them in free-hand.

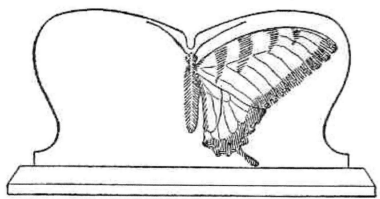

Fig. 76. A letter rack decorated with the veining tool

To a person who has not tried this work or who has not begun with simple cuts it appears very difficult, but when it is remembered that only one cut can be made at a time and that each chip is a triangle, even if its sides are slightly curved, it actually proves very easy, and within the power of any normal boy to accomplish.

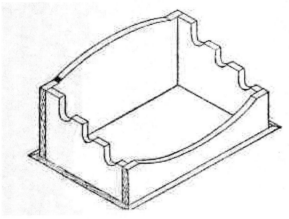

Fig. 77. The pen-holder

Harry was introduced at this time to the use of the veining tool, a fine gouge with a cross section almost V-shaped. This was used to emphasize the outlines of the designs by simply pushing ahead directly on the lines. When veining straight lines, it may be guided by a ruler or other straight edge, but for curves, a free-hand movement is necessary. A very good practice piece is the design shown at Fig. 76. This may be applied to the front of the letter rack design. (Fig. 69.)

The pen-holder shown at Fig. 77 is one of a large number which were made by the boys. The pieces were cut out with a knife to the blank forms shown. On all pieces like these, afterward to be assembled, the edges were made straight and square on the shooting board, and the carving done before assembling. This pen-holder was put together with ¾-inch brads with the exception of the front, which was glued, as it was thought best not to have nails showing on this important side. (Fig. 78.)

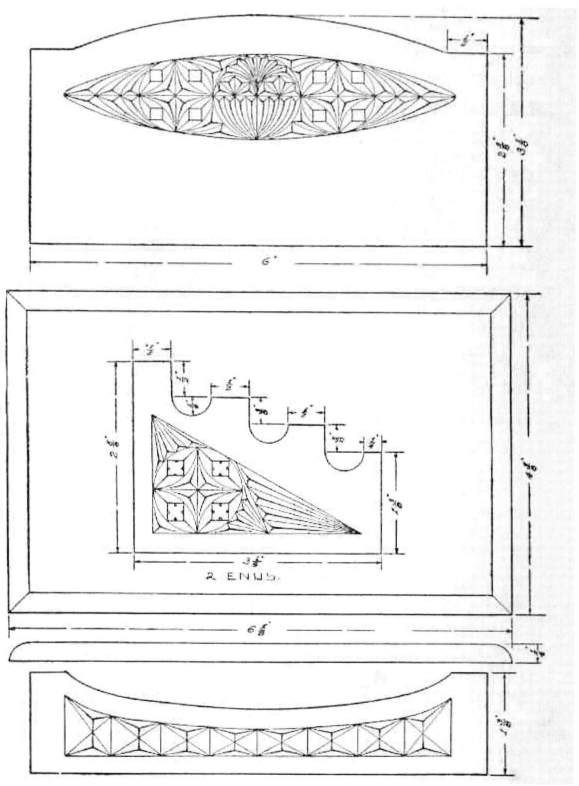

Fig. 78. Pieces composing pen-holder

Photograph by Arthur G. Eldredge
Using the Veining Tool.

XIII

CHIP CARVING AND KNIFE WORK (See 31, 109)

"I like this new work better than anything we have ever done," said Harry one day when he and Ralph were up to their ears in carving, whittling, and designing.

Ralph smiled as he remembered Harry's intense interest in making moving toys. "As I told you once before," he replied, "this is not new but old. The people of northern Europe have done it for centuries, and the reason is not hard to find. In Norway during the long winter it gets dark very early, in some places at three o'clock in the afternoon, and does not become light again until nine o'clock in the morning. The result is very, very long evenings, when it is much more comfortable to work indoors.

"At an early era the people developed this beautiful art of carving, and spent their long evenings in working at it. They became very skilful and as most of the household utensils were of wood, it was not at all unusual to see the household furniture, even to their bread boards, beautifully carved."

"By the way," said Harry, "can't I make a paper knife now? You know you said I could after I had learned to use the knife!"

"Yes, I think you might try your skill on something of that character now. It will be quite a change from this flat work we have been doing. It will require a harder wood, however, than you have been using, as a paper knife must be thin and strong at the same time.

"The Swedish carvers use apple wood a great deal for their paper knives, but as this is rare with us, suppose we try rock maple. It is white in colour, close grained, and hard."

As usual, they worked up their design on paper first and sketched in the carving shown in Fig. 79.

A piece of rock or sugar maple was first squared up and laid out in pencil as shown at *B*. In order to get the outline to conform exactly to the drawing, the form was cut out of paper and traced on the face of the wood. The blank form was then whittled out to the pencil line, and sand-papered smooth as shown at *c*.

Maple proved to be a hard wood to whittle.

Notches were cut at *d d* after drawing the edge view on front and back edges. The blade and handle were then whittled down to lines *e* and *f*.

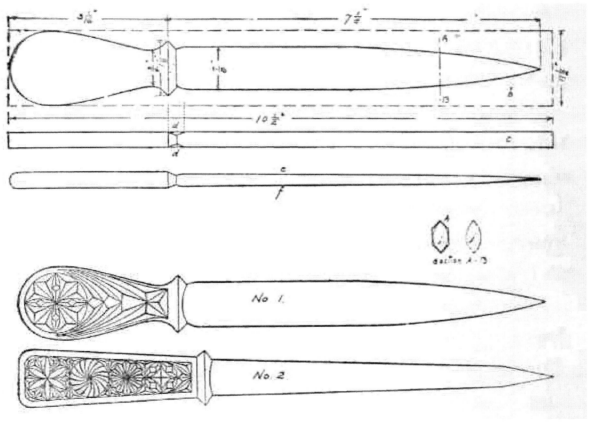

Fig. 79. Two designs for paper knives

"Whew!" exclaimed Harry, "don't ever give me any maple to whittle again."

"Well, you wanted to make a paper knife, didn't you? A paper knife that would break when it fell on the floor wouldn't be of much use, and you are not through yet. The blade must be cut down to a fairly sharp edge on both sides now."

This was done by bevelling the edges as shown in *h* and the bevel gradually cut back to the centre line, as shown at *i* and *j*. Harry concluded that this was the hardest work that he had ever done.

71

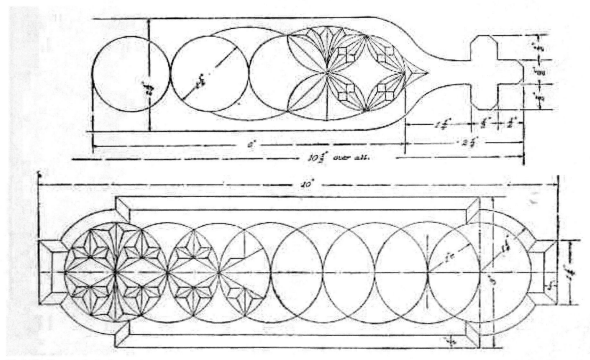

Fig. 80. Key rack designs

"Now you understand," said Ralph, "why I couldn't allow you to make a knife at first. All the training I have given you was necessary before you had the requisite skill and control of your hands. The carving will be easy for you because of all this practice. Skill is something which comes that way. Why, if I should give you the problem of making that first key rack over again, you would do it in about one third of the time, and very much better than at your first attempt. You have been gaining skill without knowing it.

"Just to show you how much you have advanced, I will give you one or two key rack designs to be decorated with chip carving. When they are finished, take them into the house and compare them with the first you made. I think you will be amused at the difference. That original piece of which you were so proud will seem a very crude affair now."

"All right," said Harry, "but I should like to make one more paper knife first if you don't mind."

"Very well; make up a new design, because no artist ever duplicates his work," said Ralph with a mischievous smile.

The smile was premature, however. The boy had not been designing woodwork for nothing. The design is shown at No. 2, Fig. 79, and even Ralph, severe critic though he was, had to admit that it was "pretty fair."

"Looks like a table knife," he said seriously. "However, it is your own design, so go ahead and make it. Try a piece of cherry this time. It makes a good wood for carving, and is not quite so hard to whittle as maple."

The different steps in the process of cutting this out were the same as in No. 1, Fig. 79.

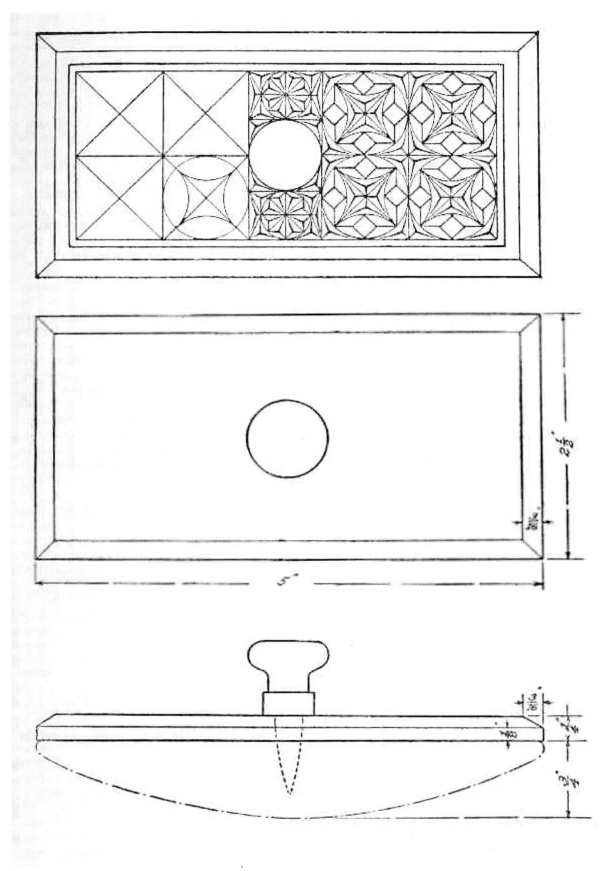

Fig. 81. The blotter pad

The key rack shown in Fig. 80 was comparatively easy after making paper knives. The bevelling of the curves at the ends was the only new feature of the knife work.

Fig. 82. Method of using the spokeshave

The making of presents went rapidly onward from this time. The next article to engage our woodworkers' attention was the blotting pad, made of two pieces of black walnut fastened together with the screw handle. (Fig. 81.) The blotter is bent around the curved face of the lower part, and the ends gripped between the two parts by tightening the screw. These handles with screw attached are of brass, and can be obtained at any hardware store.

The upper piece was bevelled, and a circular space in the centre left plain to provide for the handle, the rest of the space being carved.

The making of the curved face on the bottom was too difficult for the knife, so the boy worked it out with the plane and spokeshave shown in (Fig. 82).

When these blotter pads are finished with the brass handle, coloured blotter and hand-carved top, they are very attractive, and make acceptable presents.

Toilet boxes were next in order, and there seemed no end to them; glove boxes, collar boxes, handkerchief boxes, boxes for storing away photographs, etc. Those for collars were square, viewed from the top, while glove boxes were made long and narrow.

The construction of these called for the use of carpenters' tools, and Ralph was not ready to start his pupil on this branch of woodwork yet, for several reasons.

In the first place, it meant a halt in the fascinating work of carving, and they had not yet exhausted the possibilities of knife work. So they tried the plan of buying ready-made boxes from the stores. This was not entirely satisfactory, as most of them were of basswood, soft, and easily carved, but so white that it became soiled too readily. This difficulty finally led to a unique scheme. They stained the wood a dull ebony, and found that the design showed very clearly in gray pencil lines, easily carved.

The carving came out white on a black background, and proved quite satisfactory for the coarser designs. The finer work, however, did not show to advantage, and the method was adopted of leaving certain portions of the surface plain.

One of the glove box designs is shown in Fig. 83.

The lines made in this black and white carving by the veining tool are very effective.

Fig. 83. Design for glove box

The boys had just gotten nicely at work one afternoon when Harry remarked very seriously: "On what subject shall our lecture be this afternoon, professor?"

A block of white pine hurtled across the shop, but Harry ducked and no one was hurt.

"No," said Ralph, "you can't start a discussion to-day. I've been thinking that you will have to take up the use of bench tools pretty soon, because you are really doing this work backward."

"What do you mean?"

"Why, you should never decorate anything which you haven't actually made."

"Well, haven't I made everything we have carved so far?"

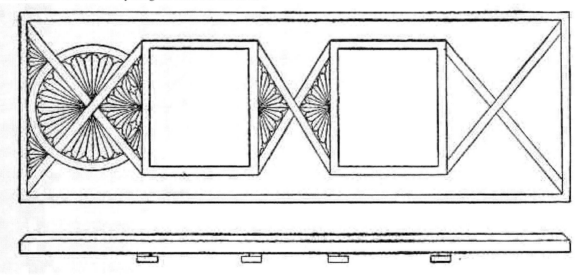

Fig. 84. Double photo frame

"All except the boxes. When we bought those boxes, that was a signal that it was time for you to begin constructive work. It has been a big problem to give you carving to do on articles in the flat that you could make with the knife. We will make a few picture frames, carve them, and then leave our carving until you can construct anything in wood. You will always be able now to design carved work for any given space; one of these picture frames, however, is going to be a rather severe test of your skill."

Fig. 84 shows the first photograph frame they took up, a simple design in one piece.

The openings for the pictures were cut out with coping saw and knife and bevelled. The bevels on the outer edges of the frame were planed.

Fig. 85. Carved picture frame

Fig. 85 shows a problem in designing for irregular spaces, and the design is a typical Swedish form. In both of these frames it was necessary to provide a method of holding the photo on the back.

This was accomplished by tacking on two strips of ⅛-inch basswood on each side, and the bottom as shown in Fig. 85, the narrow strip being ¼ inch wide, and the top one ½ inch wide, making a groove ⅛ inch deep to receive the picture. If it is designed to have glass in front of the photo, the narrow strip must be ¼ inch thick in place of ⅛ inch.

The problem of polishing carved work is rather a difficult one. Ordinary varnish or shellac cannot be used to advantage, as on flat surfaces, because it fills up the spaces and ruins the effect. Perhaps the best method is to dissolve a small quantity of beeswax in turpentine, and rub in with an old tooth or nail brush, which is comparatively soft. This will not injure the carving, and will protect it from dampness and dust, as the wax hardens. It should be put on when about the consistency of soft putty.

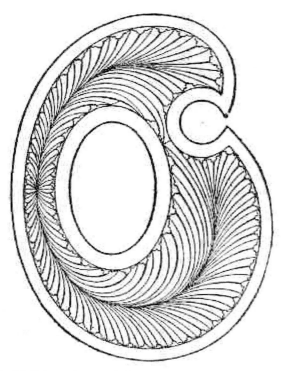

Fig. 86. Palette photograph frame

The photo frame shown (Fig. 86) was the last form our boys attempted in the flat.

It has the advantage of simplicity, only one kind of cut being used; but the long flowing lines, which must be first drawn on the wood free-hand, require all the patience and skill one can command.

The form in outline is the artist's palette, and the opening for the picture an ellipse.

All the lines in the carving converge to a point to the left of the centre of the opening.

XIV

THE SHOP

The man who is most successful is the one who is best prepared for his work. In beginning to learn how to use woodworking tools, the average boy is very often hampered by the lack of facilities. The place he is to use for his shop should at least have good light. Many of the lines he uses are knife lines, which are harder to see than pencil lines, so that light at least is an essential.

The tools should be as good as he can obtain. This does not mean that it is necessary to have elaborate sets of chisels, gouges, etc., but the cutting tools should be of well tempered steel. It is far better to have a few very good tools than an elaborate equipment of poor ones, such as the boy's ready-made tool chest often contains.

A good workman is one who can do a large variety of good work with a few well-selected tools.

One reason for our having given so much space to knife work was to illustrate this very fact. Very often the carved pieces described in previous chapters are salable at good figures, and from the money thus obtained a supply of bench or carpenters' tools can be bought.

Next to a well lighted place in which to work, a fairly good bench is essential. This can be made by the boy himself, if he cannot secure one already built, but as the construction of a bench presupposes some previous practice with tools, we will assume that our readers receive their first tool practice on a bench already built, just as Harry did.

Several forms of benches on the market are shown in Fig. 87.

The bench to be of any use must have a vise of some description, as very often both hands are required to guide the tool, and the wood must be held rigid.

The old-fashioned screw vise is cheap, and a cheap vise may be made at a cost of half a dollar, by purchasing the screw and nut and making the jaw and guides by hand, but this again calls for the use of a bench. So taken all in all it will pay the young woodworker to save his money and buy a good vise even if the bench is home-made.

This is just where our boys had their first argument; Harry wanted to begin by building a work bench.

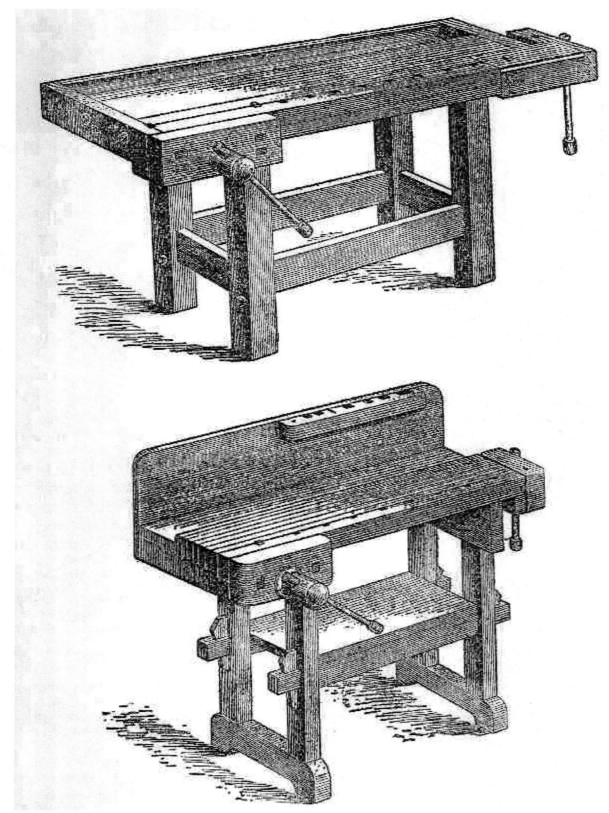

Fig. 87. Types of work bench

"That is where you are wrong," said Ralph. "Perhaps you remember that you wanted to begin knife work by making a paper cutter, and as a matter of fact it was very nearly the last thing I gave you to do. It required all your skill and previous practice to accomplish it. It will be just the same with the bench and vise. You will be able to construct them, but only after considerable experience with tools. You might as well insist on making all your tools before starting to use them or you might insist on going into the woods, cutting down trees and ripping out your own planks for stock. Just wait a minute."

He went into the house and came out with a pamphlet on lumbering, which he opened at the picture shown in Fig 88. It represents the old style of sawing out planks by hand before the coming of the saw-mill.

The man in the pit is called a pit man, the one on the log, the sawyer. This method of cutting lumber was in vogue up to about fifty years ago.

"This," said Ralph, "is what your line of reasoning would lead us back to, so if I am to be your instructor you must leave these things to my judgment, and my advice is to start work with a good bench having on it a good vise."

Fig. 88. The old way of getting out lumber

To let you into a family secret, the boys' work in carving had been admired by several friends and they had worked up quite a trade in making and selling their carvings. From the money they had saved they purchased the bench shown in Fig. 89. It was very well built, having a heavy top of 3-inch maple and a modern quick action vise. The seven drawers underneath were not really necessary, but the boys found them very handy for storing tools, nails, screws, unfinished work, etc.

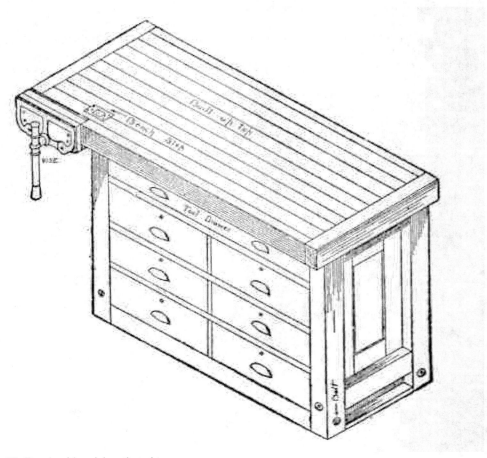

Fig. 89. Bench with quick action vise

The space under a bench is very apt to become a catch-all and a nuisance, so as time went on they concluded that the extra cost of this bench was justified, although at the time the price seemed very high. Some of the cheaper benches they looked at are shown in Fig. 87.

The quick action vise was a great time saver, as it could be pulled wide open or pushed back without turning the handle, as in the old screw vises.

A dozen of these quick action vises are on the market, and may be had at hardware stores for from four dollars upward.

This flat topped bench had no tool rack, and could consequently be worked on from any side. At first, the owners kept most of their tools in the large drawer at the top, but later on they made a good sized tool cabinet, which was fastened to the wall and will be described later.

The iron bench stop also proved a valuable feature, as it could be fastened at any desired height by a set screw, or dropped down out of the way below the level of the bench top. When planing thin wood, one end of the board is braced against the bench stop. Ralph found that starting with a new bench had another advantage. It helped his pupil to take good care of the bench. Harry was very careful not to saw or cut it as he might have done with an old bench, and to foster this spirit of carefulness, Ralph gave him for his first problem the making of a bench hook. (Fig. 90.) The tools used in its construction were:

24-inch rip saw	Brace and ¼-inch bit
20-inch cross cut saw	Countersink bit
Marking gauge	1½-inch flat head screws
Try square 6 inches	Piece of maple, planed to ⅞-inch
15-inch jack-plane	thick, 12 inches long, 10 inches wide

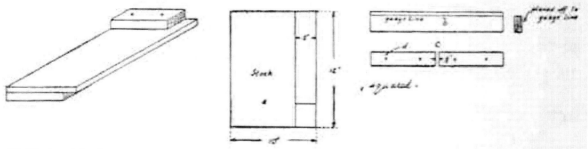

Fig. 90. The bench hook

The maple board was first laid out as shown at *a*, a pencil line being drawn 2 inches from one edge. The piece was placed in the vise horizontally, and both long edges planed straight and true and tested with the try square.

The block was then placed upright in the vise, and the ends planed square with the block plane. This required much explaining and practise, as the block plane has a bad habit of breaking off the farther corner.

Ralph showed Harry how to use this tool safely by planing only part way across the end and then finishing from the other side. Both ends were tested with the try square.

The piece was now sawed in two by using a rip saw on the pencil line, the wood being held in the vise in an upright position.

This made two pieces of stock 12 inches long, one 2 inches wide, the other 8 inches nearly, as the saw cut had removed some of the wood.

The 2-inch piece was laid out as shown at *b*. The marking gauge was set at $1\frac{3}{4}$ inches and from the joint edge—that already planed—a line was gauged on each flat face, and the sawed edge planed to these lines as at *b*.

It was then laid out as shown at *c*, two knife lines being squared around the four sides $\frac{1}{8}$ inch apart. The piece was then sawed apart carefully between these two knife lines, and the ends block planed and tested.

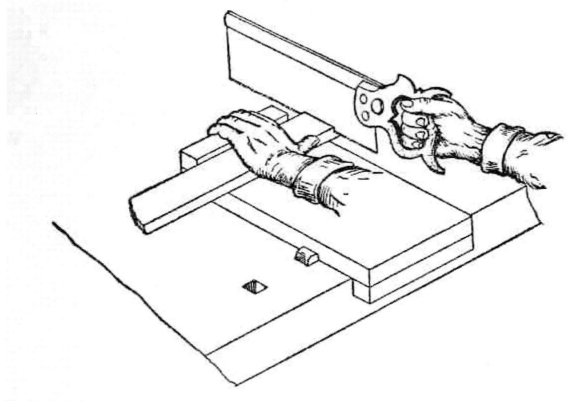

Fig. 91. Method of using the bench hook and back saw

Two $\frac{1}{4}$-inch holes were bored, as shown at *d*, in each piece, and countersunk with the countersink bit. This makes a place for the screw heads, so they will be below the surface where they cannot be in the way of tools or scratch the bench.

The wide piece was next planed on its sawed edge, and the blocks screwed on. That the bench hook might always be handy and have a definite place of its own, a half-inch hole was bored as shown in the illustration, and it was hung on a nail, set in the end of the bench.

The bench hook is designed to protect the bench from saw marks and the cuts of chisels, gouges, etc. The method of using it with the saw is shown in Fig. 91. Wherever possible, it should be made of hard wood.

XV

THE EQUIPMENT FOR A SHOP

Nothing is so necessary to the saving of time and energy as an orderly shop. Our boys had bought a quantity of white pine to begin operations and it was lying in a pile on the floor where it was always in the way.

To cut a piece of stock from one of these 12-foot boards it was necessary to use two kitchen chairs for trestles, so it was decided to construct two saw horses, and as soon as they were finished, to build a lumber rack against the wall where their little supply could be stored out of the way.

"We will carry out our regular practice by first making a drawing," said Ralph. "We know from experience that it saves time."

Fig. 92 shows the proportions of the trestle at a, and the mechanical drawing with all dimensions at b.

The body of the trestle was built up of four pieces, two long and two short ones. The open space in the centre, Ralph explained, would make a convenient tool rack where hammers, chisels, etc., could be placed while they were working, especially at outdoor work, instead of being dropped on the ground. The body then called for two pieces 3 feet long by 4 inches wide, and two pieces 10 inches long by 4 wide.

These were sawed from a rough plank with the rip saw by using the chairs as trestles. A pencil line was laid out $3\frac{1}{4}$ inches from one edge, and the saw cut made directly on the line, 8 feet long.

The cross cut saw was used to cut the strip off and this strip was then sawed with the same saw into four pieces of equal length for the legs. Another strip $4\frac{1}{4}$ inches wide, 7 feet 8 inches long, was ripped out and taken off with the cross cut saw, for the body, and divided into two pieces 3 feet 10 inches long, for convenience in planing.

Harry now had his first real experience in planing. All the pieces were of 1-inch rough lumber, with sawed edges, and had to be planed down to $\frac{7}{8}$ inch in thickness.

To plane six pieces of stock straight and true, with squared edges and of definite size, was no easy task.

"How do you like manual labour?" asked Ralph, mischievously.

"I like it all right," replied the perspiring boy, "but we won't need any gymnasium work for exercise while we are doing this."

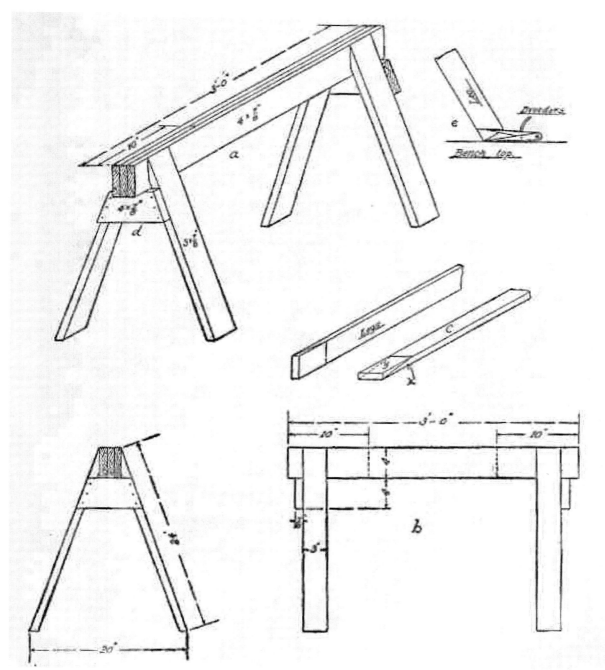

Fig. 92. The trestle or saw horse. By permission of Carpentry and Building

"Wouldn't you like to make a bench in hard wood right away?" asked Ralph.

"No, I guess you were right after all."

Ralph showed him the proper way to stand, and how to hold the jack-plane so as to get the best results. He promised to show him how to sharpen and adjust the plane as soon as the lumber was stored away on the lumber rack.

Harry's business was to dress down one of the flat faces of each piece till it was smooth, straight and true both with the grain and across it. He tested it by his eye and the edge of his plane and when he thought it was about right, passed it over to Ralph for criticism.

Ralph was a very exacting instructor, but made allowance for the boy's inexperience. He was making the second trestle at the same time and it was exasperating to Harry to see the ease with which he turned out his work.

"Never mind," said Ralph, "you can do as good carving now as I, and in a few weeks you will be able to do just as good joinery or carpentry. The first day is always the hardest. You are all impatience and want to get through right away. After a while you will learn by experience that you can only do one thing at a time, and will not rush so."

83

Photograph by Helen W. Cooke
Using the Jack Plane.

Finally, one face on each of the six pieces was pronounced finished, and the next step was to "joint" or "dress down" one edge straight, smooth and square with the working face—the first planed surface. This seemed easier after the experience of making the bench hook, and Harry knew how to test for squareness with the try square.

Working on the two long pieces for the body, both edges of each were squared up, a 10-inch piece was marked off on one end of each with pencil and try square, and sawed off with cross cut saw.

It was decided to leave the inner faces rough, as they would be inside the trestle, and out of sight. These four pieces forming the body were now nailed together with $2\frac{1}{2}$-inch wire nails, as shown in a.

The four pieces for the legs were dressed on all four sides, and it only remained to cut the angle at top and bottom.

This brought into use a new tool, the bevel. The angle x was found by laying the bevel on the mechanical drawing, and fixing it at the angle by tightening the set screw provided for the purpose. The line was carried across the face by means of the try square, and the bevel used on the farther edge. When this laying out was finished, the piece looked like c, the triangular piece y being removed by sawing directly on the pencil lines.

After the four legs were laid out in this manner and cut, they were nailed to the body with 3-inch wire nails.

The saw horse was now complete with the exception of the two braces, and the final truing up.

The braces were made by holding a piece of stock 4 inches × $\frac{7}{8}$ inch in position and marking the slope with a pencil, sawing to pencil lines and nailing in position d.

The final process of truing up was an interesting one to Harry, and he used it many times afterward in finishing pieces of furniture, such as tables, tabourettes, etc.

The horse was placed on the bench, and a pair of dividers set as shown at e.

A line was scribed on each leg wherever the compasses point touched it, holding the latter upright and going around all four sides of each leg. By sawing to the lines made in this way, the trestle was found to stand on the floor perfectly true. This is a method much used in truing up articles that rest on three or more legs, and it overcomes any inaccuracies that may have arisen in the process of assembling; but it is very important that the surface on which this truing up is done shall itself be perfectly true. The bench used in this case was new and had not yet warped at all, but an old bench might not have been suitable. This can be ascertained by testing the surface in several directions with a long straight edge.

The facts of warping and shrinkage in wood must always be taken into consideration.

The saw horse is an important part of every shop equipment, and the boys now relegated the clumsy chairs to the kitchen, where they belonged, and were prepared to saw out stock from their longest boards.

XVI

BUILDING A LUMBER RACK

Ralph had painted two signs and fastened them in prominent places on the wall. One read: "One thing at a time"; the other, "A place for everything, and everything in its place."

"Those are very old-fashioned," he said, "but they are none the less absolutely true. Many boys fail to accomplish anything in tool work because they do not heed the first, and more time is wasted than we ever realize, particularly among mechanics, by failing to observe the second. It often seems a waste of time to put a tool or piece of stock away in a definite place, but, on the other hand, one often spends ten times as many minutes in looking for a thing as he would putting it in its place where it could be found instantly."

"What's the answer?" said Harry absent-mindedly.

"The answer is that we will make a rack for our lumber before we do anything else.

"It need not be very fine work, but it will make our shop much neater, if the surfaces of the wood are planed instead of being left rough, and to give you practice in planing and to develop your muscles, I am going to let you do most of the planing, while I lay out the work."

The rack as finally constructed is shown in Fig. 93. The shop was not sheathed on the inside, the framework or studding being exposed. The short cross pieces were nailed to the studding with ten-penny wire nails, but where they joined the uprights they were let into the latter to a depth of $\frac{1}{2}$ inch before being nailed. Harry wanted to know what this was for, and Ralph explained that if the cross pieces were simply nailed to the uprights, all the weight would be carried by the nails. By letting or "gaining" them part way into the uprights, the weight was carried by the latter without so much strain on the nails.

"Then why don't you let them into the wall studs too?" asked Harry.

"Because the studs are in position and we couldn't saw them out without breaking through the outside of the building; therefore we are obliged simply to nail them on."

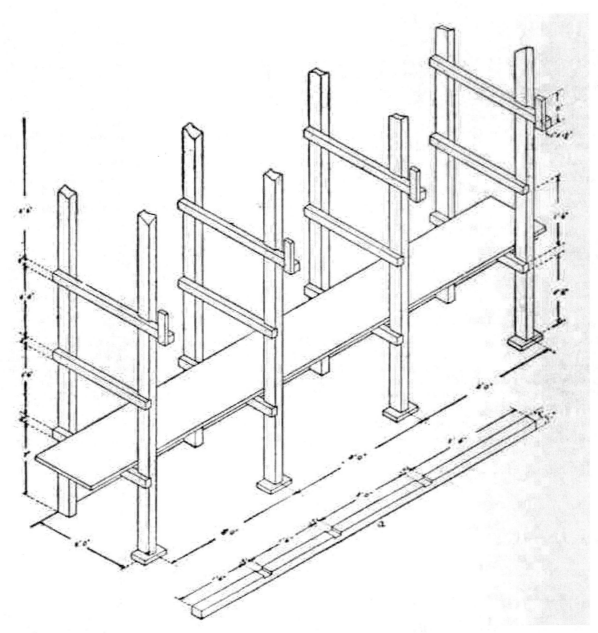

Fig. 93. The lumber rack

Four of the uprights were spaced three feet apart, and held in place at top and bottom by blocks nailed to the ceiling and floor. A carpenter would have simply "toe-nailed" them by driving nails at an angle through the ends of the uprights into the floor, but the boys were not yet skilled in carpenters' methods. An ideal lumber rack is made of galvanized iron pipe. It is indestructible, fire-proof, rather expensive, and the joints are regular pipe fitter's joints, elbows, tees, crosses, and floor plates.

This was beyond our boys' pocket-book, as it would have required the services of a pipe fitter.

One of the uprights laid out and partly cut is shown at a, the openings having been taken out with cross cut saw and chisel.

On one of the upper tiers the cross pieces were made eight inches longer than the others, and where they extended beyond the front of the rack pieces of pine 6 × 2 × ⅞ inches were nailed to the ends, making a convenient hook for hanging hand screws, which are always in the way on the floor. It also made a very convenient shelf for storing narrow waste strips of lumber, which should not be destroyed, as one can never tell when they will be needed.

In the case of a rack made of iron pipe, the ends of these long cross pieces need be only ordinary pipe elbows.

The labour of building a lumber rack was much heavier than anything the boys had done before, but it brought the larger muscles into play, seemed like real carpenter work, and was an excellent preparation for the finer tool work to follow. A boy who has never carried out a piece of large work successfully cannot realize the satisfaction of looking at a really good piece of construction and being able to say, "I made that all myself!"

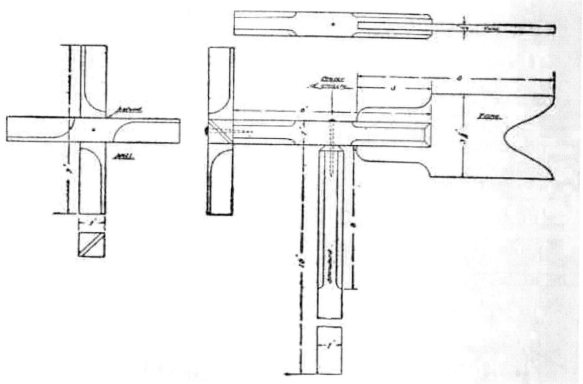

Fig. 94. First wind vane

Ralph suggested that one or two things more were needed to make their equipment ship-shape—one was a tool cabinet, and another was some arrangement for storing small pieces of stock; but as both of these required considerable tool practice, they were recorded in a notebook as among the things to be done later on.

It was agreed that the shop needed a vane to show the direction of the wind, and the boys' design for this is shown at Fig. 94. It included a weather vane and windmill.

The whole combination required five pieces of wood. The two short pieces, 7 inches long by 1 inch square, were first dressed to size, cut out and halved together as shown. They were then taken apart and cut to the lines shown, with a knife, making propeller blades similar to those made for the aeroplane. When both were finished, they were again put together, and a hole drilled through the centre a trifle larger than a flat-head wire nail 2½ inches long. This nail is to hold the mill to the horizontal piece. The nail is to be tight in this horizontal piece, but the windmill must revolve freely about the nail. It is for this reason that the hole in the mill must be slightly larger than the diameter of the nail.

The horizontal piece is bevelled on one end with the knife and has a ¼-inch slot sawed out at the other. The slot is to receive the wind vane. The vane was sawed out of ¼-inch wood, fitted into the slot and nailed with brads.

When all these parts were assembled, it was necessary to find the centre of gravity of the whole combination, as it is important that it be perfectly balanced.

To find the correct point, a light string was slipped under the horizontal piece and moved back and forth until the vane hung horizontally. The spot where the string touched the wood was marked with a pencil and a ¼-inch hole drilled at this point for the pivot. A corresponding hole was drilled 3 inches deep into the bevelled end of the standard.

A piece of ¼-inch maple dowel was used as a pivot, the upper end being sand-papered until the vane swung freely. The boys found that by placing a metal washer between the vane and its standard, much of the friction was removed. A wire nail driven into the standard through a hole drilled in the horizontal piece would have answered the same purpose as the dowel. When the centre of gravity is not found for the pivot, the vane is apt to tilt forward or backward and not only look badly, but bring considerable friction on one end, so that it will not revolve freely with the wind.

XVII

MILLS AND WEATHER VANES

The subject of windmills and weather vanes opened up a field that seemed inexhaustible, and for a while there was a perfect furore of designing and experimenting. As usual, Harry wanted to try great schemes that Ralph knew were impracticable, and it required all his diplomacy to keep the boy down to earth, on something simple and within his power to do successfully.

One of his earliest attempts was a scheme to make a windmill on the principle of a water-wheel, placed horizontally to catch the wind.

Ralph knew that it would not work, but after arguing for some time, he decided to let the youngster learn by experience. While Harry was working at his project, Ralph sketched out and made a vane which he considered an improvement on the first one. It is shown in Fig. 95; and it was made without a mill and composed of four pieces. The horizontal piece had an arrow head at the forward end. At the rear end, two pieces of ¼-inch pine were fastened with two small bolts. From the point where they were bolted they curved outward as shown in the top view, and were held in that position by two small strips nailed on with brads, one on the upper and one on the lower side. The centre of gravity was found as before, and the vane pivoted to its standard.

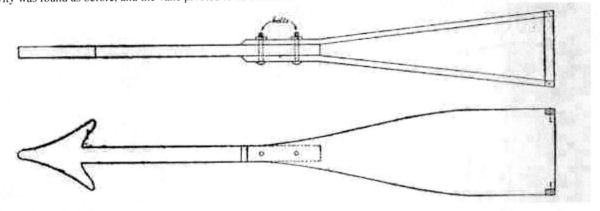

Fig. 95. Second wind vane

In the meantime, Harry had found out to his own satisfaction that his water-wheel windmill would not work.

"What have you curved those ends out for?" he exclaimed on catching a sight of Ralph's vane.

"Why, to make it more sensitive to the slightest breeze. Those curves catch the wind quicker than flat surfaces; have you never noticed that on the weather bureau vanes they are always curved out like that?"

"No," said Harry. "By the way, do you know why my mill doesn't work?"

"I have told you about six times that a water-wheel receives the water on one side only, while your mill receives the same pressure on both sides of the centre. The two forces balance, so your mill can't very well turn. If you could cut off the wind from one side, it would go all right."

"Well, why can't I box in one side?"

"You can, but then you will have to shift it every time the wind changes. You could construct a combination mill and vane, and arrange it so that the box would be shifted by the vane, but honestly, I don't think it worth the trouble. It would be clumsy, top-heavy, and hard to balance. I have a scheme for a horizontal mill, but we will take it up later. In the meantime, let's make a happy jack windmill!"

"Happy jack?"

"That's what they call them, but we will try to be original and I propose an Indian with war clubs."

"Whew! That sounds interesting!"

Ralph's sketch of the Indian is shown in Fig. 96. The figure was sawed out of ½-inch pine, a ⅜-inch hole bored for the arms, and a ¼-inch hole bored for the dowel pivot at the feet. The arms were made of a piece of dowel, six inches long, with ³⁄₁₆-inch holes bored near the ends to receive the "clubs." These were whittled out of pine, each club being a propeller blade. When fastened into the dowel they formed a complete two-bladed propeller, but this was not done until the dowel had been inserted through the Indian's shoulders, and a brad driven through on each side of the body to keep the arms in place.

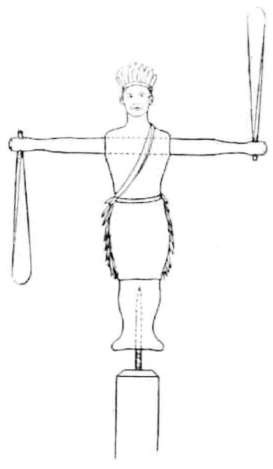

Fig. 96. Happy jack

Harry was so anxious to see it work that he came near spoiling it, and had to be restrained by the older boy, as in making these toys a well balanced figure is very important. When it was finally finished, and placed out in the wind, the antics of the Indian made Harry laugh till the tears ran down his cheeks.

"That's the finest thing we ever made," he said. Ralph smiled. It seemed that he had heard something like that several times before.

An athlete was suggested, and a bold figure with outstretched arms was sketched, as shown in Fig. 97.

The Indian clubs he is supposed to be swinging were propeller blades, and to give them more uniform motion than in the case of the Indian, the hands were drilled and a piece of ¼-inch dowel inserted. At each end of the dowel was fastened a blade which had been drilled to fit. Brads were driven through the dowel on each side of the hand to keep the clubs swinging freely.

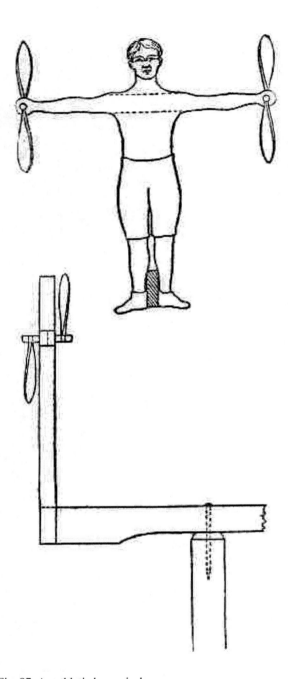

Fig. 97. An athletic happy jack

The body and arms were cut from a piece of ½-inch pine and halved together across the chest, and after the joint was made the form of the body and the arms whittled out with a knife. The two parts were then fastened together with brads.

It was important that this figure face the wind, so into the space between the ankles was fitted the small end of a wind vane and the figure securely fastened to it with brads. The centre of gravity was then found and the whole combination pivoted on a generous piece of ¼-inch dowel.

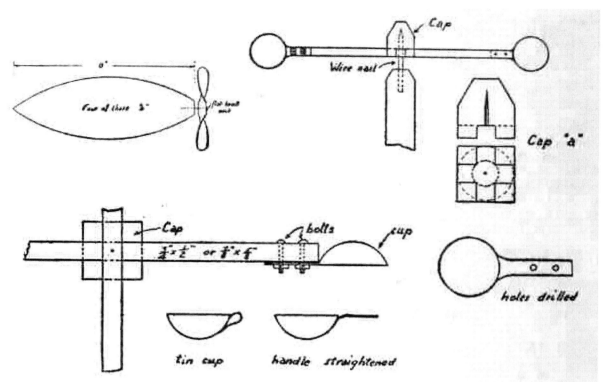

Fig. 98. The anemometer

This athletic weather vane is painted in bright colours, the clubs being gilded to make them realistic Indian clubs.

"What was that scheme of yours for a horizontal windmill?" asked Harry after he had watched the athletic club swinger until he was satisfied.

"Why, to make one on the principle of the anemometer," replied Ralph.

"How do you spell it?"

"Never mind the spelling, it's like this," and Ralph rapidly sketched out Fig. 98.

"This is the wind gauge of the weather bureau," he explained, "and I figure we can use ordinary tin cups for the buckets. You go down to the hardware store and buy four small round bottomed tin cups while I start the woodwork."

Having secured the cups for five cents each, they cut the handles with a pair of tinners' "snips." The cut was made next to the cup at the lowest point and the handle straightened out even with the top of the cup.

Two pieces of pine, 16 inches long, 7/8-inch wide, and 5/8-inch thick, were halved together at the centre, where a 1/4-inch hole was bored straight through the joint.

A block of wood cut to the shape a was fitted over the joint, and fastened to the four arms with 1-inch brads. The 1/4-inch hole was now continued almost through this cap to give a long bearing for the pivot—a ten-penny wire nail with the head filed off. Two 3/16-inch holes were drilled through the handle of each cup and corresponding holes through the wooden arms. The cups were made fast by passing 3/16-inch bolts through cup handles and arms and tightening the nuts.

This made a very strong and rigid construction and on testing it by holding the pivot in the hand out in the breeze the instrument revolved rapidly.

Altogether it was one of the most substantial and satisfactory things that they had made, but Ralph was not yet satisfied.

"We might as well have a Coney Island of our own as not," he said. "You whittle out four propellers, 4 inches long and 1/2 inch across, and I'll show you something," he said.

While Harry was doing this, Ralph sawed out four wooden dirigibles shown at b, 8 inches long, 3 inches across at the widest part, and 1/4 inch thick.

A hole was drilled through the centre of each propeller and another in the flat stern of each air-ship. The pivots for the propellers were flat-head wire nails small enough for the blades to revolve freely, but driven securely into the air-ships.

These were now fastened at the ends of the arms of the anemometer by attaching two strips of basswood to each ship by wires. The strips were to hold the ships in the proper position facing in the direction of motion, which was always the same, no matter in which direction the wind was blowing.

The upper ends of these strips were brought together, and securely fastened under one of the bolts by wires.

As the anemometer revolved, centrifugal force sent the air-ships out as far as the basswood strips would allow.

91

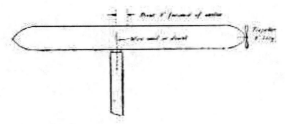

Fig. 99. The Zeppelin wind vane

It was a very interesting fair weather toy, but the first gale, while having no effect on the anemometer other than to make it spin around at terrific speed, nearly wrecked the ships by slamming them against the standard. So the boys always took the ships off at night, and put them on again when they wanted to give an exhibition.

The propellers were gilded and the ships painted in bright colours.

A very simple vane may be made to represent a Zeppelin air-ship (Fig. 99) by cutting out a piece of white pine 2 feet long and 2½ inches wide with the ends pointed to the shape of a Gothic arch. The hole for the pivot should be bored 2 inches deep and be placed well forward of the centre. To make the vane balance, the rear portion from the pivot to the stern should be planed thin and rounded with the spokeshave.

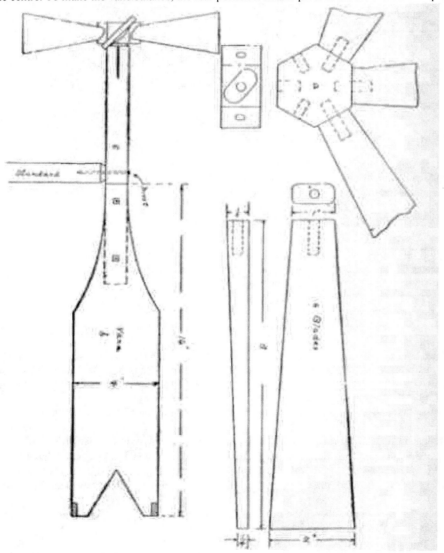

Fig. 100. A six-bladed mill

At the stern should be a small two-bladed propeller, pivoted on a flat-head wire nail. If the stern is still too heavy, the balance can be restored by driving into the forward point a round-headed screw, or by attaching another small propeller. In fact, if the hole in this propeller is made large enough, the screw can be used as the pivot; in any event, the vane must be balanced by adding some kind of weight at the bow.

92

These typical forms of wind vanes will suggest others and the young woodworker should try to be original, to design new forms, ships, submarines, air-ships, etc.

One form which the boys made was especially substantial and reliable. A six-bladed mill was constructed as follows:

First: a piece of $\frac{7}{8}$-inch pine was cut to the form of a hexagon 2 inches across the points.

Second: a $\frac{1}{4}$-inch hole was bored in the centre of each of the six edges and a $\frac{3}{16}$-inch hole through the centre of the hexagon. (Fig. 100.)

Third: six blades were formed from $\frac{1}{2}$-inch pine 8 inches long, 2 inches wide, tapering down to 1 inch at one end.

Fourth: in the small end a $\frac{1}{4}$-inch hole was bored at the centre, about an inch deep.

Fifth: the blades were tapered in thickness from $\frac{1}{2}$-inch at the small end to $\frac{3}{16}$-inch at the wide end, the tapering being done on one side only, that away from the wind, the side facing the wind being perfectly flat.

Sixth: dowel pins were glued securely into the holes in the hexagonal block and into the blades, the latter being turned on the dowels at an angle of about 30 degrees—$\frac{1}{3}$ a right angle—from the front face.

Seventh: after the glue had hardened over night, the whole mill was painted, special attention being given to covering the joint where the glue held, to prevent the rain from loosening it.

Eighth: two pieces of $\frac{1}{4}$-inch white wood were cut out to the form shown at b. These were fastened to the square piece c by two small bolts.

The wide ends of the vanes were spread and fastened by two small strips of white wood, by brads as shown.

Ninth: last came the locating of the centre of gravity, after the mill had been attached by a ten-penny flat-head wire nail. The pivot was made of a similar nail into the standard, as on previous wind vanes.

XVIII

TOOLS: SAWS

The boys now took up the systematic study of tools, as Ralph suggested that they had spent time enough on toys and curiosities.

A cutting tool must be constructed with reference to the material it is to cut. In the machine shop, we find the angle of the cutting edge large—often 80 degrees—while a razor has a cutting edge of about 5 degrees. All cutting tools are wedges, whether saws, chisels, planes, axes, or knives, and the angle depends on the hardness of the material in which it is to work. The action of the tool may be a chisel action, a knife action, or both. In the rip saw, the teeth are really a series of chisel edges cut in one piece of steel, while in a cross cut saw we have a knife action for cutting the fibres, followed by a chisel action for removing the wood.

The side view of a rip saw is shown at a (Fig. 101), the end view at b.

The chisel-like edges are bent outward to right and left alternately. This is called the "set" of the teeth and its purpose is to make the cut wider than the body of the saw, to prevent friction. As the saw teeth pass through the wood, the fibres spring back against the saw blade or body, and the friction makes the work almost impossible without "set" to the teeth. All woodworking saws must be set, and special tools called "saw sets" are sold for the purpose of bending out the teeth.

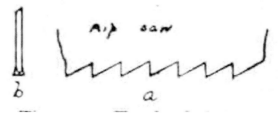

Fig. 101. Teeth of rip saw

The rip or slitting saw should only be used for cutting with the grain. When used across the grain, the action is exactly like that of a narrow chisel, and it will tear the fibres instead of cutting them.

The teeth of a cross cut saw are shown in Fig. 102. At a is the side view, and at b the end view. The teeth are set and filed to a knife edge. This gives two parallel lines of knife-like teeth which cut the fibres in two parallel lines, while the body of the tooth cuts out the wood in the form of sawdust. All woodworking saws belong to one of these two classes, and the cutting angles of the teeth are shown in Fig. 103.

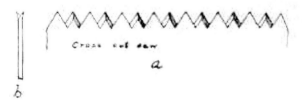

Fig. 102. Teeth of cross cut saw

Photograph by Helen W. Cooke
Learning to Use the Cross Cut Saw.

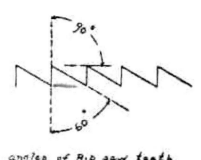

angles of Rip saw teeth

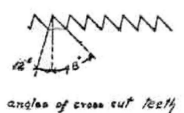

angles of cross cut teeth

Fig. 103

We are very apt to regard the saw not only as a very commonplace article, but as a fixed quantity which has always been the same and always will be. As a matter of fact, the saw has gone through a process of evolution the same as the electric motor, automobile, and aeroplane. New methods of its manufacture are constantly being invented and improvements made in its construction. Some of the steps in the process of making a hand saw are: rolling the steel plate of which the body is made, hardening, tempering, hammering or smithing, grinding, polishing, filing, setting, etching, handling, and blocking.

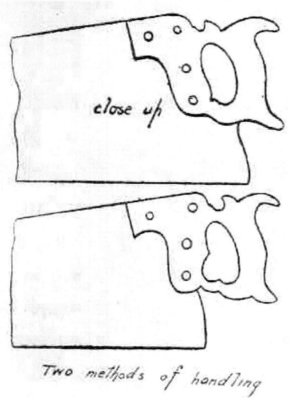

close up

Two methods of handling

Fig. 104. Two methods of handling

95

The handling refers to the placing of the wooden handle and some idea of what it means is illustrated in Fig. 104, showing two methods of attaching the apple wood handle.

Some idea of what the grinding means is shown by the tapers, or difference in the thickness of the steel, as shown at Fig. 105, the thickness in one thousandths of an inch being given at the different points. It will be noticed that not only does the blade decrease in width from the handle out to the end of the saw, but the thickness decreases from the teeth to the top and also from the handle out to the end. This represents ideal saw construction, and it is found only in the good makes.

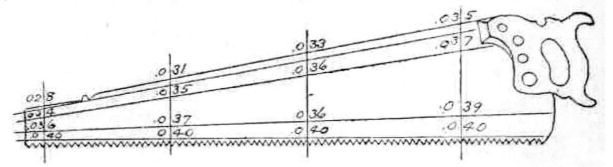

Fig. 105. Thickness of saw blade

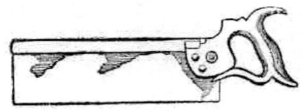

Fig. 106. The back saw

The back saw, being strengthened by a heavy piece of steel along the top, is made of thinner material, and the tapers are not necessary, for the back piece gives rigidity. It removes less wood, but is limited in its action by the back. It is used chiefly by pattern makers, and for finer bench work, such as cabinet making, but should be part of every boy's outfit.

The compass-saw shown at Fig. 107 is used for general purposes, but is not so necessary as the back saw. It is useful for cutting out small openings, though it is not as valuable for this purpose as the turning saw.

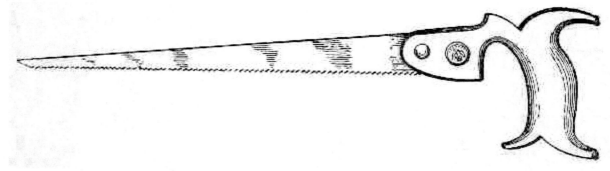

Fig. 107. The compass saw

One end of the turning saw can be released from the frame by removing a pin, passed through a small hole. This is fastened in the frame again and made to follow a curved line like a fret or coping saw.

Fig. 108. The turning saw

The number of teeth to the inch varies, and saws are rated as four-point, five-point, etc., according to the number of points or spaces to the inch. For very hard woods, a saw with small teeth, *i. e.*, with more points than ordinary to the inch, should be used; but a boy who possesses one saw of each kind—a rip, a cross cut, a back saw, and a turning saw—has all that will be required for ordinary woodwork.

Fig. 109. Using the rip saw and trestles

In working with the board on trestles, the saw should be held at an angle of about 45 degrees to the surface. When sawing a board held in the bench vise, this is not so easily done, but the cut should at least be started with the tool in the correct position. (Fig. 109).

The hack saw is used for cutting metal, and while not essential for woodwork, is often valuable for cutting pieces of pipe, rivets, bolts, screws, and nails and should be added to the outfit when the finances will allow. (Fig. 110).

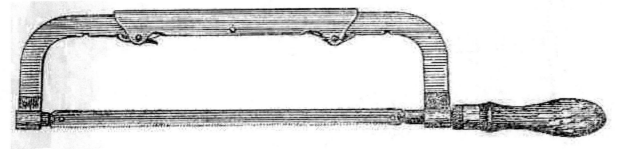

Fig. 110. The hack saw for cutting metal

In fact, there is no such thing as a set of tools. Good tools only should be bought, and the outfit at first should be simple; new ones can be added from time to time, as they are needed. In this way one learns the possibilities of his kit much better than by starting with an elaborate collection.

XIX

TOOLS: PLANES

A boy buying his tool outfit is often bewildered by the array in the hardware store. He is further confused by the advice of the salesman, and his own little store of money.

In selecting planes, only three are really necessary for ordinary work, and this number may even be reduced to two.

Wooden planes are still the favourite tools of some woodworkers, but iron planes have largely superseded them. A 15-inch iron jack plane, a 9-inch smoothing plane, and a block plane make a very good combination for a beginning.

Special planes can be added later, as the finances will allow.

The iron plane with its various parts is shown in Fig. 111. These refer to either the jack or the smooth plane.

In the block plane there is no cap iron, the cutter or plane iron being placed with the bevelled side up. There is frequently found on this tool an adjustment for changing the amount of opening in the mouth for hard or soft woods.

The plane iron and cap are fastened together with a set screw, and the cap is removed when it is being ground or sharpened on an oilstone.

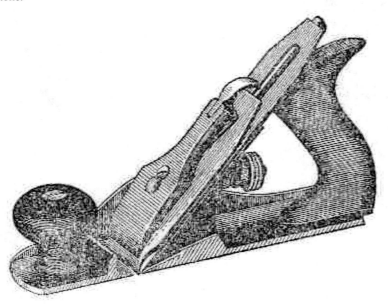

Fig. 111. The smoothing plane

This set screw, which is loosened with a screw-driver, or the edge of the clamp used as a screw-driver, also allows the distance from the cutting edge to the cap to be changed for soft or hard woods. These two irons are fastened into the throat of the plane by the clamp.

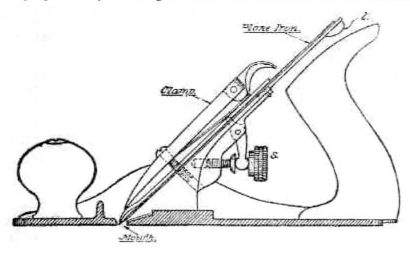

Fig. 111b. The smoothing plane

The lever (1) is for straightening the plane iron, and the screw s is for adjusting the depth of the cut.

The difference between the jack and smooth planes, aside from the size, is in the shape of the "cutter" or "bit." In the jack plane, the bit is ground with a slightly curved cutting edge. This enables the tool to remove coarse shavings, but leaves a slightly corrugated surface which must be smoothed with the smoothing plane.

The jack plane also tends to straighten the work, owing to its greater length. The greater the length, the more does it straighten. The old-fashioned jointers were made several feet long for this very purpose.

If a boy can afford only one plane, it should be a jack plane, but the cutter should be ground straight to act as a smooth plane.

The block plane can be dispensed with better than any of the others, because the smooth plane can be used on a shooting board for truing up end grain, the original purpose of the block plane.

The latter plane has no cap, as it works on the ends of the wood fibres with a shearing or paring action. This is helped by holding the tool at an angle with the wood, a position not advisable with the other two tools.

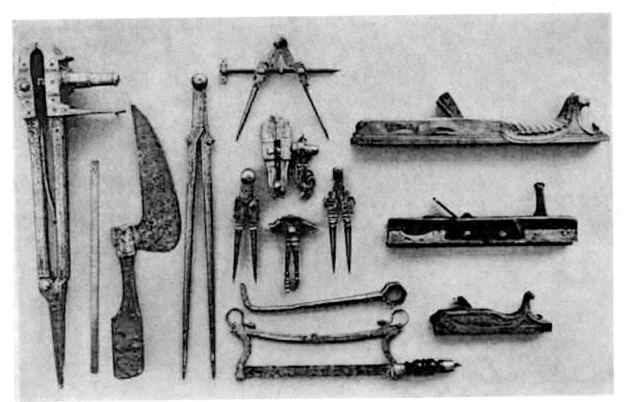

By the Courtesy of the Metropolitan Museum of Art

Tools of the Seventeenth Century.

Showing how little progress has been made in tool construction. In this collection is a jointer plane, a smooth plane, rabbit plane, straight edge, dividers or compasses, a bench vise, hand vise, wrench, hacksaw and combination tool.

The proper position for planing is with the right side to the bench, the plane held flat on the work. Each stroke should, wherever possible, be the full length of the board, unless one part is higher than the rest of the surface. This may be ascertained by using the edge of the plane as a straight edge. High spots should be marked with a pencil, and then planed off, till the full length strokes can be made, and the edge planed straight and true. In surface planing, if the surface be warped, the amount of wind may be determined by placing two "winding" sticks—two straight pieces of the same size at the two ends—and sighting with the eye along their top edges. To take out wind, it may be necessary to plane diagonally across the grain from corner to corner. This defect is common in lumber not properly piled or seasoned, and is more noticeable in such woods as gum or chestnut.

The sharpening of plane irons is a very important part of one's knowledge of tool work, and of course applies to chisels, gouges, and all cutting tools.

Remember that the cutting edge or bevel is a wedge, the angle of a plane-iron bevel being from 25 to 35 degrees, the smaller angle for soft wood, the larger for hard. This angle is not measured by the woodworker often, but is a matter of experience. If the young mechanic will keep his tools ground to the same angle as he finds them at the time of purchase, he will not go far astray.

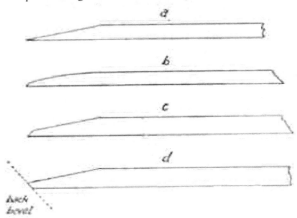

Fig. 112. The cutting angle

This angle should be a clean-cut one, however. Fig. 112 shows some correct and some incorrect ways of grinding. At *a* is shown the right way, *b* is not an angle at all, and *c* is a waste of time and material. At *d* is shown the worst fault of all—a "back bevel." This occurs when the tool is carelessly turned over and ground on both sides, which renders it useless until all the steel in front of the dotted line has been removed; in other words, until the tool is reground.

This mistake is sometimes made in using the oilstone, by rubbing the tool on both sides instead of on one only. All the grinding and sharpening must be done on the bevelled side. As the plane iron is only a thin chisel, the sharpening of the latter tool is performed as in the case of the plane iron, and the same care should be taken to keep the bevel clean cut.

A good grindstone is a shop necessity, and, one might add, a household necessity, because every household uses knives, and the dull knife is an altogether too common nuisance.

Our boys hung up another sign at this stage, and it read, "Keep your tools sharp." This ought to go without saying, but it is a fact that many people make failures of their work and become disgusted with it because they do not keep their tools in order. The satisfaction of using fine, sharp tools cannot be explained; it must be experienced.

Like other things about the shop, there are many kinds of grindstones on the market. The old-fashioned stone with a wooden frame (Fig. 113) worked by hand or a treadle may be good—it depends on the stone—and the new one with a small stone, iron, or pressed steel frame is handy. The last stone is provided with a bicycle seat, and is worked by both feet, so that the hands are free to hold the tool. This stone has ball bearings, is noiseless, and occupies less space than the other.

A stone that is soft and gritty, rather than one that is hard like a piece of granite, should be selected.

In holding the tool against the stone, some common sense is necessary. The harder one presses, the quicker the grinding, but if there is not plenty of water on the stone, the tool may be "burned." When a black place appears, you have destroyed the temper, showing that there has been too much pressure, or too little water, or both.

Fig. 113. Two types of grindstone

The tool may be moved back and forth across the stone to keep its face true, but never up and down. This up and down motion is careless and gives the defective edge shown at *b* (Fig. 112)—very bad grinding.

It is an easy matter to test your grinding by occasionally placing the blade of a try square on the bevel. If it is not straight, your grinding needs more care. Too much stress cannot be laid on the importance of this subject of grinding. It is the key-note of success. If you are careless in this particular, your work at the bench cannot be a success. "A good workman is known by his tools."

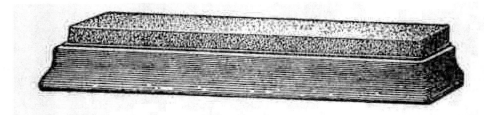

Fig. 114. The oilstone

A teacher of drawing once said, "I don't care to see your drawing; all I want is to see your pencil. I can tell just what kind of work you are doing by observing the care you give your pencil."

This is peculiarly true of the worker with tools. Find a man very particular about them, and you may be sure he is a careful workman.

After grinding comes sharpening. This is done by rubbing the bevelled side back and forth a few times on an oilstone, lubricated with a few drops of sperm or light machine oil.

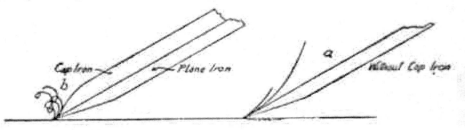

Fig. 115. The action of the cap iron

The stone should be wiped off, afterward, and should never be saturated with the oil. If this is allowed to happen, the surface becomes gummed (Fig. 114) and loses its cutting edge. This rubbing will sometimes turn over a thin wire edge, which is removed by laying the tool with the flat side on the oilstone and drawing it toward you. The wire edge can be further removed if necessary by stropping on a piece of leather.

Before replacing the cutter in the plane, the cap iron is fastened on the flat side about $\frac{1}{16}$-inch from the cutting edge; but this distance may be varied for different woods.

The object of the cap iron is to prevent a splitting action by bending the shaving forward, as shown in Fig. 115. At *a* is shown the effect when there is no cap, and at *b* the splinter bent over giving a shaving.

XX

SQUARING UP STOCK

Having prepared Harry for the serious work to come by his explanation of the plane and its operation, Ralph prepared to start his pupil on the most important and difficult problem in shopwork—squaring up stock.

"Anybody," he said "can hack away at a piece of wood with tools, and get some kind of result, but if this work is worth doing at all, it is worth doing well, and to be able to square up stock is perhaps the most important operation you will ever do. It is like mathematics, the answer is either right or wrong. When you finish, the stock is either square or not square.

"To square up stock means to reduce it to three definite dimensions, length, breadth, and thickness, with all adjoining edges or surfaces at right angles. It sounds easy.

"Suppose we want a piece 12 inches × 2 inches × $\frac{7}{8}$ inch. First, saw out your stock about $12\frac{1}{4}$ inches × $2\frac{1}{4}$ inches × 1 inch. This allows something each way for the tools to remove in the process—for sawdust and shavings. It is considerably more than necessary, but on the first trial you waste more than later, when you have become skilled in this work.

"Second. Dress down one of the flat faces with the jack plane; follow with the smoothing plane and test, with straight edge, with the grain, across it, and diagonally across corners. When this face is finished it constitutes the foundation of the process, and is called the 'working face.'

"Third. Make a pencil mark on the working face near one of the edges. This is called a witness mark, and it indicates that the edge it touches is to be the next face dressed.

"Fourth. Dress down the edge, making it square with the working face, and testing its whole length with the try square. This is the 'joint edge' (Fig. 116).

"Fifth. Set the marking gauge, as shown in Fig. 117, holding it in the left hand and the rule in the right, to two inches, the width of the finished piece. The reason for this is that the scale on the gauge stick is sometimes inaccurate.

"With the gauge block against the joint edge, gauge a line the entire length of the working face. In doing this, the gauge may be used in either hand, and in fact it is well to practise so as to be able to use either at will. The tool should always be pushed from you, and at the same time tilted from you, until the steel point makes only a fine line. If it is held upright, the point will try to follow the grain, which is very seldom parallel with the edge.

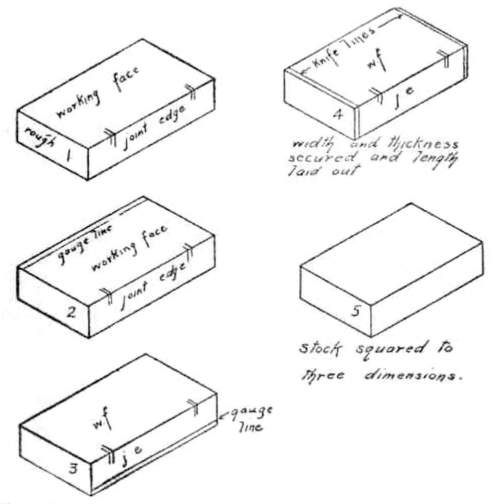

Fig. 116. Steps in the process of squaring up stock

"You have now laid out on the working face your first dimension—the width.

"Sixth. Plane down the edge opposite to the joint edge, almost to the gauge line just drawn. Remember that the tendency is always to take off too much, and when a piece is too small there is no way of making it larger, but if it is left a little too large, it is a simple matter to take off one more shaving. In other words, always be on the safe side, and take off too little rather than too much. Test this edge to see that it is square with working face before reaching the gauge line. Get into the habit of marking all high spots with a pencil, and planing out the marks.

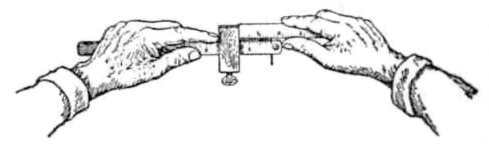

Fig. 117. "Setting" the marking gauge

"Seventh. Set the gauge at the required thickness, in this case ⅞ inch—and with gauge block against working face, make a line full length on both of the squared edges.

103

"Eighth. Dress down the remaining rough face to or near both gauge lines just drawn, and test with straight edge, as in the working face. The stock is now to the second dimension—thickness.

"Ninth. Secure the last dimension—length. As near one end as possible make a line across the working face with a knife and try square, and continue it around the four sides back to the starting place. If it does not come out exactly at this point, the stock is not square.

"From this knife line, measure off the length on the working face, and square a knife line on the four sides, as on the first end. Block-plane both ends to the knife lines, and test.

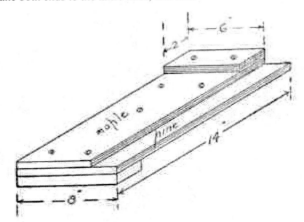

Fig. 118. The shooting board

"If these nine successive steps are carried out accurately, the answer is correct," as Ralph remarked after Harry had worked faithfully throughout the whole explanation.

The boys realized that they needed a shooting board as a necessary part of their equipment, and after Ralph had worked out the drawing shown in Fig. 118, Harry was told to square up the four pieces of stock to be used in its construction.

"Now let me show you a new trick," said Ralph. "It is always a good plan after making a drawing to write out a bill of material something like this:

1 pc. pine 14 × 8 × ½   1 pc. pine 6 × 2 × ½

1 pc. maple 14 × 6 × ½   4 1¼-inch f. h. screws

1 pc. pine 8 × 1½ × ⅞   5 ¾-inch f. h. screws

"There you have in a nutshell all the items needed for the shooting board, and you can proceed to square all your pieces to these dimensions without consulting the drawing until you are ready to assemble the parts. The five ¾-inch screws are for fastening the maple pieces to the flat piece of pine, and the 1¼ screws to fasten the cleats. All the holes for screws are to be bored and countersunk."

"What's countersunk?" asked Harry.

This led to a talk on screws and boring tools, and as it is valuable to the young worker in wood, we will give it as fully as possible.

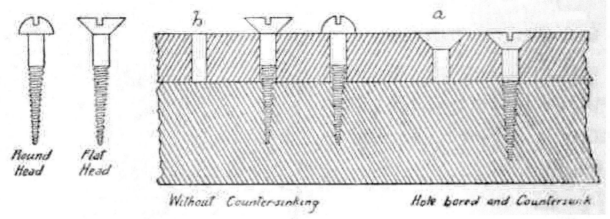

Fig. 119. The use of screws

"There are several kinds of screws," began Ralph, "but the two most commonly used are flat heads and round heads. (Fig. 119). Flat-head screws are those we generally think of, but unless the hole which has been bored or drilled is reamed out at the top, countersunk as we call it, the screw head will stand out from the surface ready to tear your clothes and to scratch anything it may come in contact with, so you can readily see the importance of sinking them below the surface.

"On the other hand, there are often cases where we have no desire to hide the screw. The round heads are used for such cases, and because of their shape they do not catch hold of things. These screws are usually blued—treated with acid to give them a dull, more artistic colour. Screws treated in this way do not rust as readily as the bright ones. You can buy brass screws in both flat and round head forms; in fact you can get tinned, Japanned, lacquered, bronzed, copper, nickel, and even silver plated screws—if you have the money.

"In buying them, you must always give two numbers—the length, in inches, and the diameter. This is the diameter of the wire forming the body and runs from 0 to 30, number 0 being about $\frac{1}{16}$ inch.

"A one-inch screw No. 8 would be fatter or larger in diameter than a one-inch No. 6, which is of comparatively slight or thin proportions. They are sold in boxes containing a gross.

"In fastening two pieces of wood together, they should be prepared as shown at a (Fig. 119) for a flat head and as at b for a round head. The screw slips through the first board, and the screw threads engage only in the second in each case."

XXI

BORING TOOLS

"Boring tools are very interesting," said Ralph. The brace and bit for soft woods have practically taken the place of the old fashioned augers, gimlets, etc. The reason is not hard to find. An auger or gimlet could bore but one size of hole, while with a brace and set of bits almost any diameter can be secured. A little later on, I'll tell you about a Yankee invention along this line.

"The brace is a sort of universal tool holder, and any tool designed to fit into it is known as a bit, as for example a countersink bit, or a screw driver bit, and several varieties of drills.

"The shank, or part that fits into the brace, is usually square and tapering, and the part of the brace which engages this shank is called the 'chuck.' (Fig. 120.)

Fig. 120. Gimlet bit and centre bit

"The centre bit, an old-fashioned form, had all the necessary features of a good boring tool but one. It had a sharp centre for accurately locating the hole, a knife edge for cutting the fibres, and a chisel for removing the wood, but it lacked the spiral screw thread of the modern tool, and had to be forced through the wood by main strength. On a modern auger bit, this spiral screw relieves the worker of a large part of the labour; all he has to do is to turn the brace and keep it straight, supposing of course that the bit is sharp. (Fig. 121.)

"The auger bit is most commonly used by woodworkers. It has two knife edges and two chisels besides the spiral spur in the centre. A short form of this tool, called the dowel bit, has the advantage of bending less readily than the ordinary auger bit. The size in sixteenths of an inch is stamped into the metal shank, but if this number is not distinct or for any reason is missing, the diameter may be measured by holding the rule across the knife edges."

Fig. 121. The auger bit

"What's the Yankee invention you were going to tell me about?" interrupted Harry.

"Well, suppose you wanted to bore a large hole, say $2\frac{1}{2}$ inches in diameter, the probabilities are that you wouldn't have a bit that size. In fact, to have a full set of bits from $\frac{3}{16}$ inch up to 3 inches would mean a very expensive lot of tools. This difficulty has been overcome by a very clever invention called the extension or expansive bit. (Fig. 122). On this tool the knife edge and chisel are part of a moving lip, which may be fastened at any desired point by means of a set screw.

"Besides being adjustable in diameter, the lip of the bit has a scale, and the body a single line engraved on it. By bringing this line to the various measurements on the scale, you can set it to a definite size without the trouble of measuring it.

106

Fig. 122. The expansive bit

"The tool has certain limitations, of course. It is made in two sizes; one will bore holes of any size from ½ inch up to 1½ inches, and the other any size from ⅞ inch to 3 inches, while extra lips or cutters are made to bore as large as 4 inches, but if you ever try to bore a hole of this size you will want all your muscle."

The screw-driver bit is simply a screw-driver with a bit shank instead of a wood handle, and the countersink has a cone-shaped end with enough grooves cut in it to give one or more cutting edges. Its use was illustrated in making the bench hook and shooting board.

Fig. 123. The Forstner bit

The gimlet bit may be used for boring holes for screws. It is made from $\frac{2}{32}$ inch up to $\frac{12}{32}$ inch, and is valuable for preparing articles for the smaller-sized screws where the auger bit would be too large.

We find for sale drill bits for electricians, warranted to go through a nail if necessary, and dozens of special bits.

In working with thin wood, the auger bit is very apt to split it, especially brittle woods, like red gum. Even this contingency is provided for in the Forstner bit, which will bore a hole in a sheet of paper (Fig. 123), and is therefore very valuable for work in veneering or other very thin material.

The brace is represented by several styles and makers, but the beginner must look for the same qualities in the brace as he would in any other tool—good workmanship and material, simplicity and durability.

The old-fashioned Spofford brace was strong, simple, and reliable. For working in corners or any place where a full revolution of the tool is not possible, a ratchet attachment is necessary. This is found on most of the modern tools, and may be obtained at any hardware store. (Fig. 124).

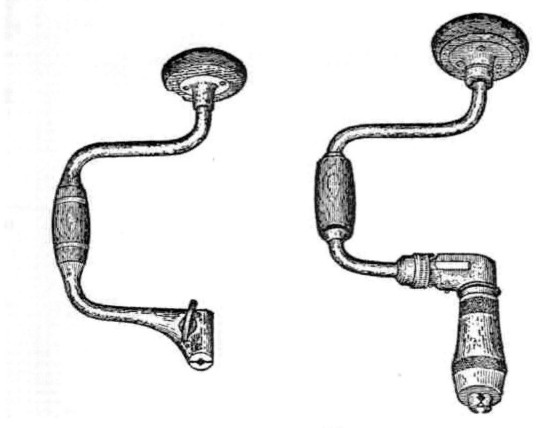

Fig. 124. Common types of the brace

The hand drill (Fig. 125) is one of the most useful tools any one can have about the shop or the house. To be able to make holes in soft or hard wood, tin, zinc, brass, copper, or iron is certainly a great advantage, and some form of the tool should be in every establishment. Our boys found it useful in making moving toys, wind vanes, anemometers, and dozens of other pieces, and never regretted its cost. It may be bought for fifty cents and upward, a very good one costing about $1.50. The drills designed to be used with this tool vary by $\frac{1}{64}$ inch, beginning with $\frac{5}{64}$ inch up to $\frac{3}{8}$ inch. Above this a larger chuck is required. They have round shanks instead of the ordinary square bit shank.

Fig. 125. The hand drill

XXII

MISCELLANEOUS TOOLS

THE SCREW-DRIVER

The need of a screw-driver is too obvious to require special mention. They are made with blades from two inches up to thirty inches long, and have round, flat, or corrugated handles. The best grip is obtained on either a flat or corrugated one, and two sizes are desirable, a small one with about a three-inch blade, the other with an eight or ten. (Fig. 126.)

Some of the magazine brad awls containing a dozen awls and screw-driver are very convenient, but the combinations supposed to contain a whole tool outfit, including saws, are poor investments.

Ratchet screw-drivers, from which the hand is not removed during the operation of driving or withdrawing a screw, are on the market, but they are luxuries rather than necessities.

Pliers with wire-cutting attachments are convenient, and should be added to the kit when possible; some of them are powerful enough to cut a heavy wire nail. (Fig. 127.)

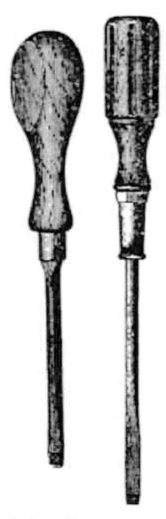

Fig. 126. Screw-drivers

The Mallet. This simple tool is made in a dozen different forms for various trades. The round-headed kind is perhaps the cheapest. It is made of hickory or lignum vitæ. (Fig. 128.)

The best form for woodwork has an oblong or square head of lignum vitæ. The handle should pass clear through the head and be fastened with a wedge.

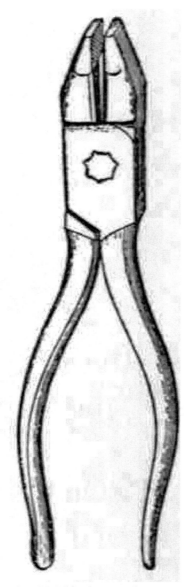

Fig. 127. Pliers

A blow from this tool does not shatter the tool handle as would a blow from a hammer. A comparison of the two blows might be likened to the action of gun powder and dynamite. The slow burning powder represents the action of the mallet. The hammer should never be used on a chisel or gouge.

Hand screws for holding glued-up work together, sometimes for holding special work on the bench top, are made of wood, with either wood or metal spindles. For ordinary work, the jaws should be parallel, but special forms are on the market which will hold irregular forms, as shown in Fig. 129.

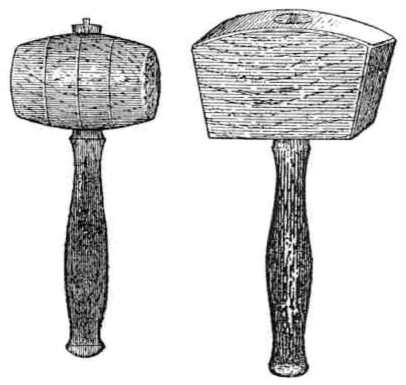

Fig. 128. The mallet

They are made in several sizes, from little ones with 4-inch jaws up to 22-inch jaws. For large and heavy work, clamps of wood or metal may be had as large as eight feet in length. They are useful in the making of drawing boards, doors, etc., but are not a real necessity for boys' ordinary woodwork. Clamps in the form of trestles for specially important large work are made as large as twelve feet in length.

For ordinary purposes, a pair of 6-inch and a pair of 12 or 14 inch wood hand screws will answer. The ingenuity of the young woodworker will suggest other ways of holding glued-up work in the absence of hand screws, such as winding with heavy twine or rope, and twisting a stick through the strands, after the old method of tightening a buck saw or turning saw. In building up a drawing board and gluing the strips together, the requisite pressure may be obtained by laying it on the floor between blocks temporarily nailed there, and wedges driven in, after the method described for picture frames.

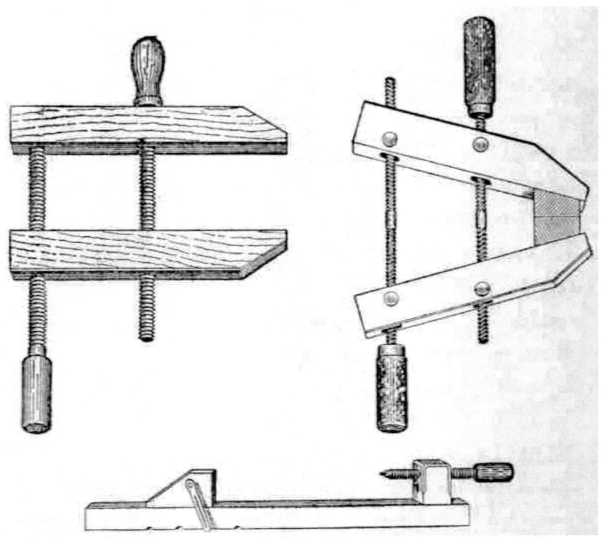

Fig. 129. Clamp and hand screws

A large part of the value derived from woodwork is in the exercise of ingenuity required to meet unexpected contingencies. Just so the owner of an automobile learns more about mechanics and the construction of his machine by being obliged to make repairs on the road, miles from any repair shop, and with a limited number of tools and appliances.

THE HAMMER

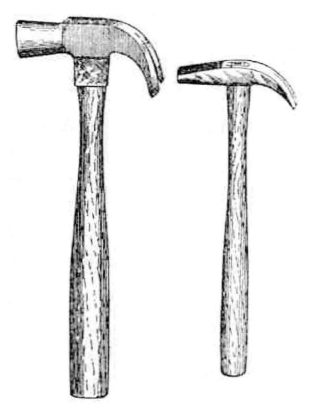

Fig. 130. Hammers

This common tool is made in at least thirty different forms, and some styles in nine or ten different weights. For woodwork, the adze-eye claw hammer, weight sixteen ounces, will answer all requirements. For use with brads as small as ⅜ inch, a brad hammer of three or four ounces is desirable. Both of these forms are provided with claws for withdrawing nails. (Fig. 130.)

Claw hammers are comparatively modern inventions, and there are men now living who, when serving their apprenticeship, were obliged to withdraw their nails with a pair of pinchers. At that period all nails were wrought by hand, and houses are standing to-day on which the clapboards are still held in place by nails forged on an anvil by hand.

THE FILE

A volume might be written about the various shapes, sizes, and methods of cutting of this tool. Its place in woodwork is limited, and it should never be used where another tool will do the work. Like sand-paper, it has a tendency to lead to bad habits and slovenly work. On certain pieces of curved work in hard wood it may be used to remove the sharp edges left by chisel or gouge, especially the latter, but its action even there is apt to tear away the fibres.

An eight-inch, half-round, cabinet wood file and an eight-inch, round, slim No. 0 cut Swiss pattern file are sufficient.

For sharpening bits, a special auger bit file is made, and this may be used for sharpening the marking gauge point and such small work. For sharpening saw teeth, triangular saw files are sold at all hardware stores.

THE SPIRIT LEVEL

This is necessary on outdoor structures which are to be placed on foundations, in securing level or horizontal timbers, and in plumbing the uprights. The human eye is not equal to the task. Masons and builders make use of wooden plumb rods, but as the level is necessary to secure the horizontals, it will be at hand for the uprights, the two glass tubes being at right angles. (Fig. 131.)

Fig. 131. The spirit level

RULE

A two-foot, four-fold, boxwood rule, graduated to eighths outside and sixteenths inside, will answer all ordinary requirements. (Fig. 132.)

113

THE STEEL SQUARE

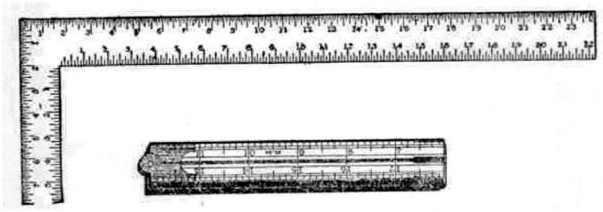

Fig. 132. Steel square and rule

This simple but valuable tool, about which volumes have been written, is necessary for building construction, but is not needed in the making of furniture or cabinet work.

XXIII

MAKING NAIL BOXES

The boys now became very busy completing their shop equipment, and the first project was a box for holding different sizes of nails. This was to be kept on the bench where it could be reached conveniently, and it is shown in Fig. 133.

After studying the sketch, Harry made out the bill of material:

2 pcs. pine 15 × 1¾ × ½

2 pcs. pine 3 × 1¾ × ½

2 pcs. pine 3½ × 1¾ × ⅜

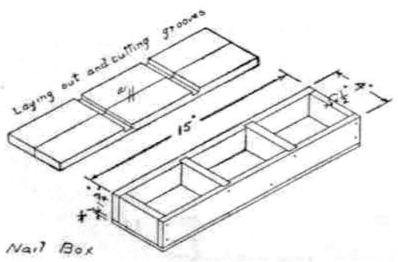

Fig. 133. The nail box

These six pieces were squared up, and the joints for the two partitions laid out by placing them edge to edge in the vise. Pencil lines were drawn across the faces at random, *a*. Ralph explained that by fitting these pencil lines they could at any time bring the two pieces together in the original position.

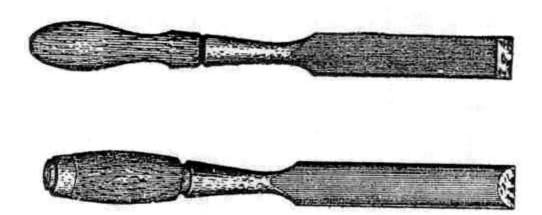

Fig. 134. Socket chisels

The four knife lines representing the edges of the grooves were next drawn, and squared half-way down on each edge, using the face with the pencil lines as a working face. The bottom of the groove was laid off with the marking gauge set at $\frac{1}{4}$ inch. The wood inside the lines was removed by making a saw cut just inside the knife lines, and cutting out with a $\frac{3}{8}$-inch chisel.

This led to a talk on chisels. Ralph explained that for fine work a "firmer" chisel was used, having a comparatively thin body.

There are two kinds of handles, known as "socket" and "tang." The chisels having "tangs" should never be hammered, as the tang acts as a wedge and splits the handle. Where blows are to be struck with the mallet, a socket handle should be used. (Fig. 134.) For heavy work, where hard blows are to be struck, as in house-framing, and out-of-door work generally, the heavy framing tool should be used. The handle of this chisel has a heavy iron ring near the top to keep it from going to pieces.

Our boys' equipment at this time consisted of one half-inch and a one-inch firmer chisel with tang handles, a $\frac{1}{8}$-inch and $\frac{3}{8}$-inch socket firmer, and one $\frac{1}{2}$-inch framing chisel. Later on they added a $\frac{1}{4}$-inch firmer with tang handle.

The grooves for the nail box were cut with the $\frac{3}{8}$-inch chisel without the aid of the mallet.

Ralph showed how, by inclining the tool at a slight angle, a paring action could be obtained, and by working from both ends of the groove no corners were destroyed.

When the four grooves were finished, the box was ready for assembling. This called for hammer and nails.

Wire nails are so cheap now that the old-fashioned cut nails have been largely driven from the market.

The nails used on the box were one-inch brads.

The holding power of flat-head nails is of course much greater than bung head, but in this case the box was to be squared up after nailing, exactly as if it were a solid block of wood. This meant planing the sides and ends, and as the nails would ruin the plane iron, they were all sunk below the surface with a nail set or punch. (Fig. 135). This is a useful tool, but not absolutely necessary, as for light work a wire nail, with the point ground flat on the grindstone, will answer the same purpose. A carpenter frequently uses the edge of a flat-head nail instead of the punch.

Photograph by Arthur G. Eldredge
The Correct Way to Hold the Chisel.

The box was assembled by nailing together the sides and ends. The bottom was next put on, holding the try square along one side and end to make sure everything was square, and last of all the two partitions were pushed down into their grooves, and tied in place by one brad from each side. Next, all nails were set, and the outside tested with the try square and trued up with the plane.

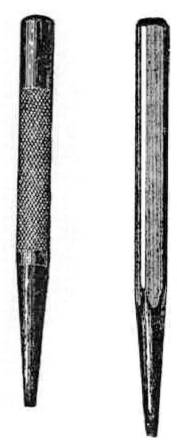

Fig. 135. Wire nails and nail sets

Fig. 135a Wire nails and nail sets

The cabinet of drawers shown in Fig. 136 was next designed to keep the assortment of screws and nails, which the boys knew would soon accumulate. As far as possible, they were kept in their original paper boxes, on which the sizes were plainly printed.

The twelve drawers were simply boxes without covers or partitions, and Ralph suggested that it was not necessary to make them all at once, but that they could often fill in spare time that way, and gradually complete the dozen.

117

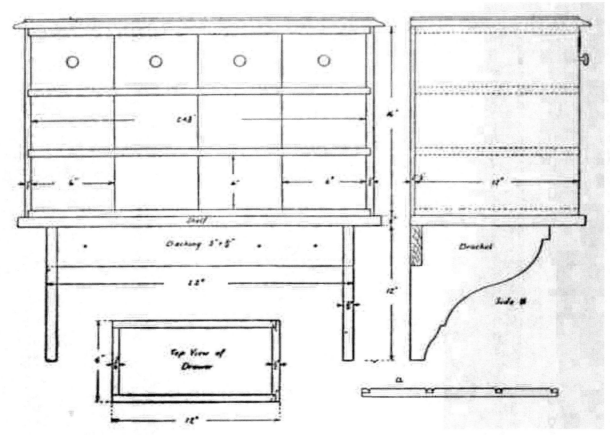

Fig. 136. Cabinet for nails and screws

After making the nail box with partitions, this was a simple job, it being only important that they all be of the same size.

The construction of the cabinet, however, brought new problems. The shelves, being short, did not require any vertical support except at the ends, where they were gained into the sides, and to give Harry practice the top and bottom were to be "rabbeted" into the sides. The sides then were the most important parts. All six pieces were first squared up to the dimensions called for in the drawing. The list of material was as follows:

4 pcs. $24\frac{5}{8} \times 12 \times \frac{1}{2}$
shelves

2 pcs. $14 \times 12 \times \frac{1}{2}$ ends

1 pcs. $25\frac{1}{8} \times 14 \times \frac{1}{4}$ back

"The grain must run the long way," said Ralph, "so the grooves will be across the grain."

The four grooves were laid out with knife and try square, and the lines scored as deeply with the knife as possible.

Then another cut was made with the knife inside of the first, and with the knife held at about 45 degrees, cutting out a V-shaped groove, as shown at a.

In each of these grooves a cut with the buck saw was made down to the line, and the wood removed with the $\frac{3}{8}$-inch chisel. There are special planes, called rabbet planes, and plows for doing this kind of work, but it is good practice for beginners to use the chisel.

The grooves finished, the cabinet was put together with $1\frac{1}{2}$-inch brads, except the back. This being of thin material, and having no special strain on it, was nailed on with 1-inch brads. The total width of the drawers in each tier was $\frac{1}{8}$ inch less than the space. This gave clearance, so that they could be moved in or out easily.

Later, when all twelve drawers were finished, the boys bought a dozen simple drawer pulls, and screwed one in the centre of each box.

The centre was found by drawing the diagonals in light pencil lines. The front and ends were sand-papered, and given two coats of dark-green stain, and the cabinet was placed on a shelf against the wall.

XXIV

BIRD HOUSES

The boys felt that they were ready for business, and Ralph suggested that they had provided enough weather vanes and windmills, but had made no provisions for the birds.

The cat, that arch enemy of the native birds, had driven the robins, martins, and wrens all away. Each year some of these brave little birds started homes in the trees near the house only to have their families devoured as soon as they were hatched.

A bird house to be attractive need not be very pretentious, but it must absolutely be cat-proof, or the birds will inspect it carefully from all points of view and leave it severely alone. A nest well hidden in the tree foliage or shrubbery is not nearly so conspicuous as a brightly painted house fastened to the limbs of a tree. The side of a barn or outhouse, far enough down from the roof so that the cat cannot reach it, or a tall pole covered on the upper part with tin, so that the feline bird hunter cannot gain a foothold, are about the only safe places for a house which the birds will actually adopt. The first house our woodworkers manufactured is shown in Fig. 137.

This was a single or one-family house, and its construction was very simple.

The list of material follows:

One pc. ½-inch pine or white wood 10 × 6½ ins.

Two pcs. ½-inch pine or white wood 7½ × 3 ins.

One pc. ½-inch pine or white wood 9½ × 5 ins.

One pc. ½-inch pine or white wood 9½ × 4½ ins.

Two pcs. ½-inch pine or white wood 5¼ × 4½ ins.

The first piece, 10 × 6½ inches, was simply squared up for the bottom. The two pieces for the sides, 7½ × 3 inches, were squared up, and one edge of each planed to a 45-degree bevel, to engage with the roof boards.

The latter were squared up, and nailed together at right angles with 1¼-inch brads.

The two ends, 5½ × 4½ inches, were carefully laid out as shown in the drawing, sawed, and planed to the lines with square edges.

In the end which was to contain the circular door a hole 1¾ inches in diameter was bored with its centre two inches from the bottom line. This required the services of the extension bit, and, to avoid splitting the wood, as soon as the spur of the bit showed on the further side, the wood was turned about, and the hole finished from the other side.

The house was next turned upside down, and fastened in the bench vise. Holes were drilled along the sides of the bottom piece ¾ inch in from the edge—three on each side—countersunk, and the piece fastened to the sides with 1-inch No. 8 screws. The top pieces already nailed together were now nailed in position on the sides and ends with 1-inch brads.

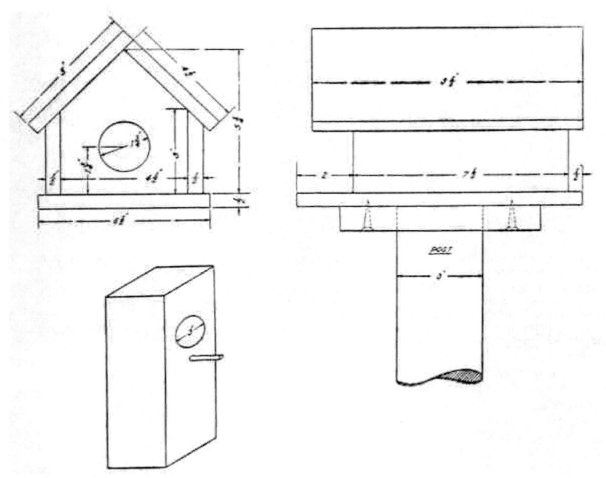

Fig. 137. One family bird house, and house for high-hole

The pole they used was 13 feet long and about 3 inches in diameter at the small end. It was rounded at this end by using a draw knife. (Fig. 138). A block of ⅞-inch pine was bored out, and fitted snugly over the end of the pole. This block was then removed, and four holes bored through it for screws.

Fig. 138. The draw knife

Before replacing the block on the top of the pole a cut was made across the end of the pole about two inches deep, by means of the rip saw.

The block was replaced, and wooden wedges driven into the saw cut. This fastened the block securely on the end of the pole, and after making sure that it was level, the bird house was fastened to the block by four 1¼-inch screws from the under side.

A piece of sheet tin was wound around just under the house to discourage pussy, and the pole set into the ground about three feet, bringing the under side of the house ten feet above the ground.

A double or two-family house of similar proportions was built next, as shown in Fig. 139. The list of material called for:

One pc. ½-inch wood 18½ × 6½ (bottom)
One pc. ½-inch wood 18½ × 5½ (roof)

One pc. ½-inch wood 18½ × 4½ (roof)

Two pcs. ½-inch wood 15½ × 3 (sides)

Three pcs. ½-inch wood 5¼ × 4½ (ends and partition)

The construction was the same as before, each end having a door, and the partition of course being solid. The block for supporting the house on the pole was larger, being 8 × 5 × 1¼ inches, and called for six 1½-inch No. 10 screws, to secure it to the under side of the floor. Harry wanted to make it more complete by adding a small wind vane, but Ralph said it might frighten the birds, so it was omitted.

Of course larger and more ornamental houses may be built, but where there are too many families in such close proximity there is apt to be trouble, while houses that are too conspicuous do not appeal to the beautiful American wild birds that we want to attract. With the English sparrow it does not matter so much. For these birds, a tenement house against the side of a barn may be built easily, in the form shown in Fig. 139.

This may be made any length, each door leading to a compartment separated from the others by partitions. Make as many pieces plus one as there are to be compartments, apartments, or flats; have the bottom project as shown in side view for a perch and walk, and have the roof also project to shed rain.

If not fastened from the inside of the barn by stout screws, this house must be secured to a shelf, or by brackets.

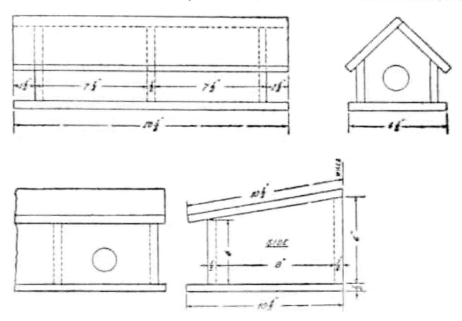

Fig. 139. Two family house and tenement

The side view shows a simple shelf made of a back piece secured to the side of the barn by screws or nails, a plain shelf nailed to this back piece, and two wooden brackets. If iron brackets are used, both the shelf and back piece may be omitted, the brackets being fastened to the under side of the bird house and to the siding of the barn by screws.

For birds like the high-hole, or flicker, a piece of hollow log, or an elongated box fastened securely to the side of a pole, made cat proof, is very acceptable. This should not be painted, but should be provided with a door on the side and a perch. (Fig. 137.) The opening should be about three inches for these large birds, and the location should be as secluded as possible. Any number of devices will suggest themselves, but always remember the cat, and study the location from the bird point of view. The martins and swallows are especially to be encouraged, as they are wonderful destroyers of insects.

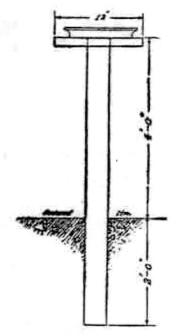

Fig. 140. The bird bath

One device, especially grateful to these feathered friends in hot weather, is a pan of water, in a place where they can drink and bathe without being eternally on the watch for that crouching enemy, who is always stalking them—Tabby.

A pedestal with a platform about four feet above the ground will do nicely, and it can be placed so close to the house that you can watch them, and enjoy their ablutions almost as much as they do. (Fig. 140.)

The construction is too simple to require an explanation.

XXV

SIMPLE ARTICLES FOR HOUSEHOLD USE

The boys thought it was about time to pay some attention to the wants of the family, who had been clamouring for weeks to have this article or that for the kitchen, dining room, and in fact for every part of the house.

Ralph was a wise teacher, however. He knew that the cause of ninety out of every hundred failures was due to the young mechanic's trying some problem too far advanced.

It seems strange that people cannot learn this lesson. We have seen hundreds of boys led along, say in carving, from one simple lesson to another, until at the end of five or six carefully graded exercises, these boys could carve beautifully any design given them.

On the other hand, we have seen boys start in on their own hook, without any direction from older people, and ruining everything they tried, simply because they wanted to do the most difficult thing first, before they had developed any skill.

Ralph was determined that his boy should be an expert and successful user of tools, so he paid no attention to the clamours of the family, and allowed Harry to make only those things which were within his power to do well. Each time a piece of work was finished, and inspected by the family, the universal chorus was something like this:

"Well, if he can make such a fine bird house, I don't see why he can't make half a dozen picture frames for these water colors," or, "If he can make such a fine pen tray, I don't see why he can't make a new stool for the piano!"

In vain Ralph explained that these things could be made in due time, that a picture frame required much more skill than a bird house, etc.

Their household articles commenced with a bread board for the kitchen. (Fig. 141). This gave Harry his first experience in planing a broad surface. He used jack and smoothing planes for the working face, and squared the rest of the board as he had smaller pieces. This required some time. The wood about the semi-circular top was removed with saw and chisel, the board held for the chiselling flat on the bench hook. After getting this curve as true as possible with the chisel, it was finished with a sand-paper block. A ½-inch hole was bored at the centre of the semi-circle to hang it up by, and the two lower corners were rounded with chisel and sand-paper. No sand-paper was used on the flat surface, as Ralph explained this was a board for cutting bread, and the grit from the sand-paper would become more or less embedded in the wood, and it would spoil the bread knife. Sand-paper is made of ground quartz, and it soon dulls the edge of a cutting tool.

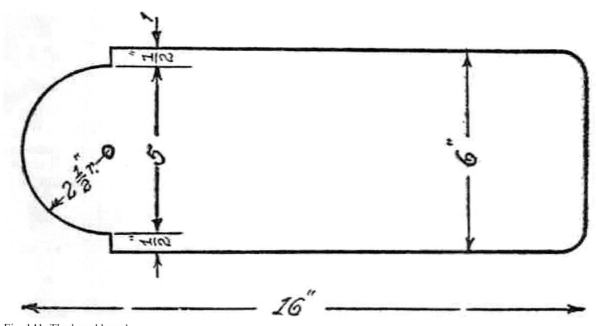

Fig. 141. The bread board

The knife and fork box (Fig. 142) brought new problems. The list of material was:

1 pc. $11\frac{1}{2} \times 3\frac{1}{4} \times \frac{1}{2}$ 2 pcs. $7 \times 1\frac{1}{2} \times \frac{1}{2}$

2 pcs. $14 \times 1\frac{1}{2} \times \frac{1}{2}$ 1 pc. $12 \times 6\frac{1}{2} \times \frac{1}{4}$

It was made of white wood, and, after being assembled, was stained a rich brown by receiving two coats of bichromate of potash. This is a chemical, which may be bought at a paint or drug store in the form of crystals. These are dissolved in water, until the solution looks like pink lemonade. It can be applied with a brush, but each coat must be allowed to dry completely before the whole is sand-papered smooth with No. 0 sand-paper. A deeper brown can be obtained by adding one or two extra coats of stain.

123

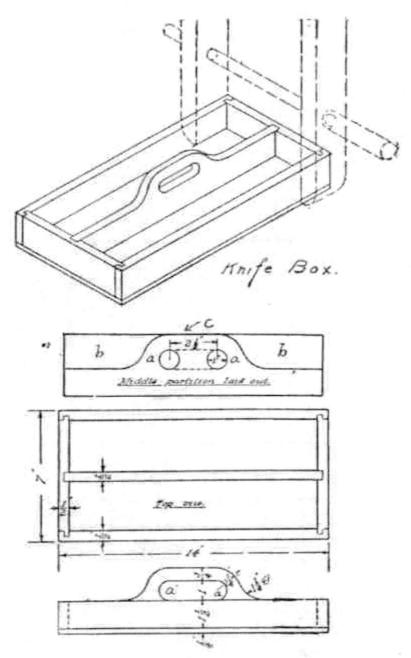

Fig. 142. Method of using hand screws in the construction of a knife box

The middle partition containing the handle was made first. The drawing was laid out on the wood after it had been squared up, and two holes 1 inch in diameter were bored out at *a a*. The wood between was taken out with a key-hole saw, and finished to the line with chisel and knife. A turning saw can be used to advantage on this handle, but it is not absolutely necessary. Spaces *b b* were removed in the same way, but a knife was used in the concave part of the curve. If it is handy, a small spokeshave can be employed on the whole upper line of this handle.

Anything in the nature of a handle should be rounded to fit the hand. Edges *c c* were therefore rounded with the knife, and finished with coarse, followed by fine, sand-paper.

The two sides were laid out together as in the nail box, and the groove cut with back saw and ⅛-inch chisel.

The end pieces were made in a similar manner, and the bottom piece squared to ¹⁄₁₆-inch of finished size. The assembling consisted of first gluing together the sides and ends. Two hand screws were used to hold them. This was Harry's first attempt at using hand screws, and Ralph showed him the importance of keeping the jaws parallel.

The box remained in the hand screws over night, and the next day it was found to be securely fastened. The most convenient kind of glue for boys is the liquid sold in cans. It is always ready for use, and very handy where only a moderate quantity is needed.

Dry glue in the form of flakes, or granulated, must be soaked over night, and then heated in a pot having a double bottom with water in the lower part.

It should be put on hot with a brush or a small flat stick. The best glue is none too good, yet a good quality has wonderful holding power and should last indefinitely.

After removing the hand screws, the unfinished box was placed in the vise, tested with the edge of the plane, and made perfectly true, top and bottom.

The ¼-inch bottom piece was now put on with one-inch brads, the sides and ends made square, the handle partition slipped into the grooves, and fastened with two brads at each end.

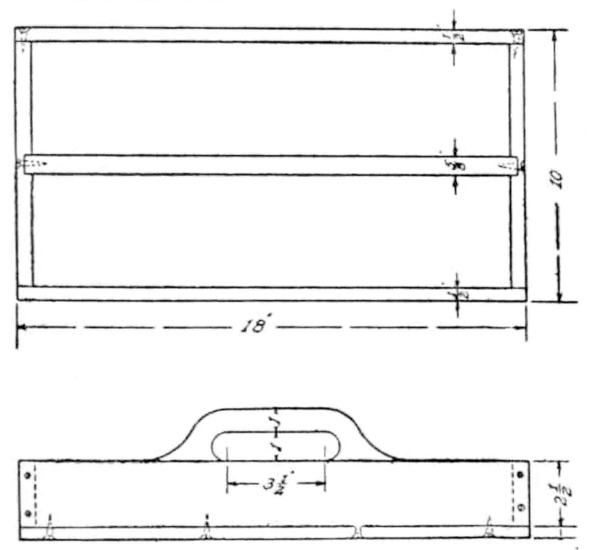

Fig. 143. Tool box

This knife box was so satisfactory that our young carpenters resolved to have a large one for tools. Whenever they had a job to do in the house, they were constantly running out to the shop for something, so that a tool box became a necessity.

The construction was similar to the knife box; but this was larger and heavier, and the dado joints at the ends were replaced by a butt joint fastened with flat-head screws. (Fig. 143). The bottom and partition were also put on with screws, on account of the weight to be carried.

125

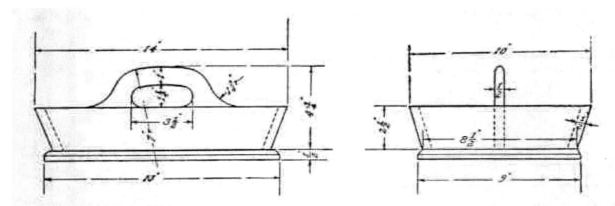

Fig. 144. Another tool box

These tool boxes are frequently made in the shape shown in Fig. 144, with sloping sides and ends called the hopper joint; but aside from the tool practice it affords, it is doubtful if the shape has advantage enough over the other form to warrant the extra time it takes. Man is an imitative creature, however, and what one carpenter has, the others copy.

The principal features about this useful article should be size and strength, especially in the handle, which should be of about ⅝ or ¾ inch stock.

XXVI

THE MITRE BOX AND PICTURE FRAMES

It seemed to Harry that the shop was fairly well equipped, but Ralph insisted that they must have a mitre box before making anything else for the house.

The mitre box is, or should be, an instrument of precision, and although simple in construction, must be perfectly accurate, or it is useless. (Fig. 145.)

The illustration shows the common form, but elaborate affairs of iron and wood can be bought ready made. Every boy should make his own, for the practice, if for nothing else. The sides should be made of oak ⅞ inch thick, 18 inches long, and 3½ inches high, the bottom of ⅞-inch pine or other soft wood, the same size.

When squared up, the two sides must be tested by standing them side by side; then reverse one end for end, to see if they are alike. If not, find where the trouble is, and correct it.

It is especially important that the edges of the bottom piece be square and the sides perfectly parallel. This test can be made with the marking gauge. Sides are fastened on by boring and countersinking for three screws on each. After assembling, the whole thing must be tested as if it were a solid block. Top edges must be true and parallel.

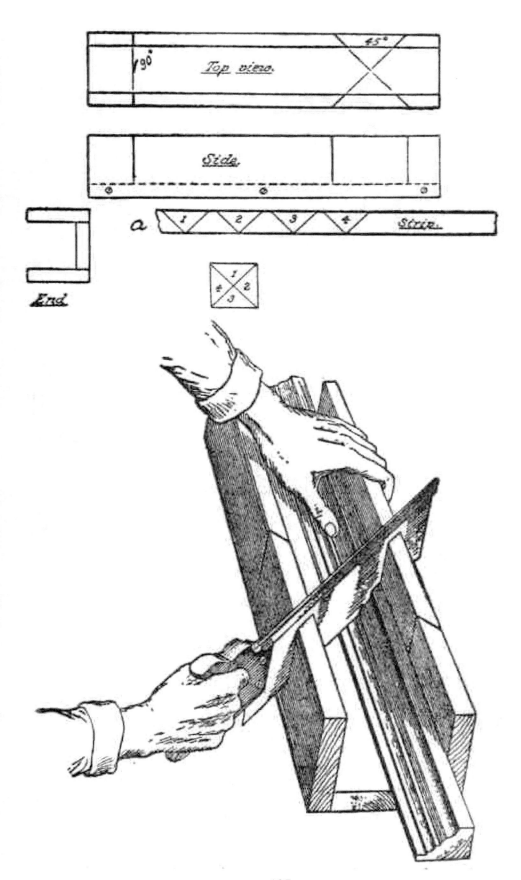

Fig. 145. The 45° mitre box and test pieces

Near one end—about two inches in—lay out across the top with try square a line 90 degrees with the sides. Carry the line down each side, square with the top edges. For 45-degree angles, lay out a square by drawing two pencil lines across the top, as far apart as the finished mitre box is wide. Draw the two diagonals and square lines from their ends down both sides, taking care that their position is not over the screw in the bottom; because as the saw cuts deeper it may reach this screw and ruin its teeth.

Make the three saw cuts directly on the lines laid out with a cross cut or back saw, with the utmost care. If this is not done accurately, all the labour of preparation is wasted. The blank end of the mitre box may have an additional 90-degree cut, or be left for new cuts in the future, as a mitre box of this description wears out and becomes inaccurate.

Other angles may be used, as 60 degrees or 30 degrees, but it is better to have these on another box as they are used less, and for special purposes. (Fig. 146.)

The mitre box is not ready to use until it has been thoroughly tested. Prepare a strip of soft wood—pine or white wood—1½ inches wide and ½ inch thick. Cut four pieces from it on the mitre box, using the back saw as shown at a, with only one of the slits. Place these four triangular pieces together to form a square. All the four mitre joints of this square must fit perfectly. If they do not, mark the slit "N. G.," and test the other slit in the same way. If all right, mark "O. K." It often happens that one may be perfect and the other inaccurate. If they are both O. K., the box is ready for use. If one slit is useless, lay out and cut another on the blank end of the mitre box in the same direction, and test again.

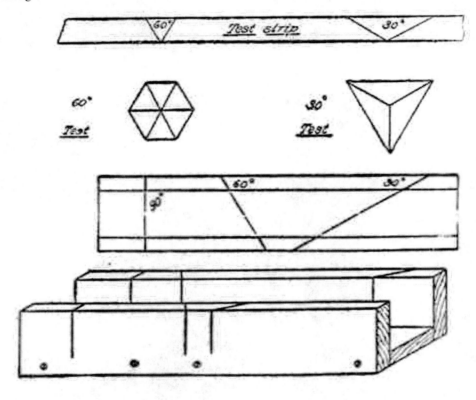

Fig. 146. 30-60-90 mitre box

In testing a 30-degree cut three pieces of the strip should be sawed out, and when placed together they should form a perfect equilateral triangle, while from a 60-degree cut, six pieces are needed to form a hexagon.

These angles are valuable in inlaid work, and for getting out geometrical designs.

The 45-degree cut is indispensable in making the mitred corners of picture frames and in cabinet work.

In making picture frames of simple cross section, it is first necessary to cut the rabbet (Fig. 147) with a rabbet plane. If this moulding is made by hand, the size of the picture should be measured, the length of all four sides added, and a liberal allowance made for waste.

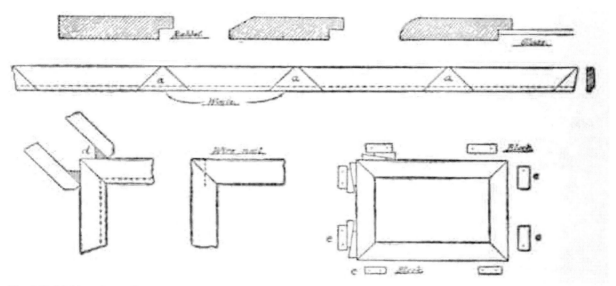

Fig. 147. Making picture frames

In the figure, the triangles *a a* are waste, the rabbet being indicated by the dotted line. After the four pieces have been sawed out on the mitre box, they should be placed together on a flat surface, such as the bench top or floor, to see if the mitres fit perfectly. If they do not, one of them can be block planed to make a perfect fit, and the other three laid close together, as shown in the illustration.

The assembling is the hardest part of the operation, and many devices have been tried and some patented to hold the parts together while the glue is drying.

Perhaps the surest way is to drill a hole in one piece of each joint large enough for the passage of a wire bung-head nail.

The undrilled piece is placed vertically in the vise. The drilled piece, after receiving a thin coat of glue, is brought into position horizontally, and the nail driven home.

Theoretically, the nail should catch at the first blow, but the horizontal piece will sometimes slip, even with the best of care. It is wiser to place this piece about $\frac{1}{16}$ inch above its final position, to allow for this slip.

A method sometimes used is to glue near the ends of each piece a triangular block of wood, as shown at *d*. These must be left over night to harden.

The next day the whole four pieces can be glued and held together by four hand screws, as shown, until the glue is thoroughly hard. This method, of course, can only be used with plain moulding or that which is square on the outside.

Our boys tried another way that is commonly practised. They nailed oblong blocks to an old drawing board, as shown at *e e*, and then placed the picture frame in the centre, after gluing the joints, and driving wedges in between the blocks and the frame. Paper placed under each joint prevented the frame from being stuck to the drawing board by the glue forced out by the pressure.

This paper plan was learned by experience, as the first frame the boys tried had to be pried up from the board, and in so doing they broke it at two of the joints, so that it had to be made again.

It is well to remember in gluing mitre joints that end grain absorbs more glue than a flat surface. A priming coat should be applied first, and allowed to remain a few moments to fill up the pores. The second coat should hold fast and make a strong joint, but an excess of glue should always be avoided, as it must be removed after hardening, and glue soon takes the edge from the best of tools.

Very fancy frames should be avoided. A bevel on the outside or inside, or both, is about all the young woodworker should attempt in the way of ornamentation. Depend on the natural beauty of the wood, as a fancy frame draws the attention from the picture, which after all is the main thing. We should admire the man, not his clothes, the picture not its frame, although the latter should be neat and well made.

The finishing and polishing of frames is taken up in Chapter XLIX.

XXVII

MAKING TOILET BOXES

To make a wooden box sounds like a simple proposition; but in making the drawing, the questions of size, proportion, joints, hinges, etc., immediately come up.

The size of course depends on the purpose of the box. If it is for ladies' gloves, it should be long and narrow; if for collars or handkerchiefs, square or nearly so. The height is nearly always made too great. In fact, the whole question of proportion is one which can hardly be taught; it must be felt, and different people have different ideas as to what constitutes good proportion.

Some hints, however, may be given: A box perfectly square does not look well. Again, dimensions that are multiples do not look well. A box 4 × 8 × 12 inches would not be nearly so pleasing as one 3 × 5½ × 12 inches.

The proportions are also affected by the constructive details. Is the box to be flat on the sides and ends or is the top to project? etc.

Our boys argued and sketched and finally drew the design shown at Fig. 148. This was to hold ties. The top was to project and have a bevel, or chamfer, also the bottom. No hinges were to be used, but the cover was to have cleats fastened on the under side to keep it in place, and to prevent warping.

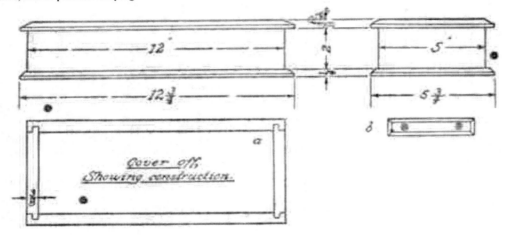

Fig. 148. Dado joint used in box design

The next question was the manner of fastening the sides and ends. On unimportant work, a butt joint with glue and brads can be used, but for a toilet article, the holes made by the brads, even if they are filled with putty, are not satisfactory.

So it was decided to use the dado joint as shown at *a*. This meant more fine work, but, as Ralph suggested, it was to last a lifetime, and should be made right.

Sides and ends were squared up, and the grooves on the side pieces laid out as in the nail box. The rabbets on the end pieces were cut out with the back saw and chisel. After the joints had been carefully fitted, the four pieces were glued together and placed in hand screws over night.

While the glue was hardening, the two pieces for the top and bottom were squared up and bevelled with the smoothing plane on the long sides, the block plane on the ends.

The cleats for the top were next made, drilled and countersunk for the screws as at *b*.

A careful full-sized drawing of half of the top was made, and a chip carving design drawn for it. The cleats were not put on until the carving was finished and short screws had to be used so they would not come through and spoil the surface.

The next day the body of the box was removed from the hand screws and squared with a smoothing plane. The top and bottom were put on with 1-inch brads. These were "set" with a nail punch to prevent any possible scratching and the whole box was rubbed down with wax dissolved in turpentine.

For fine cabinet work, the dovetail joint makes the most satisfactory method of fastening, but Harry was not yet skilled enough to do the fine work it demanded.

The second box was for handkerchiefs, dimensions 8 × 7 × 3 inches outside, and no overhang at either top or bottom. The construction brought in several new features. Sides and ends were dadoed together as in the first box.

The top and bottom, after being squared, were rabbeted on all four sides until they fitted snugly into the opening top and bottom. They were glued in these positions and placed in hand screws over night. (Fig. 149.)

"How are you going to get into that box?" asked Harry. "You've closed it up solid and glued the top on."

"Wait and see," was all the satisfaction he got.

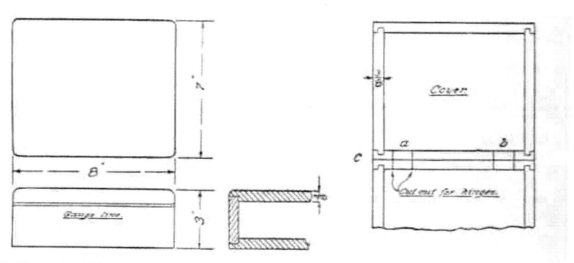

Fig. 149. The handkerchief box

The next day the hand screws were removed and the box squared up exactly as if it had been a solid piece of wood. Ralph then made two gauge lines around the four sides, ¾ inch from the top and ⅛ inch apart. Then he cut the box in two between these two lines with a rip saw, after slightly rounding all corners except the bottom ones with a plane and sand-paper.

By this method, the box and cover must be exactly alike in outline, and by planing to the gauge lines, they will fit perfectly.

It only remained to hinge the two parts together, but this operation proved to be no slight task.

The body was placed in the vise and the cover laid upside down on the bench top. The two parts were brought together as shown at *c*, and the four knife lines laid out as shown with knife and try square.

The distance between the lines at *a* and *b* must be equal to the width of the hinge, and the wood between these lines removed to a depth equal to half the thickness of the hinge at its joint when closed. If too much is removed, the box will be "hinge bound" and will not close in front. If too little is taken out, it will close in front and have an open joint at the back. In the former case, a thickness or two of paper placed under the hinge will often be enough to make it close in front. In the latter case, of course more material must be cut out. It is a delicate operation, as the depth of these cuts for 1-inch hinges is only about 1/16 inch. It is a question of accuracy, pure and simple.

Holes for the screws can be made with a brad awl.

The boys made several boxes of various sizes and styles, some plain, some decorated with carving. Pyrography, or burnt work, is frequently used for decoration, and the best wood for this purpose is basswood, because of its white color, softness, and freedom from pitch.

Other woods may be burnt, but pine, which has veins of pitchy sap, is not suitable.

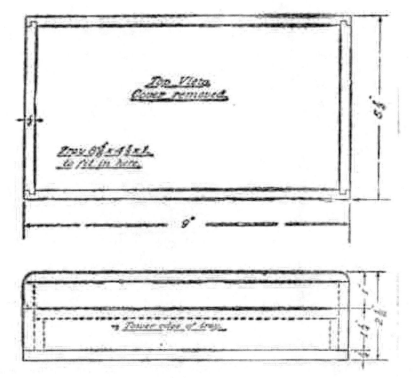

Fig. 150. A box for drawing instruments

A box for drawing instruments is shown in Fig. 150. Its outside dimensions are 9 × 5¼ × 2½ inches. Our boys made theirs of gum wood because of the beauty of its colouring and its suitability for carving. The joints used and the method of construction were the same as in the handkerchief box, but it was provided with a tray for the instruments. This was one inch deep over all, and rested on two thin strips fastened to the ends inside. These strips were 4¼ × 1 × ¼ inches, and, by raising the tray one inch from the bottom, left a space convenient for holding triangles, protractors, pencils, etc. The cover was decorated with a border and centre piece in chip carving.

The making of dovetailed boxes is taken up in Chapter XXXV.

XXVIII

BRACKETS AND BOOK RACKS

Brackets are often required about the house for many purposes, and their size, shape, and decoration are infinite. There is even more fun in designing them than in making them. Tastes differ in this respect, as in everything else, and, given the problem, no two people will bring out the same design unless they simply copy something they have seen, which is not designing.

When our boys started to make brackets in response to urgent demands from the family, Ralph blocked out the sketch shown in Fig. 151 at *a*.

"There is a bracket," he said; "it consists of three pieces, and properly put together it will hold what it is designed to hold. It is not a thing of beauty, and we must improve it. How? By changing its outline without impairing its strength. In other words, we must '*design*' a bracket constructed of three pieces of wood put together at right angles. There's your problem; now take paper and pencil and let us see what you can do."

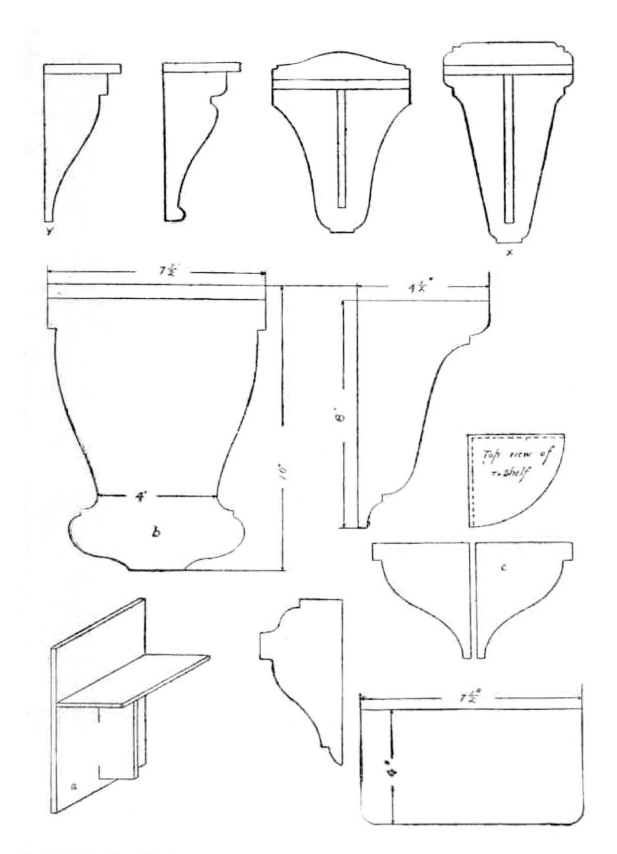

Fig. 151. Designs for wall brackets
"What size?" asked Harry.

133

"Oh, in this case, I'll leave it to your judgment."

For fully an hour, no sound was heard in the shop but that of two lead pencils. Harry was getting experience.

"Let me give you a pointer," said Ralph. "Don't try to draw both sides alike, as it is very difficult where you have free-hand lines. Draw a vertical line representing the centre. Sketch one half of the design, and when you have it about right, fold the paper on this centre line and trace the other half."

Harry went to work again and at the end of another hour produced the sketches shown in Fig. 151.

Ralph criticised them all rather severely, and as Harry was tired, this treatment made him sulky.

"Don't get mad," said Ralph kindly; "you know designing is hard work and the only way you can learn is to have me help you by pointing out your weak spots. Artists are obliged to pay for criticism; you know I'm not finding fault."

"All right," said Harry, brightening up, "which one shall I make?"

"I think the one marked x is the best. Work it up more carefully, design the shelf and bracket and put on all the dimensions."

"The bracket? Why, what is this I have drawn?"

"That's the back piece that goes against the wall; the bracket piece supports the shelf, and remember when you make it in wood, the grain must always run the long way of each piece."

"Why?"

"I'll show you," said Ralph.

He cut out two pieces of wood about $8 \times 1 \times \frac{1}{2}$ inches, one with the grain running lengthwise and on the other the grain running the one-inch way. Handing the first piece to Harry, he said, "Let me see you break it with your hands."

The boy tried and failed. Handing him the second piece he said, "Now try this."

It broke so readily that Harry was astonished.

"That's why," said Ralph, "and that's all."

The three pieces as finally drawn are shown in Fig. 151 at x. They were all cut out of gum wood with a coping saw, finished to the lines with chisel, spokeshave and sand-paper block, and put together with ¾-inch brads. The nails were driven through the back into the bracket, the latter piece being held in the vise in a horizontal position. It was then shifted to a vertical position with the back piece to the left of the vise and the shelf nailed to the bracket. Two brads were also driven through the back into the shelf.

Brackets may be ornamented in many ways; by chip carving, pyrography, or by staining, but the decoration should be put on before assembling.

Another form is shown at b in which the back piece is not carried above the shelf, the latter piece resting on the top of the back. From a constructive standpoint this is a stronger form than the other, as part of the weight is carried by the back instead of by the brads alone.

Corner brackets are sometimes used and may be made in the form shown at c. Here we have two wall pieces and a V-shaped shelf, the V being a right angle. Again, the form may be so long as to require two brackets and it may then be considered a shelf.

In fastening any of these forms to a plastered wall, considerable care must be taken in placing the nails or screws so that they will engage in a stud instead of just in the plaster. The location of the studs can be found by tapping on the wall with the knuckle or lightly with a hammer. A surer way, however, is to find the nails in the picture moulding or base board and plumb from either of these places with a small weight—such as a nail—on a string.

The designing and making of book racks offer an almost endless field for the imagination. The rack may have a fixed length or be adjustable and either of these forms may have fixed or folding ends, and again the shapes of the ends may be varied in form and decorated in several ways.

134

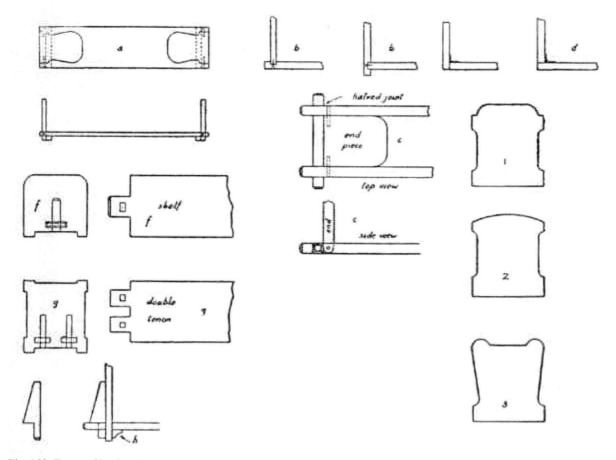

Fig. 152. Types of book racks

Perhaps one of the simplest forms of folding book rack is shown in Fig. 152, at *a*. The ends are sawed out of the bottom piece, pivoted with two ¼-inch dowels and when stood upright the lower part strikes against a cleat, which acts as a rest for the rack and a stop for the end piece.

The weakness of most book racks lies in the gradual weakening of the ends at the joint so that the weight of the books makes them lean outward. This should be considered carefully in working up the design. One of the weakest forms perhaps is shown at *b*. Theoretically, this is all right, but in practice the ends soon bend or lean out. A skeleton form, making use of the halved joint, is shown at *c*.

The two long sides and two short ends are squared up and halved as shown. All the ends are bevelled. Holes are bored for the pivots—¼-inch dowels—a distance from the cross pieces equal to half the thickness of the folding ends. This is to insure the ends standing perfectly upright against cross pieces. If this distance is greater than half the thickness, the ends will lean out, and if less than half, the ends cannot be gotten in place. The bottom of the ends must be rounded, or they will not fold over.

The construction is very simple, and requires little material. Another very ordinary method is shown at *d*. It is as common and simple as it is weak and unsatisfactory. The ends are placed on the bottom piece and hinged. If a cheap and quick method is desired, it would be better to place the hinges as shown at *e*, because then the tendency to tilt out is prevented by the pressure against the bottom piece as long as the screws hold.

A far better method is to mortise the shelf through the end pieces and fasten it with a good, healthy pin or wedge, as shown at *f*; and a still better plan is to have two mortises and two wedges, as shown at *g*.

In constructive design, nothing is lost by honesty. The ends in this case are held in place by pins, so instead of hiding the fact, emphasize it by making these pins big and strong enough to do their work. The rack may be further strengthened by adding corner brackets at *h*.

Having decided on the construction, the form of the ends may be taken up. This is affected somewhat by the construction, but some of the outlines tried by our boys and suggestive to other boys are shown at 1, 2, 3.

They used two distinct kinds. One was characterized by straight lines. These they decorated with chip carving. The other style was distinguished by curved outlines, and decorated by outlines made with the veining tool, and by staining the figures in various colours.

The stains they used were oil colours thinned with turpentine so as to bring out the grain of the wood, rather than to hide it, as in painting, and care was taken to tone down these colours to dull reds, browns, greens, and grays. For staining and polishing, turn to Chapter XLIX.

XXIX

CONSTRUCTION

Fig. 153

The study of construction includes many items such as strength, proportion, joints, etc. If we look at the roof timbers shown in outline at *a* (Fig. 153), the interesting parts of the construction are the three spaces enclosed by circles. The straight lines between these circles do not interest us very much, but the parts enclosed do. Immediately the question arises, how are the timbers fastened at these places? In other words, what kind of joint is used? The joint then is the critical part, or we might say the cream of the construction.

A very large number of joints are in use, but many of them are rare. Our grandfathers, who built their houses and barns from oak timbers hewn out with the axe, commonly used the mortise and tenon, fastened with a generous hard wood pin, and many of them are still standing after a century or two of hard usage. The fact that the beams were rough hewn, instead of sawed, did not in any way affect their strength, because they made good, strong joints.

Some of the more common joints are shown in the accompanying illustrations, and may be used for reference.

No. 1. A butt joint in which the two pieces are fastened together, end to end, by means of glue and dowels. It should be used only in cases where there is little strain in the direction of the two pieces.

No. 2. A dowel joint joining two pieces at right angles. One form of it is shown at No. 3 applied to the leg of a table.

No. 4. Shows two pieces fastened edge to edge by dowels. This joint is often made without the dowels; the two strips, after jointing or fitting, being glued and rubbed together—sometimes called a rubbed joint.

No. 5. A butt joint fastened by nails, brads, or screws, common in box construction.

No. 6. A butt joint where the pieces are not at right angles, owing to the slant. This is called the hopper joint and it is fastened with nails or brads.

No. 7. End lap. A joint much used in house framing.

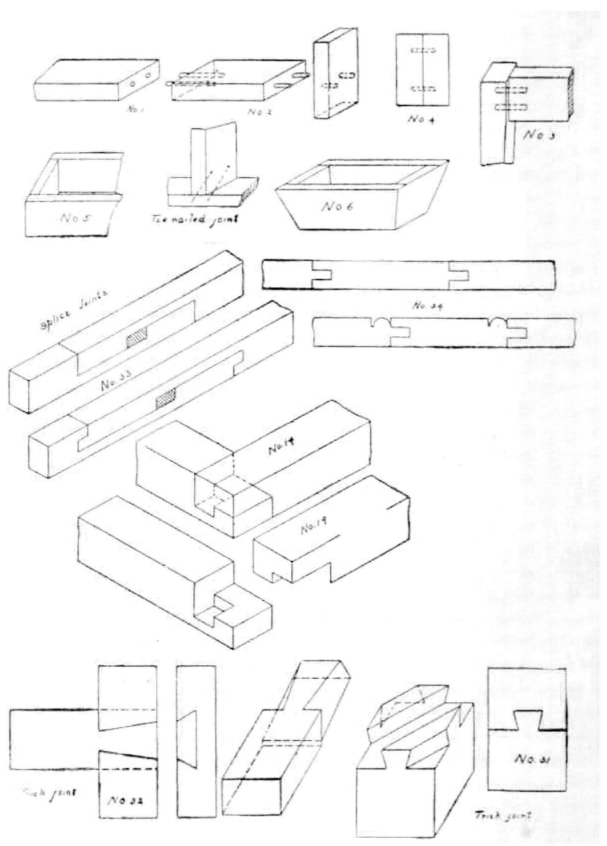

Fig. 154. Joints used in construction

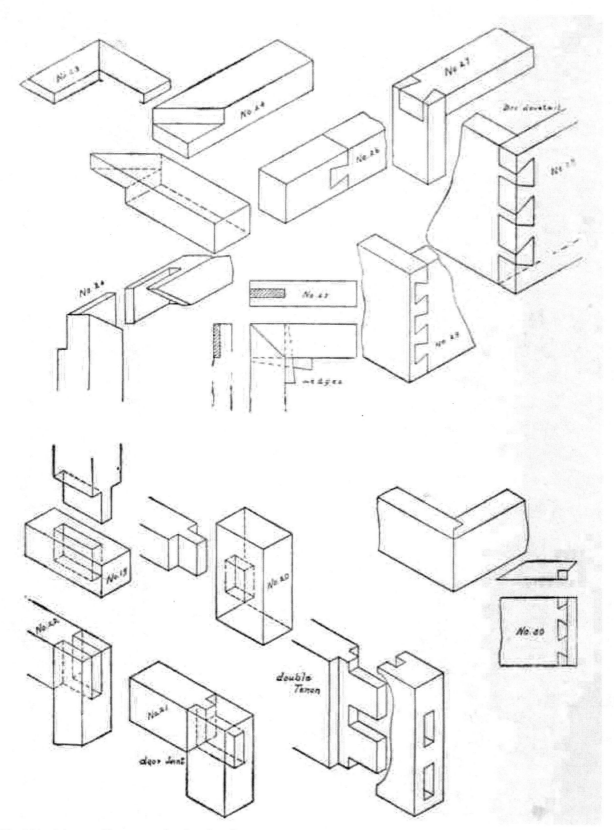

Fig. 154a. Joints used in construction (continued)
No. 8. Shows the lap joint used for splicing two pieces lengthwise. It needs to be nailed or bolted to prevent pulling apart.

No. 9. A middle lap joint.

No. 10. Dovetail lap or lap dovetail. This form resists pulling apart and is a combination of lap and dovetail joints.

No. 11. Shows a modification of the same, only one side being dovetailed.

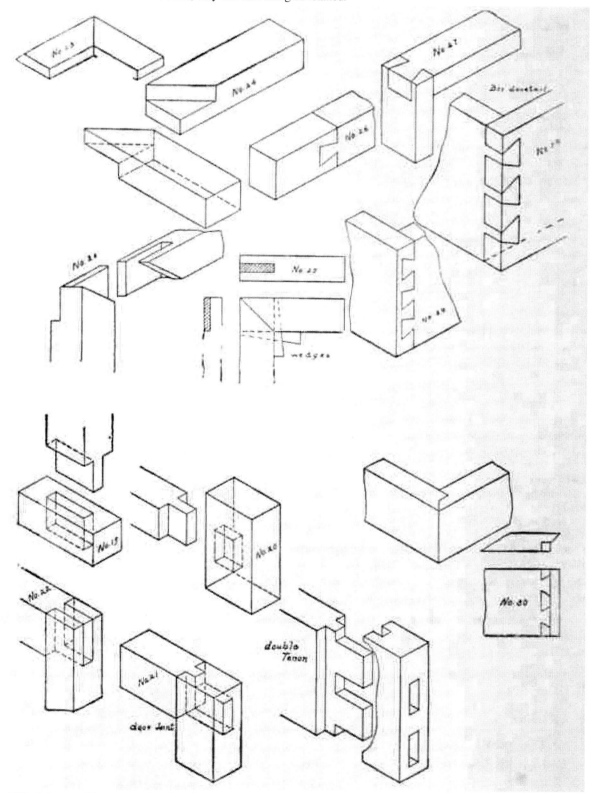

Fig. 154b. Joints used in construction (continued)

No. 12. Halved joint. Both pieces are cut out to half their thickness, and a width equal to that of the other piece. The pieces may be at right angles or some other angle, as shown at No. 13.

No. 13. Halved joint at 45 degrees.

No. 14. Lock joint. This is a form of lap joint rarely used. It resists pulling apart, but should be glued on account of shrinkage.

No. 15. Notched joint; used where two pieces cross, and where full halving is not desirable, as in the sketch of pergola.

No. 16. Rabbeted or gained joint.

No. 17. Dado joint.

No. 18. Gained or housed joint.

No. 19. Through mortise and tenon, used in furniture construction and building.

Note—16, 17, 18 are often confused, and are named differently by mechanics. They are used in boxes, and cabinet work.

No. 20. Blind mortise and tenon, same as No. 19, except that the tenon does not go through and is invisible. These two joints may be fastened with glue, and are often strengthened by passing a dowel through at right angles to the tenon. Another method is to make two or more saw cuts in the tenon, and drive wedges into the cuts.

In door construction, where the rails meet the stiles, the tenon is often divided, as shown by the dotted line. The two parts fitted into separate mortises give the appearance of two distinct tenons on the edge of the door.

No. 21. Relished mortise and tenon or door joint, a form used at the corners of doors.

No. 22. End mortise and tenon. The tenon is seen on two sides. Used for frames of various kinds.

No. 23. The mitre joint, used in picture frames, picture moulding, interior finish of houses, etc.

No. 24. Lap mitre joint; a combination of end lap and mitre; rarely used.

No. 25. Stretcher joint; a combination of end lap, mitre, and end mortise and tenon; used by artists for frames on which their canvas is fastened. The stretching is done by driving wedges from the inside.

No. 26. Dovetail; used as a splice.

No. 27. Single open dovetail for two pieces at right angles. When two or more are cut in the same place, we have the open or box dovetail.

No. 28. Box dovetail; used in cabinet work and boxes.

No. 29. Half-blind dovetail. The dovetails are seen from only one side; used in cabinet work, especially in drawer construction.

No. 30. Blind dovetail. When the two pieces are together, the dovetails are invisible. This joint calls for very accurate work. It is used in special cases, where strength is required, and yet it is desirable to hide the form of construction.

No. 31. Trick dovetail; not used in construction, and only of interest as a curiosity. The four sides of this trick combination are apparently exactly alike. It seems impossible for them to have been put together, and to bring out the effect it is well to have one piece in light-coloured wood, the other dark. The method of laying out and cutting is shown in the illustration. The dovetails that appear on the surface are only oblique sections of dovetailed-shaped tongues and grooves running diagonally from face to face.

No. 32. Another trick. This at first sight appears like a lap dovetail, but the end view shows another dovetail, making it apparently impossible to put together. The construction is shown clearly in the drawing. It is of no value in constructive work.

No. 33. Splice or scarf joint; used in framing, occasionally; of little value to boys.

No. 34. Tongue and groove joint; used in flooring and for sheathing.

Scores of other joints might be shown, but they are seldom used, and are of no value to amateur mechanics.

XXX

THE USE OF THE GOUGE

"There is one tool you have not learned to use," said Ralph, one day, "and I think that it is about time you tried it."

Fig. 155. The gouge

"What tool is that?" asked Harry.

"The gouge ground or bevelled on the outside." (Fig. 155.)

"What is it used for?"

"For cutting concave curves, especially those below the surface. Suppose you practise on a piece of white wood."

A piece of white wood was squared up, a foot long and 1½ inches square. The lines shown in the figure were laid out with the pencil. The marking gauge is not suitable for this work, as it makes a sharp cut in the surface just where the edge is to come, so that after the gouge work is finished, it would show this edge split by the gauge mark. (Fig. 156.)

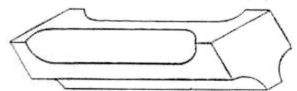

Fig. 156. Practise cuts with the gouge

The two grooves from end to end were first cut, removing a quarter circle, the curve being drawn on the ends by a pair of compasses or dividers. This gave excellent practice in freehand work, calling for good control over the hands, and a constant watching of the grain to prevent splitting.

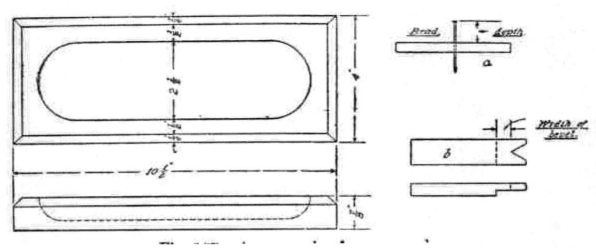

Fig. 157. An example of gouge work

The other two grooves or coves were next tried. Extra care had to be exercised here to prevent taking off the ends.

To give the boy further practice, the simple pen tray shown in Fig. 157 was sketched out, and the stock squared up.

The gouge work in this exercise was entirely beneath the surface, and to make the tool work true to the drawing, a depth gauge was made as shown at *a*. This was simply a straight piece of waste wood with a brad driven into it, carefully, until the head was the same distance above the surface as the depth of the groove called for in the drawing.

By inverting the gauge and running the brad head along the bottom of the groove, the depth could be gauged accurately. The wooden strip must rest on the surface at both sides of the groove, and the brad head just touches the bottom at the same time.

After the gouge work had been carried as far as possible, the groove was finished by sand-papering, first with No. 1½ and then with No. 0 sand-paper.

In laying out bevelled edges on a piece of this character, the same objection to the marking gauge holds as for gouged grooves. Ralph showed the boy a simple method of making a gauge for pencil lines to overcome this difficulty. He cut out a piece of white pine shaped as shown at *b*. The distance from the shoulder to the point of the V was equal to the width of the desired bevel or chamfer. The stock must be held in the vise, as both hands are required in the drawing of the lines. To make the width of the bevel greater, simply cut the shoulder further back with a knife, and to reduce the size, cut the V further in toward the shoulder. This is a very convenient and inexpensive device, quickly made.

A more pretentious project was tried next (Fig. 158, *a*), which provides for a round ink bottle, and demands some nice chisel work. In the first pen tray the bevels had been all planed. On this second one, only three could be cut that way, as the one on the back had to be chiselled. The successive steps in the construction were as follows:

1. Square up stock.
2. Lay out the drawing on the wood.
3. Bore the hole for ink well half way through the wood with extension bit.
4. Smooth the bottom of the hole with chisel, holding it bevel down.
5. Gouge out the groove and gauge the depth.
6. Sand-paper the groove.
7. Cut out the outline of the back with the back saw and chisel.
8. Cut all the bevels, doing the back part—the most difficult—first.
9. Draw chip carving design.
10. Do the carving.
11. Rub down with wax dissolved in turpentine.
12. Insert ink well.

Design No. 3, shown at *b* (Fig. 158), called for molded edges, places for two square ink wells, and a simple carved design in the flat space between them. The process in this case was as follows:

1. Square up.
2. Lay out the work from drawing.
3. Cut out squares ¼ inch deep with socket chisel and mallet.
4. Gouge groove.
5. Make moulded edges by first gouging the quarter circle shown in detail drawing, and doing the long sides with the grain first. Next remove the rest of the wood outside the curved outline with smoothing plane on long sides, block plane on ends. Sand-paper the groove and moulded edges.
6. Lay out and execute carving.

7. Rub down with wax or raw linseed oil.

8. Insert ink wells.

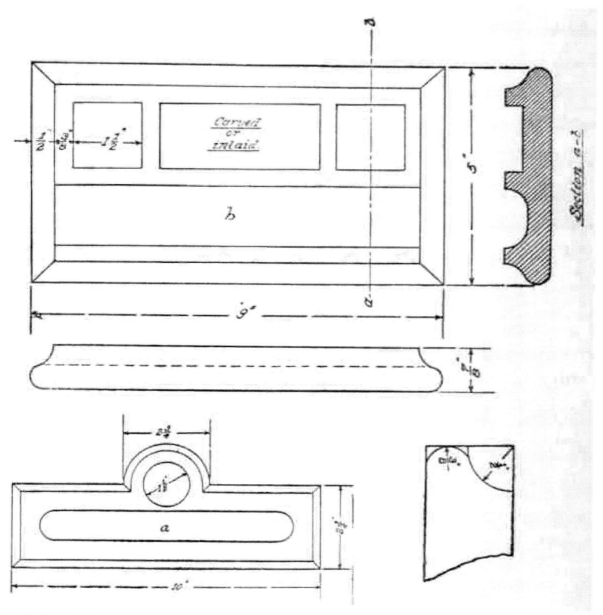

Fig. 158. Pen and ink trays

In place of carving this inkstand, an inlaid design could have been used, and the whole piece highly polished, but our boy had not yet had any practice in inlaying or polishing, so he used sweet gum wood and a chip carving design. Later on he made others out of black walnut and mahogany, and gave them a high polish. See Chapter XXXVI for inlaying and XLIX for polishing.

A very nice little problem in gouge work is shown in Fig. 159, a pen tray pure and simple, with no provision for ink wells.

The only new feature is the under cutting of the outside. The steps for this are:

1. Square up.

2. Lay out from a centre line, drawn completely around the block lengthwise, and draw with compasses and rule both top and bottom.

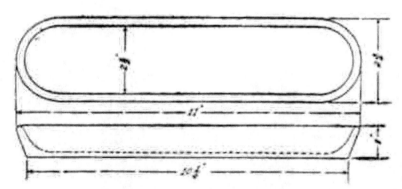

Fig. 159. The pen trap

3. Gouge groove.

4. Plane the long sides to outline of top and bottom lines.

5. Cut ends with back saw and chisel to semicircles on top and bottom.

6. Round upper edge with spokeshave, chisel and knife.

7. Sand-paper with coarse, followed by fine, sand-paper.

8. Polish or wax finish.

Perhaps the most severe test for gouge work is the pin tray shown at Fig. 160. This is something which could be made more cheaply and in less time from metal, but a skilful and careful boy can do it successfully in a hard wood, such as maple. The process is similar to the pen tray. The drawing is laid out on the squared stock, and the bowl cut out with the gouge.

The outside is best executed with a template, or better, two—one for the lengthwise section and one for the width. A template is a form cut out of thin wood or metal; in this case $\frac{1}{8}$-inch wood should be used. By frequently holding these templates to the work, it may be quickly seen where the material is to be removed.

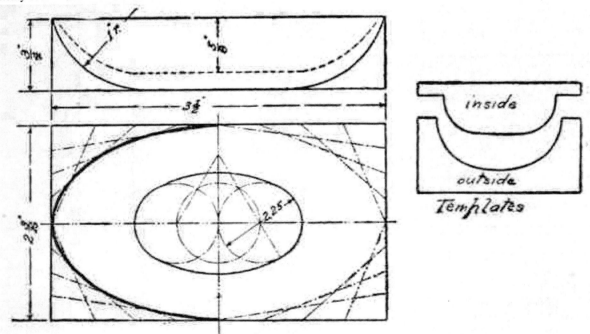

Fig. 160. The pin tray. A fine test of gouge work

When the outside of the tray fits the templates, it is ready for sand-papering, and not before. To make the tray perfect, an inside template can be used. This template method is used in forming boat models.

XXXI

COAT HANGER AND TOWEL ROLLERS

The coat hanger is a convenient thing in every household, and also a good example of spokeshave work.

A soft wood, like pine, or white wood, is suitable, and after squaring up two faces and one edge, the design may be drawn on one or both of the faces with a sharp pencil. Cut close to the lines with a turning saw, and finish to lines with spokeshave.

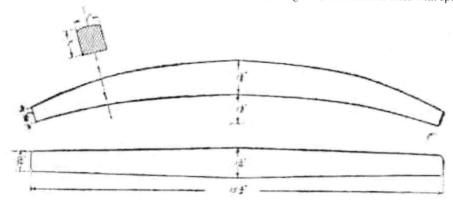

Fig. 161. The coat hanger

The upper edge is next rounded with the spokeshave (Fig. 161), and finished with sand-paper to the cross section shown in the drawing. Bore a hole for the hook with a gimlet bit, and make the hook from strong brass wire, shaped by bending with a pair of pliers. For finishing, two coats of shellac can be used. The first coat after hardening is sand-papered flat with No. 00 sand-paper; the second may be treated in the same way, or rubbed down with ground pumice stone and linseed oil. (See polishing chapter.)

For the kitchen, the towel roller is still used to some extent, especially in the country and suburbs. It consists of four pieces, a back, two brackets, and the roller. These essential parts are shown in Fig. 162 and the back and brackets may be modified and improved as shown at *b* and *c*.

Carving can be used in a simple form on the ends, as shown at *c*. The back and ends are cut out with the usual tools, but it is wise, in cutting the outline of the ends, to glue them together with a piece of paper between, cutting both at the same time. This insures their being exactly alike, and when finished they may be easily separated by inserting the blade of a knife between them. The paper will split, half coming off on each piece.

After the paper and glue have been planed off, a hole is bored half way through each end from the inside. On one end it is necessary to cut a groove of the same width and depth as the hole, clear up to the top, so that the roller can be inserted after assembling, and a towel be put over it. The ends are fastened with two flat-head screws each, by boring through the back, and countersinking.

Two holes should also be bored through the back for fastening it to the wall.

The roller may be turned on a lathe or made at the bench by the following method:

1. Square up the stock to the diameter of the roller called for in the drawing.

2. Find the exact centre of each end by drawing the diagonals with a pencil.

3. Draw a circle on each end from these centres of full diameter.

4. Bore a hole at each of these centres $\frac{3}{8}$-inch diameter, and about an inch deep.

5. Plane off the four corners down to the circle to produce an octagonal form.

6. Plane off the eight corners, using as a stop a small piece of wood fastened in the vise. Hold the roller against this stop, and allow the stock to rest over the open space in the vise. Continue to plane off the edges as long as they are large enough to see or feel.

7. Sand-paper with coarse, followed by fine, sand-paper.

8. Glue into the holes in the ends pieces of dowel long enough to project out about half an inch.

9. Allow the glue to harden over night, and saw off the dowels next day to the proper length. Cut a slight bevel on the end of each dowel with the knife.

If any carving is to be done on the ends, it must be cut before they are screwed to the back piece.

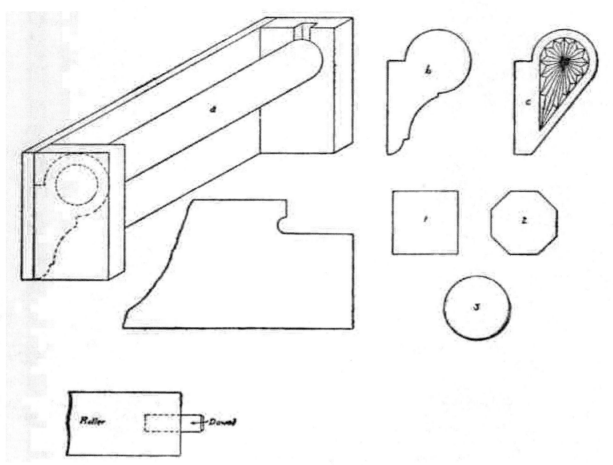

Fig. 162. The towel roller

This method of producing a cylinder without a turning lathe can be used in a number of ways. For example, boys living in the city, where a pull-up bar has to be located in the house, can easily make one in this way, and fasten it between the door jambs at a convenient height.

The blocks for supporting it can be made, as shown in Fig. 163, three inches each way and ½ inch thick. Oak is the best wood for this purpose. It is strong enough, and can be stained to match the door frame.

Bore and countersink four holes for 1¼-inch flat-head screws.

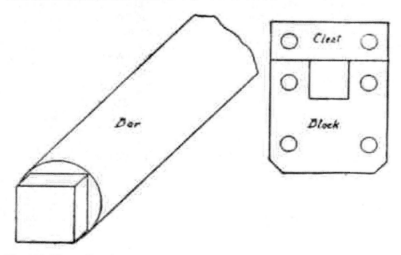

Fig. 163. The pull-up bar

To prevent the bar turning, after it has been planed round and about ⅛ inch shorter than the space between the jambs, lay out a one-inch square on each end. Cut out with a back saw, and chisel until it just fits the square opening in the blocks. This bar can be taken out and stored in a closet, when not in use, and the blocks will never be in the way.

If the bar is so loose in the blocks that it has a tendency to spring out when you jump for it, a flat piece of oak can be screwed across the top, as shown in the illustration.

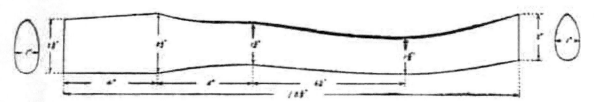

Fig. 164. The hatchet handle. An example of spokeshave work

This is an excellent, if limited, gymnasium for those who get little exercise and whose time and space are limited. Every boy ought to be able to "chin the bar" at least six or seven times without letting go.

Round objects with a taper, such as pointers and musicians' batons, can be made by this method, always getting the taper in the square form first, then planing off corners, etc. It is really work for a turning lathe, but one must work with such tools as he can afford to purchase.

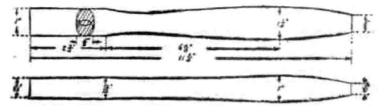

Fig. 165. The hammer handle

Many useful articles of oval or elliptical cross section can be made at a bench which could not be made on an ordinary lathe. The hatchet handle shown in Fig. 164 is a good example. The wood used should be strong and tough, such as hickory or maple. After squaring up the stock to the over all dimensions, the outline is drawn on both flat faces, and sawed close to the lines with turning saw, finished with drawing knife and spokeshave. The oval or elliptical forms are then drawn on the ends, the corners rounded with spokeshave to these curves, and the whole finished with sand-paper.

The hammer handle (Fig. 165) is made in the same manner.

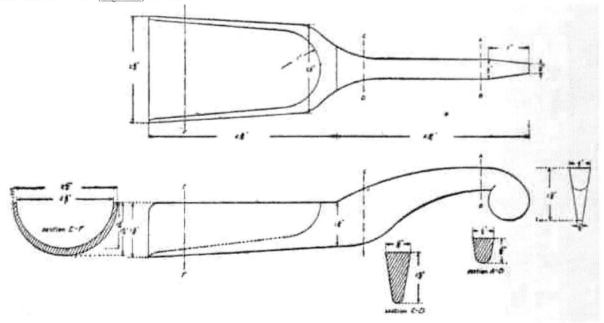

Fig. 166. Sugar scoop

The woodworkers of Northern Europe make many household utensils in this way. The sugar scoop and the wooden ladle, shown in Figs. 166 and 166 a, are familiar examples. In these two cases, the bowl is work for the gouge, while in rounding, some of the surfaces are done with the file. On general principles, it is not wise to get into the habit of using a file on wood, except in rare cases where the material is very hard, such as maple, beech, and similar woods.

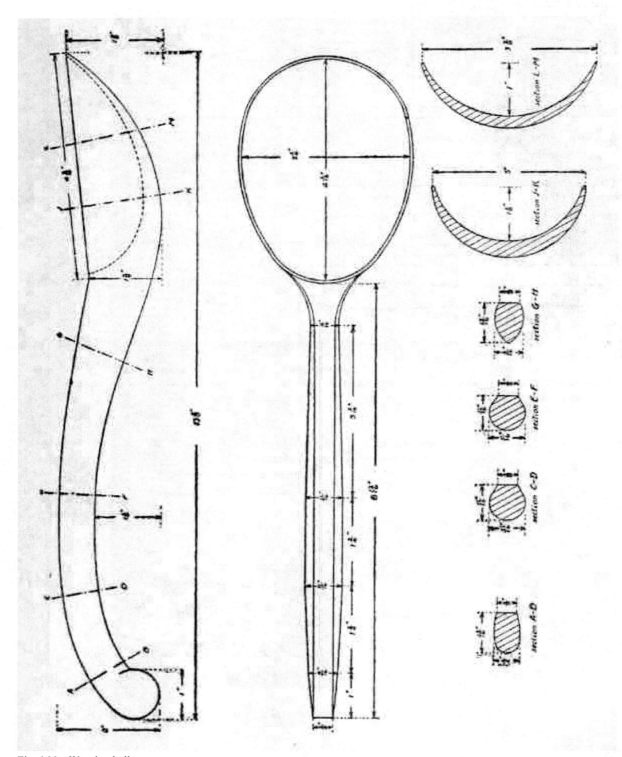

Fig. 166a. Wooden ladle
The towel rack shown in Fig. 167 is suitable for the bath or bed room, and can readily be made by any boy.

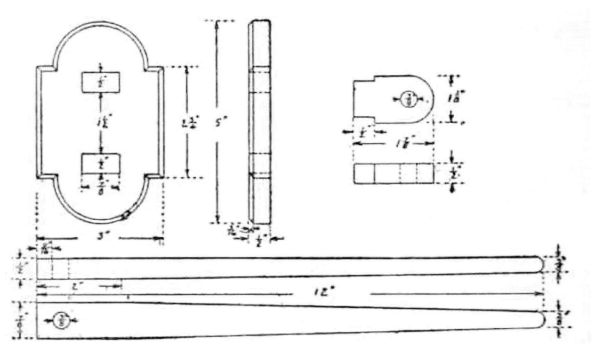

Fig. 167. The towel rack

The back piece is made with plane and chisel. The straight bevels are cut with the smoothing plane, and the curves with the chisel. The two openings or mortises should be laid out and cut before the ends are rounded. The wood is removed by boring several small holes within the lines, and finishing to line with a chisel and mallet. The two supports, or brackets, involve nothing new, and after being finished are glued into mortises.

The towel sticks may be ten inches or more in length, squared up to $\frac{7}{8}$ inch × $\frac{1}{2}$ inch. The taper begins two inches from the bored end, and from this point is planed in a straight line to $\frac{3}{8}$ inch square at the small end. The rounding is done in the same manner as in the towel roller, the tips rounded with a knife, and the whole piece sand-papered smooth.

The three sticks are held between the two supports and a $\frac{3}{8}$-inch dowel passed through the five holes, which should of course be in line.

The ends of this dowel can be split before they are placed, and then in the final position small thin wedges can be driven in with a little glue.

XXXII

CLOCK CASES

Among small articles for household use the clock case is a popular model, and the designs range from the mission style, characterized by straight lines and plain surfaces, up to elaborate attempts at imitating in miniature the old-fashioned tall "grandfather's clock."

While an ordinary alarm clock may be used for the clock proper, the small size nickeled clock, $2\frac{1}{4}$ inches outside diameter, is more satisfactory and very reliable. It costs about seventy-five cents.

In designing the frame, or case, structural items must be considered first. The clock needs a platform to stand on, there must be a circular opening just large enough for the face to fit, and the structure requires an opening in the back, so that the clock may be wound or removed.

With these facts as a basis, the form can be sketched out.

Fig. 168 shows, perhaps, the simplest style, on the mission order. The design of the front becomes a matter of proportion, and the dimensions given are only suggestions which the young designer can modify to meet his own ideas, keeping in mind that on horizontal members, if there is any difference in size, the upper ones should be the smaller.

Simple as this design appears, if put together by mortise and tenon, with provision made for the panelled front and sides, it will call for fine work. As there is no great question of strength involved, the following method will do for making this case. It will be called heretical by expert woodworkers, but is practicable and easy from the boy's point of view.

Square up a piece of $\frac{1}{4}$-inch stock 4 inches wide and 13 inches long. Saw out two pieces for the panels $2\frac{1}{2}$ inches long.

Clamp the front piece to a strip of scrap wood as a backing, and bore a hole for the clock face with an expansive bit. Fasten the front to the end pieces by $\frac{3}{4}$-inch brads, as shown in a. In the same manner nail the top and bottom pieces to the front and ends, making a box of $\frac{1}{4}$-inch wood, with the back open.

The legs, made ¾ inch square with a ¼-inch rabbet cut out as shown at *a*, may now be glued on and fastened with two 1-inch brads driven in from the ends. The horizontal rails are cut and fitted to the front and ends and glued in position.

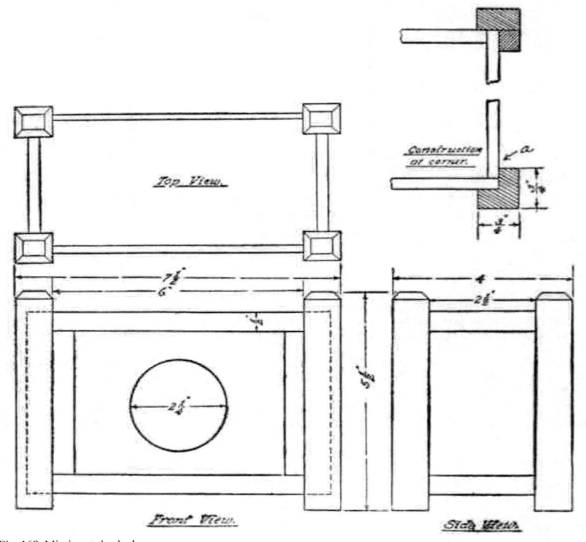

Fig. 168. Mission style clock case

If brads are used, they must be set, and the holes filled with putty, coloured to correspond with the wood used. If the legs of the clock are too short to rest on the bottom, add a shelf, or glue on a block of pine thick enough to bring the clock to the proper level.

If the case is made of hard wood, polish it to a dead flat finish. This design, however, gives a splendid opportunity to ornament ends and front with chip carving, for which gum wood will be suitable.

A clock case which can be easily upset is to be avoided, and therefore these long low designs are to be recommended, when the clock is to stand on a mantel, shelf, or bureau. If the clock is to hang on the wall the designs immediately change. The cuckoo clock is a familiar example.

Our boys wrestled with the problem of a wall clock, and their efforts to create something new brought forth considerable mental perspiration. It is always an easy matter to copy something one has seen, but that is not designing.

The result of Harry's efforts is shown in Fig. 169. After drawing the circles with a pair of compasses, the rest of the figure was sketched out free-hand about a centre line.

When it was fairly satisfactory, the two sides of the lower half were equalized and traced for the upper half. It was then measured, and the main dimensions added to the drawing.

This drawing represented only the front. The back, or wall piece, had to be a duplicate of it as far as outline was concerned, and a plain box of ¼-inch wood, to hold the clock, joined these two parts, as in previous models.

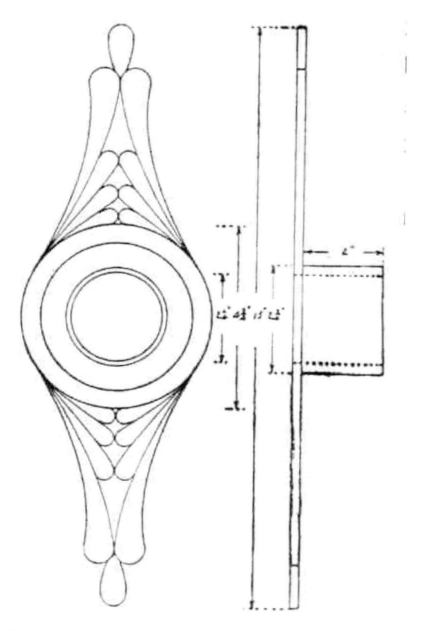

Fig. 169. The boys' first design for a clock case

This is the order of construction:

Saw out stock for front and back pieces 15 × 4¾ × ¼ inches. Draw two centre lines, one the 4-inch way, the other the 15-inch way. At the point where they cross, bore the hole for the clock face, after drawing all the circles with the compasses.

Draw outline, or trace it from original drawing, upon the surface of the wood. Saw out close to outside lines, and finish to lines with spokeshave, chisel and sand-paper block.

Bevel the clock opening ⅛ inch with knife, and smooth with sand-paper. The curved lines inside of the outer edge are worked out with a veining tool.

The back piece is made in the same way, but the central opening is bored larger than the front one, to allow the clock to be withdrawn or wound. The square box, joined to these two main pieces by means of cleats, completes the structure. On account of the long overhang of the front beyond the box, two cylindrical supports of the same material as the case can be glued between front and back, to add strength.

151

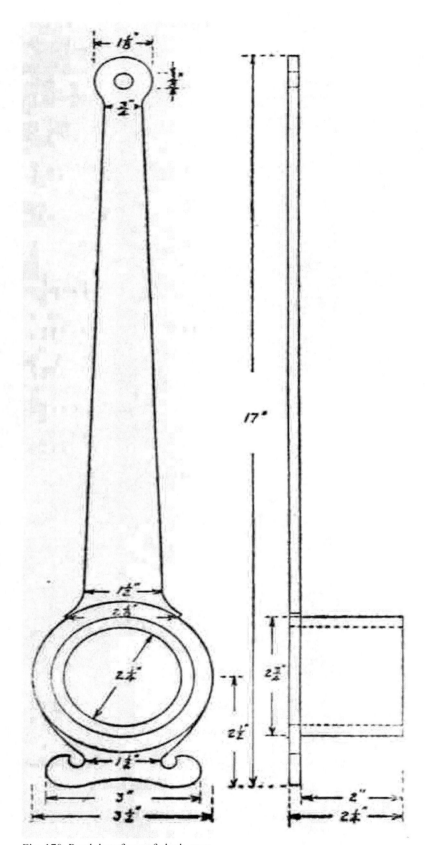

Fig. 170. Pendulum form of clock case

Owing to the symmetry of the design, this case can be hung horizontally or vertically according to the wall space it is to occupy. The method of fastening should be a screw eye at the top of the case and screw hook or nail in the wall, as it will be necessary to remove the clock each time it is wound. If placed horizontally two hooks and eyes will be needed, one at each end. Fig. 170 shows another wall design in which the clock forms the centre of the pendulum and rests in a box of hexagon shape. This is made from a strip two inches wide, the pieces cut on a 60-degree mitre box with back saw, each piece 1¼ inches long on the short side.

It will just hold a clock 2⅛ inches in its largest diameter. When the face of this clock frame is bored, and the outline finished in the usual way, it is fastened to the hexagonal box by cleats.

In order to do this accurately, turn the face upside down on the bench, place the box in position, and mark with a pencil all around the hexagon. The cleats must be fastened on the back, close up to the pencil line, with glue and brads, so carefully that the brads shall not be long enough to come through to the surface in front. When dry, insert the box between the cleats, and make fast with glue and brads. The long part of the pendulum can be either carved or polished plain. The ⅜-inch hole bored in the upper part fits over a screw hook, which should project at least an inch from the wall. To have the clock hang perfectly plumb, this hook should project 2⅜ inches.

Another form of mantel clock is suggested in Fig. 171. It is radically different from the others, and is characterized by a long, low, and massive base cut from a solid piece of wood 1¾ inches thick or built up of two ⅞-inch pieces of red gum, black walnut, or mahogany. The outline having been drawn on the planed surface, one must saw as close to the line as possible, and finish the line with chisel, gouge, file, and sand-paper. The circular piece, which is to enclose the clock, is cut from a block of the same material, two inches thick. Draw the two circles, and bore the inner one with an extension bit, unless a turning lathe is available. In that case the circular block can be turned with great accuracy. The outline can be cut with the chisel after being sawed close to the line, and finished in the same way as the base.

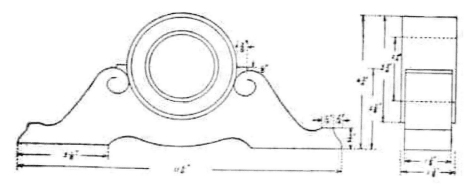

Fig. 171. Mantel clock

Glue this block in position, resting it in the semicircular opening provided in the base, and making it project ⅛ or ¼ of an inch beyond the front surface of the base. Polish to a dead, flat finish.

As the clock is to fit snugly into the opening, the legs, and the handle at the top, must be removed.

THE GRANDFATHERS' CLOCK

One of the most interesting problems in clock case designing is a miniature of the tall clock of colonial times, commonly known as the grandfathers' clock. It is a simple and satisfactory form, but it is very important to have good proportions.

The dimensions used by our boys are given in the drawing. (Fig. 172). As in all the other designs, it is based or built up around the ordinary nickel-plated clock, whose outside diameter is 2¼ inches. With a circle of this diameter as a starter, the other sizes work out as given in the drawing.

About the only fault likely to be found with this form is top heaviness, as the clock is some fifteen inches above its base. This can be counteracted by boring a hole in the back, two or three inches above the bottom, and pouring in about a pound of shot or other heavy material.

The method of construction is as follows:

All the material is ¼ inch thick, except the base and mouldings, which require ½-inch wood. Red gum is very satisfactory, but more expensive woods, such as mahogany, can be used, especially if the front panel, which in full-sized clocks is a door, is to be inlaid.

If gum wood is used, this panel can be decorated with chip carving or simply outlined with a veining tool. If an especially elaborate result is desired, it can be accomplished by a raised panel with moulded edges made of ¼-inch wood, fastened to the front with glue and small brads.

Bill of material:

Base		8½ × 4 × ½
Box	2 sides	17½ × 1¾ × ¼
	1 front	14½ × 3 × ¼
	1 back	14½ × 2½ × ¼ ¼ ˣ
Partitions		2—2½ × 2¼ ×

153

	$\frac{1}{4}$
	1—$2\frac{1}{2} \times 1\frac{1}{2} \times$
	$\frac{1}{4}$
Moulding	$18 \times \frac{3}{8} \times \frac{3}{8}$
Face	$4\frac{3}{4} \times 4 \times \frac{1}{4}$
Sides of top, 2 pcs.	$3\frac{1}{2} \times 2\frac{1}{4}$

After getting out the material construct the long box which makes the body of the design. This will be $17\frac{1}{2}$ inches long, 3 inches wide by 2 inches deep, and the method of putting together is shown at *a*. This allows only one joint to show on each side, and the back piece may be of cheap material, such as white wood.

The smallest partition, $2\frac{1}{2} \times 1\frac{1}{2} \times \frac{1}{4}$, of white wood, is inserted in the bottom, pushed up $\frac{1}{8}$ inch, and fastened with $\frac{3}{4}$-inch brads from the outside. This size of brad will not split $\frac{1}{4}$-inch gum wood, unless driven in nearer the edge than $\frac{1}{8}$ inch.

154

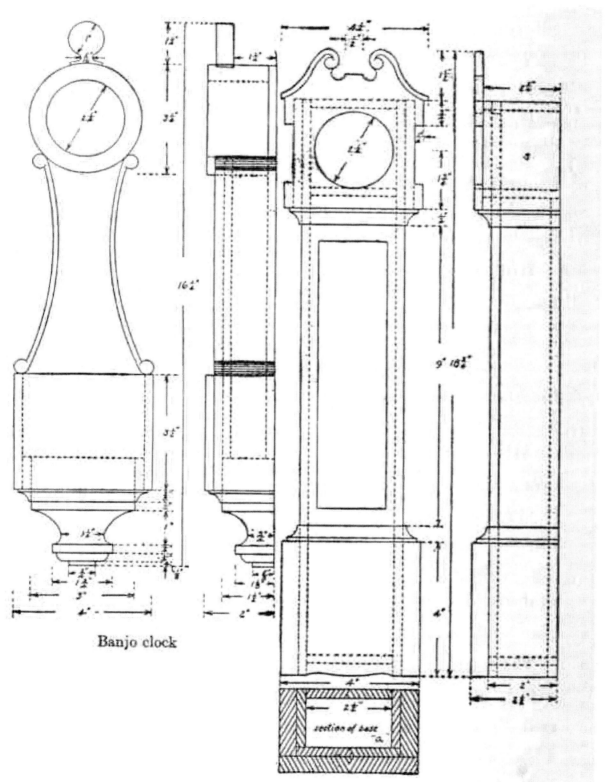

Banjo clock

Fig. 172. Grandfathers' clock

One of the remaining partitions is placed in the upper end, as in a box, one edge flush with the back. The entire back of the case must be in a straight line. The end just inserted will project out in front a quarter of an inch. Place the remaining partition $3\frac{1}{8}$ inches down from the extreme top of the box. This will bring it to rest against the front, which is only $14\frac{1}{2}$ inches high.

The compartment for holding the clock is now complete, open front and back.

155

The base may next be prepared, taking care to have the grain running up and down. The front piece of the base is $4 \times 4 \times \frac{1}{2}$ inches. Side pieces of base are $4 \times 2 \times \frac{1}{2}$. These three pieces are to be put together with a butt joint, as shown in the bottom view, and fastened with one-inch brads and a little glue. Four $\frac{3}{4}$-inch brads can be used on each of the three sides to hold the base to the box. It is very important that the bottom be perfectly square. It should be tested and, if necessary, squared with a block plane.

The cove moulding for upper and lower parts may now be prepared. Square up one piece of stock 18 inches or $20 \times \frac{3}{8}$ inches square. Draw a quarter circle with a radius of $\frac{5}{16}$-inch on each end, and remove the wood in this space with a gouge. Finish with sand-paper. This moulding is fitted around the three sides at top of base with a back saw and mitre box. Put it in place with $\frac{3}{4}$-inch brads and glue, and carefully remove any trace of glue that may appear, before it hardens.

The moulding for the upper part cannot be placed until the top is finished.

After squaring up the face, draw the outline directly on the wood. The curves at the top should be first laid out carefully on stiff paper, cut out with scissors, and traced on the wood.

The opening for the clock, $2\frac{1}{4}$ inches diameter, must be bored first. Either a sharp centre bit or an extension bit should be used. If the latter, an $\frac{1}{8}$-inch hole must be bored at the centre, otherwise the tapering spur of the extension bit will surely split the thin wood. This is the most delicate operation in the whole process, and the circular opening will need smoothing with a sand-paper block.

Having succeeded in getting a satisfactory opening, the outline is sawed close to the lines with a coping saw and finished with sand-paper.

The supplementary pieces s s, $3\frac{1}{2} \times 2\frac{1}{4} \times \frac{1}{4}$ inches, are next fastened to the sides at the top. They are flush with the top of the box and with the bottom of the face piece just described. It is to these that the front is mainly fastened. Test the bottom edges of these pieces across both the front and back with a try square. Fasten the front to these and to the top of the box with brads, and add the moulding, as shown in drawing. If the front panel is to be carved, that should be done before either the base or the top is put on; and if it is to be inlaid, the front should be increased in thickness to $\frac{3}{8}$ inches, reducing the sides to $1\frac{5}{8}$ inches in place of $1\frac{3}{4}$ inches.

After the assembling is finished, set all the brads, and fill the holes with putty, coloured to match the wood. Either an oil or wax finish can be used, but a high polish is not advisable. All lines on the front, which are not edges, can be cut with a veining tool.

Several modifications of this method can be adopted. The front panel may be made a real door, put on with small ornamental hinges. This will increase the work, make it more realistic, but result in little real gain.

The door in large clocks was necessary for getting at the weights and pendulum, but as these parts are missing in our model, the door is not necessary, except possibly for hiding things from burglars. It is the last spot they would be likely to think of as a hiding place for treasures.

As in previous designs, the ring at the top of the clock can be removed, if it prevents fitting into the opening provided.

The drawing shows a curve in the front of the base. It is not essential, but may be cut at any convenient stage of the construction with the coping saw, and sand-papered.

By comparing this design with some real old six-foot clocks, the young designer will see that we have taken some liberties for the purpose of simplifying the work. Highly ornamental tops were sometimes used, with metal and carved ornaments. It is never difficult to make elaborate designs, and the young woodworker can go as far as he likes in that direction. It is, however, sometimes difficult to simplify designs, and this we believe is at present highly desirable.

XXXIII

FOOTSTOOLS

The making of household furniture is a fascinating employment, and as there are varying styles and fashions in nearly all things which pertain to our homes, it will always be an interesting study. The savage knows nothing of furniture, for the ground is his chair, bed, and table. As we go up in the scale of civilization, we find the characteristics of a people reflected in the details of their home life.

In Japan, the house and its equipment are characterized by directness, simplicity, and subtle beauty.

In America, we find a bewildering display of ever-changing devices, styles, forms, and schemes of decoration, in keeping with our rapidly changing and, we believe, rapidly improving taste in the intimate things of life.

This condition is reflected in our furniture as much as in our clothes and in the pictures we buy. The black walnut furniture, with its hard horsehair upholstering, has been followed by antique oak, fumed oak, golden oak, forest green oak, mahogany, bird's-eye maple, French walnut, etc., and in a very few years we shall probably be using some of the beautiful but almost unknown woods of the Philippines, because fashions in woods are very materially affected by the lumber supply.

Gilt chairs—not made to sit on—have been followed by the more sensible mission style, bringing a much needed simplicity, directness, and strength, together with an unfortunate addition of weight for the housewife to move around when cleaning. There seems to be no great gain without some loss. Modern office furniture, with its simple and strong chairs, tables, and desks, can hardly be improved upon, and it is almost a pity that some of these excellencies cannot be introduced into the home, which is often overloaded, overdecorated, and encumbered with unnecessary articles.

Miss Louise Brigham gives us a fragrant breath of fresh air along this line in her interesting book on furniture made from boxes. What is needed is clear thinking. Never design nor make a piece of furniture without asking, "What is this to be used for? What will be required of it?" etc.

This is the gist of what Ralph said to Harry one day when they were about to launch out into the making of footstools, tabourettes and other small pieces of furniture. Harry would have liked very much to start with a dining-room table, but Ralph suggested diplomatically that it might be a good scheme to try several smaller pieces first.

They decided on a footstool, and this is the catechism Ralph put Harry through as they worked out their drawing:

"What is a footstool for?"

"To rest your feet on."

"Is that all?"

"What else could it be used for?"

"Never answer a question by asking another! I should say that a footstool might have to stand hard usage. For instance, suppose you wanted to reach a shelf high up in a closet. If the stool was handy, you would probably stand on it. Others would do the same, and it is easily possible that somebody weighing over two hundred pounds might some day stand on it. So I should say, that the first requisite of a footstool was strength, and the second that it should not be easily upset.

"When designing furniture, just ask yourself such questions, and you will find that your designs will be affected by them. Now I believe that most footstools are too high and too easily upset."

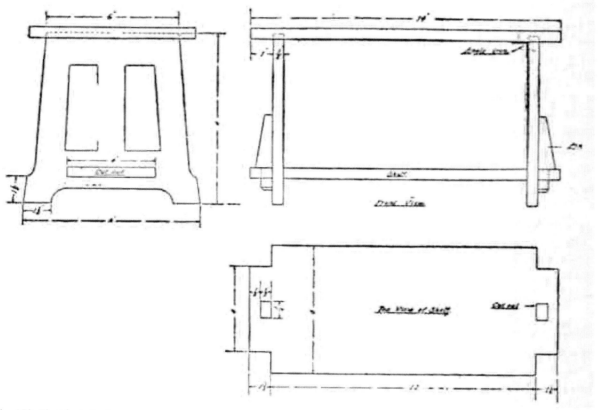

Fig. 173. First foot stool

The first design tried is shown in Fig. 173. The material used was ½-inch chestnut. After squaring up the top, the two grooves were cut to receive the upper ends of the legs. For grooves of this character, after cutting the lines as deep as possible with the knife, followed by the chisel, the router may be used. The cutter can be adjusted by means of the set screw, and a more uniform depth secured than with the chisel.

There was considerable work on the legs because of the mortise for the shelf, and the two openings above. These were cut out close to the line with the turning saw after a hole had been bored in each space, as in scroll saw work.

The outline of the legs was obtained with the same tool, and finished with the gouge, spokeshave, and sand-paper. Where hard wood, such as oak, is used, the wood file may be applied to curved edges.

To overcome the tendency to spread, the legs were made rigid by cutting the tenons shown on the drawing of the shelf. In each tenon was cut the square hole for the wedges. This shelf, when securely wedged, bound the whole structure rigidly. When the question of securing the legs to the top came up, the boys were inclined to use round-head blue screws from the top, but after considering that they would be in end grain, it looked as if this would be the weakest part of the stool. The solution was an heroic one. Four angle irons were made out of strap iron taken from a packing case, and cut with a cold chisel into pieces 2½ inches long. Each had two holes drilled in it to receive the screws, and was then bent into shape in an iron vise. A monkey wrench can be used as a vise for work as light as this. The screws used were ⅜ inch long, one fastened in the top, the other in the leg, for each of the four angle irons.

157

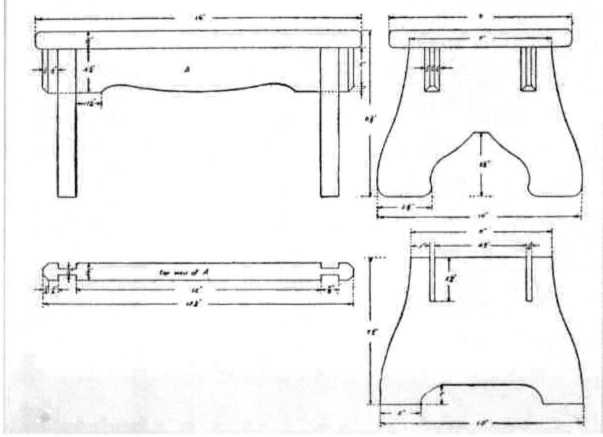

Fig. 174. Second design for footstool

Chestnut has a very open grain, and takes a stain very well. Our boys bought a small can of paste filler, coloured it with burnt umber, thinned it with turpentine to the consistency of cream, and put it on with a brush. The surfaces were rubbed down with cotton waste, and then it was left over night, to be ready for polishing in the morning.

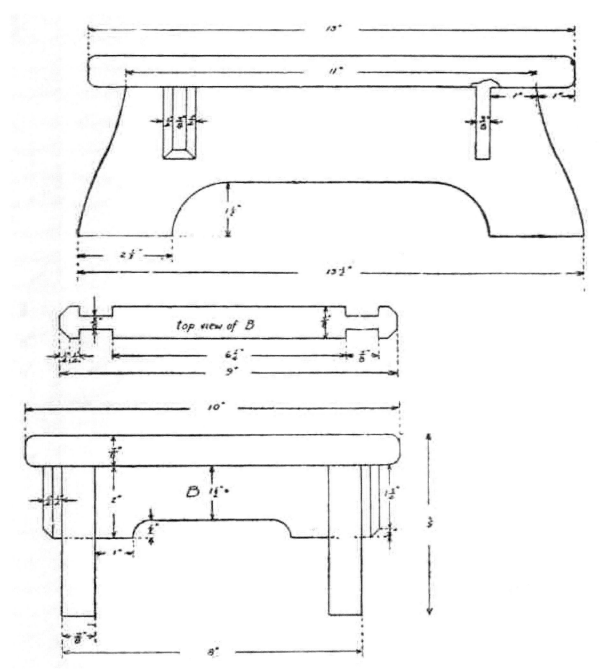

Fig. 175. Third footstool design

After this stool was finished, the boys looked it over critically, and decided that it could be improved on, that it was too high and not heavy enough.

Footstool number two is shown in Fig. 174. In this design, the shelf is dispensed with, and two stretchers or side pieces substituted; stock $\frac{7}{8}$ and $\frac{3}{4}$ inch thick took the place of $\frac{1}{2}$ inch. The two ends were glued together with paper between, cut out as one piece, afterward separated, and the paper and glue planed off. The curved outline was drawn on paper, traced on the wood, sawed out with turning saw, and finished to line as in previous work.

159

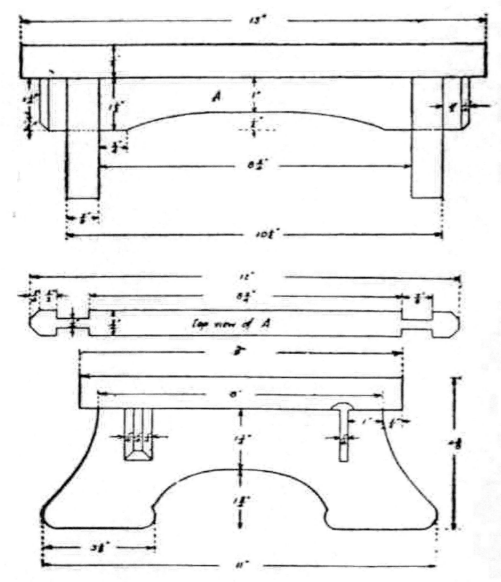

Fig. 176. Fourth footstool design

The joint for fastening the side piece to the legs is shown in the drawing. It makes a strong and rigid combination, calling for a good fit. In putting on the top piece, angle irons can be used, but the boys tried a new method. After gluing the joint, they bored holes and countersunk them through the sides, forcing flat-head screws 2¼ inches long up into the top.

Being below the level of the eye, these were invisible, and they saved the time and labour of making angle irons. Two screws on each side are enough to make a solid piece of work. The material was quartered oak with antique finish. To produce this effect, lampblack dissolved in turpentine was added to the filler, and after drying was polished to a dead flat finish. (See polishing chapter.)

Design number three is shown in Fig. 175. The legs run the long way of the stool; joints the same as number two; top fastened by screws through cross piece. The height, being much less than in the first designs, gives it a very massive and substantial appearance. All eight edges of the top have been slightly rounded with plane and sand-paper. This stool is non-upsetable in the direction of its length. Stand on the extreme end of the top and lean backward; the stool will not tilt up in the slightest degree. Harry tried this several times, but it remained on the floor with all four feet. This does not apply to the width, so the boys designed number four (Fig. 176), which would not upset from the side, where the feet are usually placed. It is even lower than number three, and as the other dimensions are practically the same, it appears even more massive.

The construction is similar to number three, but the legs are again at the ends, and the whole being made of oak, or ash, it is practically indestructible.

A very beautiful golden-brown finish may be given these stools by first coating them with bichromate of potash.

This chemical comes in crystals, which readily dissolve in water. Put it on with a one-inch varnish brush and, when dry, sand-paper down flat with No. 0 sand-paper. Two or three coats of shellac, each allowed to harden and dry thoroughly before being rubbed down with sand-paper, will give a satisfactory polish. Finish by a rub down with raw linseed oil, and wipe dry.

XXXIV

THE TABOURETTE

This is a favourite problem in woodwork for boys, because the tabourette can be put to many uses. It may hold books or magazines, serve as a pedestal for a jardinière, for vases of flowers, for smokers' sets, etc. Its forms are many, and the methods of finishing and decorating infinite.

The five styles shown in Figs. 177 and 178 are perhaps the most common ones, and they are arranged according to the difficulty of construction.

No. 1. Has a circular top supported by square legs, bound to a lower shelf.

No 2. Has an octagonal top supported by flat legs, which are held together by two strips halved together at the centre, and mortised through the legs. It is stronger than No. 1.

No 3. Is the familiar hexagonal form, with only three legs, made rigid by fastening to an hexagonal shelf.

No. 4. Is the standard square form in mission style, mortised together.

No 5. One of the simplest in appearance, is the most difficult to construct, because of the six long joints mitred at 120 degrees, the well-known Moorish style.

As it is easily possible for any boy to make any of these tabourettes with ordinary tools and ordinary patience, they will be taken up in detail.

TABOURETTE NUMBER ONE

Stock.—Four pieces for the legs, $1\frac{1}{2}$ inches square.

The height varies, usually being between fourteen and eighteen inches. It is purely a matter of proportion. Sixteen has been adopted in the drawing as a good average. The top, a circle thirteen inches in diameter, is cut from a piece thirteen inches square and $\frac{7}{8}$ inch thick. The shelf may be an exact duplicate of the top, but it appears much better, as shown in the drawing, as a square with corners cut off to fit against the legs. The method of getting this form is shown by dotted lines on the circular top.

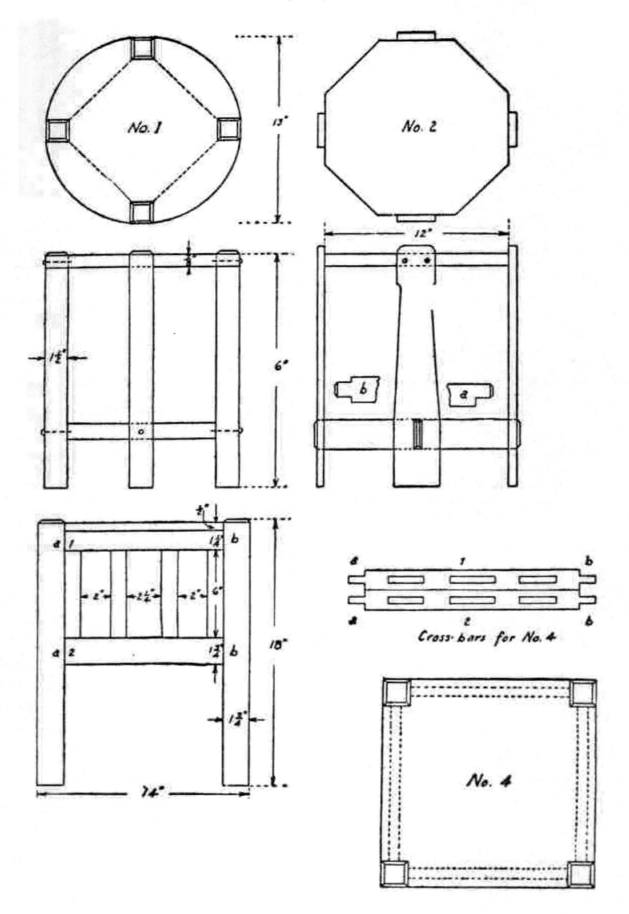

Cross-bars for No. 4

Fig. 177. Three styles of tabourettes

The method of construction is very simple. The top piece being laid out, is cut close to the line with turning saw, and finished to line with chisel and spokeshave. The square openings for legs are sawed out and the wood removed with a chisel. All chisel work should be done on a bench hook or on a piece of scrap board, as a cutting block.

In preparing to assemble, lay the four legs side by side on the bench top or fasten in the vise. Make sure they are equal in length. Four and a half inches from one end draw a pencil line with try square across all four. Half an inch from the other end draw a similar line; this end is to be the top. These pencil lines are for locating the holes for the screws, so that they will all be on the same level. Bore a hole on each line with a bit or drill, large enough so that the body of a round-head blue screw either $2\frac{1}{4}$ or $2\frac{1}{2}$ inches long will just slide through.

Before assembling, bevel or round the top of each leg about $\frac{1}{8}$ inch. Fasten the four legs to the top with the screws, slip the shelf into position, and make fast in the same manner. Stand the tabourette on a level surface, and if it needs levelling, proceed as explained in the making of saw horse.

TABOURETTE NUMBER TWO

Tabourette number two may be modified by designing legs with slight curves. Before cutting these, lay out the four mortises just as the centres for screw holes were located in previous model so that all four will be equally distant from the floor. Cut out mortises by boring several holes within the space to be cut and finish to line with chisel. These mortises should be laid out on both sides of the leg by squaring lines around the four sides.

The top needs no description, as it is just a plain octagon. The principal work in this model is on the cross pieces. They should be laid out carefully, side by side, to make sure that the distance across from shoulder to shoulder is exactly alike on both. The tenon may have two shoulders, as shown at b, or only one, as at a, but in either case the mortises cut in the legs must exactly fit the tenon. The halved joint in the centre must also be carefully fitted.

When all the parts are ready to assemble, drill two holes near the top of each leg for the round-head screws. Insert all the tenons into their mortises and fasten the legs to the top. A little glue may be used in the mortise and tenon joints and one brad should then be driven from the side or edge of each leg through the tenon. Sink the brad below the surface with nail set.

TABOURETTE NUMBER THREE

See chapter on mechanical drawing for laying out hexagon. This form will appear crude unless the legs are modified, and two or three suggestions for this are shown.

The construction consists in fastening to the under side of the top piece a hexagon of $\frac{7}{8}$-inch pine eight inches in diameter, making sides four inches long. Every alternate side of this under piece should be made with a sloping edge to conform to the slant of the legs, of which there are only three. Drill or bore four holes in each leg, two $\frac{7}{16}$ inch from the upper edge, and two to hold the hexagonal shelf. The top edge of the legs should be bevelled with a block plane to fit snugly against the under side of the top. Three sides of the shelf—every alternate one—should be bevelled in the same way to fit against the inside of the legs.

When ready to assemble, fasten pine hexagon to the under side of the top with six $1\frac{1}{4}$-inch screws.

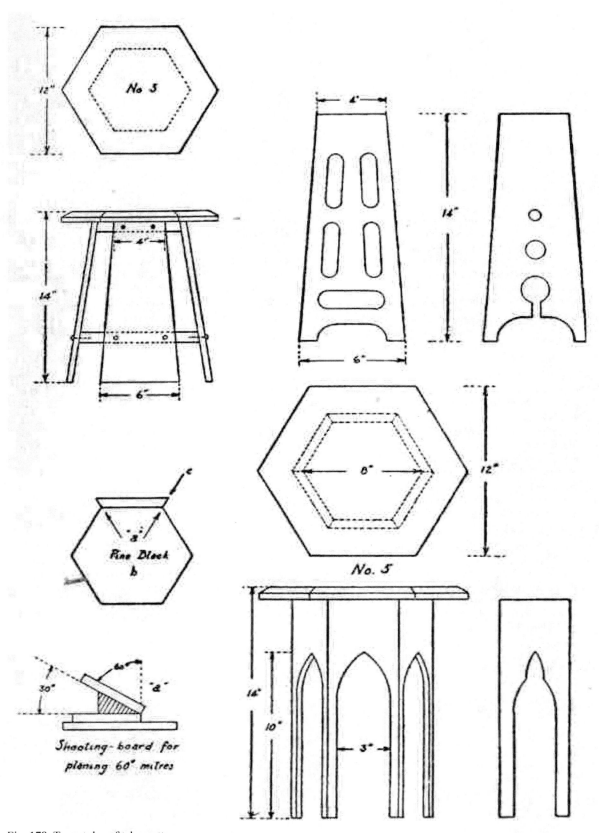

Fig. 178. Two styles of tabourettes

Attach the legs to the three sloping edges of this under hexagon lightly with round-head screws. Leave the screw heads projecting about ¼ inch until the shelf has been fastened in position, then drive them home with the screw-driver. This is one of the simplest of tabourettes to make, but it is open to criticism. The sloping legs give it a wide base so that it is less easily upset than the other forms; but the pressure from above tends to spread them and pull the structure apart. This tendency must be counteracted by a tie piece, which in this case is only a shelf held by screws, some of which are in end grain.

Of course any form may be criticised. The most beautiful of all, the Turkish or Moorish, on account of its overhanging top and small base, is the most easily upset, and in designing new forms all these points must be considered.

TABOURETTE NUMBER FOUR

This is an ideal example of the mission type taken from Mr. Fred D. Cranshaw's book, "Problems in Furniture Making." It calls for forty mortise and tenon joints, and as it is usually made in oak, it requires considerable time for laying out as well as for cutting.

Twenty-four of these joints can be dispensed with by panelling the sides in place of the lattice work. By hinging the top and putting in a bottom, the tabourette becomes a ladies' work box, a shoe box, etc.

In a project of this kind it is absolutely necessary to work systematically. Letter or number each part. Mark the legs *a b c d*, and proceed to work in pairs. After squaring up all the pieces, take side *a b*. Lay out the four joints on *a* and *b* which are to face each other, finish these ready for assembling, lay aside *a*, and lay out *b c*, etc. When you have finished all four sides around to the starting point, stand the four legs up in the position they are to occupy and check up the work to see if any mistake has been made. Treat the cross bars in the same way, marking the tenons *a1, a2, b1, b2*, etc. When you have gotten around the second time, assemble the whole thing and look again for errors.

Take apart and lay out mortises in cross pieces by pairs. Fasten 1 and 2 together in the vise with the edges which are to face each other up as shown in Fig. 177.

Square the lines across both pieces, remove from vise and gauge the horizontal edges of mortises with marking gauge.

To avoid confusion and for change of work, cut out these mortises before laying out the next set, and so for the third time work around to the starting point.

A fourth trip around, making and fitting the upright slats, and the tabourette is ready to assemble. By using liquid glue, which hardens slowly, the whole structure can be put together, fastened with large hand screws or clamps, and left over night to dry.

While the glue is setting, measure carefully for the top, to see if there is any variation from dimensions on drawing, and cut out the top piece. By this time, the amateur woodworker will have more respect for the mission style than ever, and will appreciate the difficulty of reaching simplicity.

The best method of securing the top is with small angle irons fastened to it and cross pieces on the inside. Invert the tabourette, after screwing the angles to the cross pieces, and with the top on the floor, drive home the last four screws.

No; it is not finished! There remains the polishing. See Chapter XLIX.

TABOURETTE NUMBER FIVE

This is so radically different in construction from the previous forms that it requires special consideration. Twelve edges must be planed to a 60-degree mitre throughout their entire length and the fit must be perfect. To accomplish this, first cut out two hexagons from ½-inch pine, 8 inches in diameter, and exactly alike. Construct a special shooting board, at least three inches longer than the legs. Plane a strip of white pine to the shape of a wedge whose angle is 30 degrees. Nail it to the top of shooting board, as shown in Fig. 178 at *a*. By laying the piece to be mitred on this, the edge can be planed to 60 degrees. Lay this on the two pine hexagons as shown at *b*, and with the knife make a mark at the angle *a* on both ends. Connect these two points by a sharp line drawn with a straight edge. Plane this edge on the shooting board to point *a*, giving angle *a c*. Tack this leg by brads to the two hexagons, at each extreme end, driving brads only partly in, so that they can be easily withdrawn. Fit the second leg to the first, and so on around to the starting point. Number or letter the legs, and the corresponding faces of the hexagons, so that they may be easily replaced.

Next take off the legs, lay out and cut the openings with the usual tools. These may be plain Gothic arches or simple modifications.

When the legs are finished, make the hexagonal top and prepare to assemble. Use the best glue. Fasten the first leg in its original position on the pine hexagons, using 1¼-inch brads at the top, driving them all the way into the original holes. Put a coating of glue on one edge throughout its whole length, and rub the next leg up close into position. The brads in the lower hexagon must be driven in only part way, as they are to be removed again. Put all six legs into position in this manner. To bind the legs together while the glue is drying, heavy cord should be wound around them, using strips of wood to prevent marring the angles. Let the whole stand over night.

Next day, plane off any glue that may show, removing the two brads at the bottom, dressing down one side at a time until you have reached the last leg. The pine hexagon at the bottom may be taken out, if it doesn't fall out. Sand-paper the sides with No. 0 sand-paper, wrapped around a block.

The top only remains to be adjusted.

Drill six holes in the pine hexagon at the top, and pass six ¾ or ⅞ inch screws through from the under side into the top piece by inverting, with top on the floor.

There is so much careful work on this tabourette that it is worthy of good material. Mahogany is very suitable, the light coloured bay wood being the cheapest variety; but of course other woods will do. In case bay wood is used, it can be given the appearance of old mahogany by first coating it with a wash of potassium bichromate. Polish.

XXXV

THE DOVETAIL JOINT

While most mission furniture is put together with the mortise and tenon joint, cabinet work calls for the dovetail. All the skill and accuracy possible are needed in dovetailing, and when well put together with this style of joinery, a piece of furniture should last indefinitely.

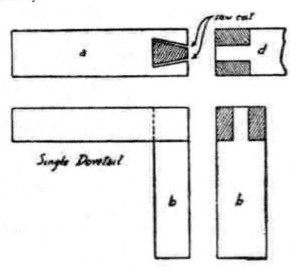

Fig. 179. The Dovetail Joint

The making of joints just for practice may not be very interesting, but in the case of the dovetail it is decidedly advisable. This is what Ralph decided in Harry's case, and he was required to make first a single open joint as shown in Fig. 179. The piece marked *a* was laid out first, after squaring up the stock, and the shaded portion removed with back saw and chisel, sawing so close to the oblique lines that no chiselling was required on these two sides. Piece *b* was next fastened upright in the vise, piece *a* being laid over *b* in a horizontal position, and the form of the dovetail scribed with a knife point. In other words, the first piece cut out was used as a template for laying out the second. The form of the dovetail appeared in knife lines on the end of piece *b*. The laying out of *b* was then completed as shown at *d*. The darkened portions were removed with back saw and chisel, and the two parts carefully fitted and glued together.

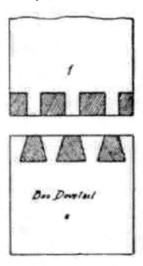

Fig. 180. The Dovetail Joint

This method of laying out dovetails is much surer than that of laying out each piece separately according to the dimensions, as any variation from the figures is duplicated on the second piece, so that they must fit.

This single dovetail was followed by a box dovetail joint comprising three dovetails on one piece, as shown in Fig. 180. The method was the same as before, the three spaces being laid out, sawed, and chiselled. After testing to see that the bottoms of the cuts were square, piece *f* was laid out, cut, and fitted. Seven-eighths pine is good for this practice work, but white wood gives better practice, in that it is harder, and the dovetails cannot be forced together without breaking, unless the fit is good. The harder the stock used, of course the more true this is.

After successfully making these two practice joints, the boy was ready to try his skill at cabinet work. He began with a toilet box in black walnut, to be inlaid later and polished. The over-all dimensions were 11 × 7 × 3½ inches, the height, exclusive of top and bottom pieces, being three inches.

The bill of material read:

2 pcs. walnut 11 × 3 × ½

2 pcs. walnut 7 × 3 × ½

2 pcs. walnut 11 × 7 × ½

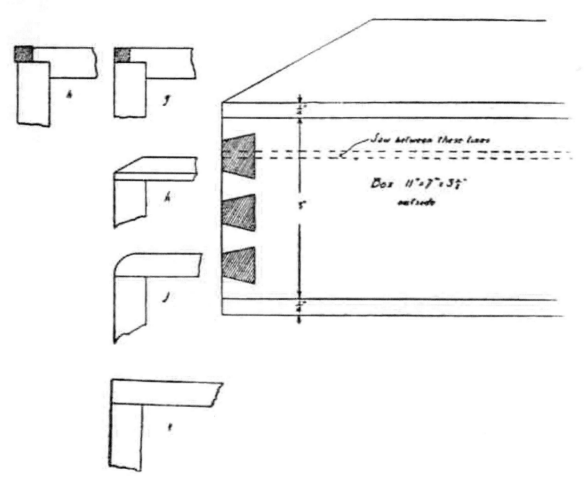

Fig. 181. The dovetail joint used in box design

The process was as follows: Sides squared up and tested. Ends squared up and tested. Sides and ends compared to see if all were exactly the same height. Dovetail joints laid out on side pieces. (The two sides can be glued together with paper between, and cut at the same time, but on this first box the boys laid out each side separately.)

Joints cut and chiselled to line and lettered *a b c d*. This was to avoid confusion in laying out the ends from the sides. Ends laid out from sides with knife. Ends cut and fitted to sides. This short description meant the fitting of four box dovetails, or twelve individual dovetail joints, and it took considerable time. The four pieces were glued and fastened in hand screws over night. Particular care was taken to see that the pressure was evenly distributed, so as not to throw the box out of square.

While the glue was hardening, the top and bottom were squared up half an inch shorter and half an inch narrower than the finished box was to be.

A quarter-inch rabbet was cut on the four edges of both top and bottom. When the box was taken out of the hand screws next day the rabbet allowed top and bottom to fit sides and ends as shown in *g* (Fig. 181). They were glued into position, and again placed in hand screws.

This construction left a quarter-inch rabbet all around the top and bottom of the box. This space was to be filled with square pieces of white holly as an ornamental feature. While the glue was hardening a second time, these little square strips were prepared. The boys found

167

that it would not be necessary to square up the four sides, for if one corner were made perfectly square, the other sides could be planed off after the strips were glued on.

When the hand screws were removed again, all traces of glue in the rabbet were carefully taken off with a sharp chisel. The strips of holly were sawed in the mitre box, and fitted around the four sides of top and bottom. The construction at this stage is shown at *h*, with the holly strips projecting beyond the walnut sides, ends and top.

The strips were fitted and glued in position, and then held in place during the drying process by winding the box in all directions with stout twine.

When thoroughly hard and dry, the whole thing was squared up, as if it were a solid block, and scraped with a steel scraper.

Gauge lines were then made for the cover, as described in the chapter on toilet boxes, sawed, fitted, hinged, and polished.

When a box like this is to be inlaid, the inlaying should be done after the squaring up, but before the cover is sawed off.

The method of ornamenting the edges by strips of different coloured woods may be omitted, and the work considerably simplified by gluing the top and bottom on, as shown in Fig. 181 at *i*, and if this seems too crude, a bevel $\frac{1}{4}$ inch on the sides and ends and $\frac{1}{2}$ inch on the top can be made with the plane. Still another method is to round the edges as shown at *j*.

Where the top is to be inlaid, either *j* or *k* is preferable, as ornamented corners combined with a decorated top is rather too much ornamentation for good taste.

XXXVI

INLAYING

In our search for the simple life with its mission furniture, etc., inlaying has become almost a lost art, but it is so easily done, and if used in moderation so pleasing to the eye, that every boy ought to try it at least.

If simple designs are adhered to, the results are bound to be satisfactory. The materials required are a few pieces of veneering of different thicknesses and two or more kinds of wood. Veneering can be obtained from $\frac{1}{8}$ inch thick down to $\frac{1}{64}$ inch, but for ordinary work the thickness should be $\frac{1}{8}$ inch, $\frac{1}{16}$ inch, and $\frac{1}{32}$ inch, and the woods, ebony, holly, walnut, mahogany.

A good collection for simple designs is:

$\frac{1}{8}$-inch ebony, holly, mahogany

$\frac{1}{16}$-inch holly, rosewood, walnut

$\frac{1}{32}$-inch holly, mahogany

The tools required are a mitre box, back saw, socket chisel, and mallet.

The process consists of building up the design, cutting out the opening, gluing the design in the opening, and dressing down.

BUILDING UP THE DESIGN

It pays to make a full-sized drawing of the design, as the relation of the inlaid work to the space it is to occupy is important. For a box proportioned like the one just described, 11 × 7 inches, the inlaid design should be in about the same general proportion. A square centre piece in such an oblong space would not look well; it should be about one and a half times as long as the width. The best plan is to draw the box top full size and then carefully work up the design.

This sort of designing will be a new experience, as the veneering is all cut in a mitre box, no tool but a saw being used, and this fact limits the designs.

Several pieces of the veneer are glued together and placed in hand screws over night.

Suppose the combination shown at Fig. 182 is used. Five thicknesses composed of two $\frac{1}{16}$-inch walnut, next two of $\frac{1}{16}$-inch holly, and in the centre one $\frac{1}{8}$-inch ebony, will make a strong combination $\frac{3}{8}$ inch thick.

Fig. 182. Inlaid designs cut in a 45-degree mitre box

The dimensions should be about 18 inches long by 3 inches wide. These five pieces when glued together make a solid piece $18 \times 3 \times \frac{3}{8}$ inches. This built up board is sawed into strips $\frac{1}{8}$ inch thick, and these strips $\frac{3}{8} \times \frac{1}{8}$ inch form the basis of the design.

In drawing the centre piece, border, or whatever form the inlay is to take, it must be constantly kept in mind that $\frac{3}{8}$ inch is the width of the pieces. Fig. 182 shows the shapes possible on a 45-degree mitre box. Four pieces like *a* make a square. To make an oblong design from this shape, ten pieces will give *b*. Four pieces like *d* will give a hollow square, in which may be fitted a piece of fancy wood such as rosewood, snake wood, satinwood, or some other South American wood.

The Greek cross is a favourite figure, and it is composed of twelve pieces, eight like *f*, and four like *a*. Some of its variations are shown in *c c*.

This design can be elaborated as shown at *e*. Some of the most pleasing combinations are extremely simple. An oblong piece of beautiful wood such as bird's-eye maple, with a simple mitred frame, is far more satisfying than the more complicated figures.

The Swastika is a favourite among boys, and it is shown at Fig. 183 applied to an oblong box design. In such a figure the border strips are not put on until all the pieces for the Swastika are cut out, fitted, and glued.

In many of these designs two, three, and sometimes four gluings are necessary. The pieces, having been cut and fitted, are all brought together on a piece of paper and glued with liquid glue. The hot glue dries too quickly. The paper holding the design is laid on a piece of pine $\frac{7}{8}$ inch thick, and wire brads driven into the pine up close to the inlay to hold the design together while it dries. Two nails should be used against each piece of the outside border. These nails may be used to exert pressure by bending them with the fingers over the design to force the pieces together.

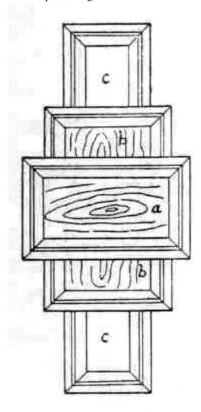

Fig. 183. The Swastika used as an inlay

When each piece has been pressed into place, allow it to stand over night. Next day bend the nails back, and lift the design, paper and all, out of its nail fence, tear off the paper and cut away any glue that projects beyond the edges with a knife or chisel.

You now have a solid inlaid design $\frac{1}{8}$ inch thick ready for use. Find by measurement the exact place where you want this figure, lay it on the surface and with a sharp knife scribe a line around the design. Place the inlay to one side, and cut out to a depth of $\frac{1}{8}$ inch the whole space inside the knife lines. This can be done with socket chisel and mallet, or with a router. The final cut should be made with the chisel, bevel side in and straight down.

You now have a space cut in the surface the exact size of the design, except possibly the depth. Coat the bottom of this space with glue, press the design down into the space and hammer it tight with the mallet and block of soft wood.

Allow the glue to harden thoroughly, plane the design down to the surface, scrape, and sand-paper.

This is one of the things much more easily done than described on paper.

Instead of the solid designs just described, an inlaid border is sometimes preferable. Fig. 182 at *g* gives a good idea of a very neat one. In this case, the groove to receive the inlay is drawn directly on the surface of the box, and cut out to the usual depth, ⅛ inch. The pieces of inlay are sawed out in the mitre box and fitted into the groove individually, but not glued until the entire border has been fitted. They are done all at one time, and then a piece of board is laid over the whole top, and it is placed in hand screws over night.

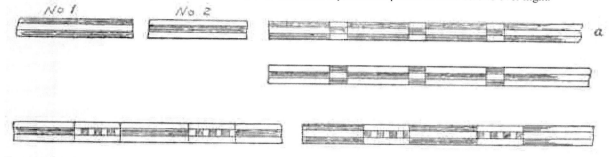

Fig. 184. Built up borders for inlaying

The number of combinations which can be obtained from three or four veneers of different thicknesses is astonishing, but perhaps the most interesting form is called built up work. Fig. 184 shows several forms of built up borders. The method of making *a* is as follows:

Ebony and holly ⅛ inch thick are required and two separate combinations are glued up, one containing two pieces of holly with one ebony, and the second two of ebony with one holly.

When dry, saw out of each combination a strip an inch or an inch and a quarter wide. From strip No. 1 saw a dozen or more pieces an inch or so long. To make these pieces exactly alike, drive a nail into the bottom of the mitre box an inch from the 90-degree saw cut. By pushing the strip up to this nail each time a cut is made the pieces must be the same length.

For combination No. 2, shift the nail to ⅜ inch from the saw cut, and saw out an equal number of pieces as from No. 1.

By gluing these pieces together alternately, border *a* will result. It is necessary on these built up combinations to add an outside retaining strip of thin veneer to hold the pieces rigidly together.

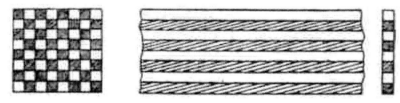

Fig. 185. Method of making an Inlaid checker-board

When the final gluing has dried, the usual ⅛-inch strip should be sawed out. This is best done on a power, band, or circular saw, but it can be done by hand if the rip saw is good and sharp.

Other built up combinations may be handled in the same way. For square spaces, the checker-board is a great favourite. It calls for a dark and light veneer of ⅛ inch thickness. Glue up four light and four dark pieces in alternation as shown in Fig. 185. When hard, saw out eight strips as wide as the veneer is thick. Glue these eight strips together, reversing four of them, so that the black and white squares come together. The result will be a solid piece one inch square, and by sawing off ⅛-inch slices, each slice will be a checker-board composed of ⅛-inch cubes.

The very best glue obtainable is needed for this work, especially if the woods are ebony and holly, as these are so hard that the glue cannot penetrate.

When a 30-60-90-degree mitre box is used to cut the strips, an entirely different class of designs is obtained. Fig. 186 shows some of the endless possibilities of these combinations. They are suitable for the top and shelf of an hexagonal tabourette, and the oblong figures are suitable for the top of an oblong box or the space between the wells of an inkstand.

Some of the simplest yet most effective forms give the impression of overlapping shown at *a*, Fig. 183, this being an oblong piece of fancy wood with a narrow mitred frame around the four sides; *b b* are pieces of the same kind of wood but different from *a*, with a narrow frame on three sides; *a* appears to be laid over *b*, and *c c*, still another kind of wood, both cut from the same piece.

It looks more uniform and harmonious if the frames of the five pieces representing three distinct kinds of wood are the same.

It is important in choosing these borders to see that the outside veneer be in marked contrast to the surface into which the design is to be set.

A very simple centre piece may be made interesting by surrounding a plain oblong or rectangle of rare wood with an interlaced border.

Inlaying of curved designs means some difficulty in accurately cutting out the opening to fit the design; but this is overcome by reverting to the ancient art called marquetry work. Three or more veneers 1/16 inch thick are glued together at the corners and the design drawn or glued on the top layer.

171

Suppose the figure is that of a butterfly. Assume that the veneers are holly, mahogany, and rosewood. With a fine fret saw cut or saw directly on the lines. The three thicknesses being sawed at one time, the pieces must exactly fit. The rosewood may be used for the outer edge of the wings, the holly for the main part of the wings, and the mahogany for the body. As all these parts fit accurately, they may be glued to a ¼-inch backing piece and dried under the pressure of hand screws. Flowers, birds, etc., in infinite variety, and even landscapes, can be cut out and used in this way. Veneers coloured green are on the market and may be used for leaves or foliage effects.

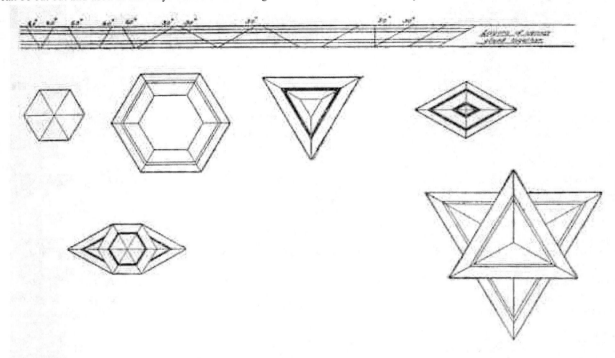

Fig. 186. Designs cut on 30-60-90-degree mitre box

A great deal might be written about this old style of ornamental woodwork, but it would deal almost entirely with questions of design, as the method would be practically the same in every case. One form of this interesting art is called buhl work, in which sheet brass, German silver, or even the precious metals are used. Brass and ebony were a favourite combination at one time, the two layers being glued together with paper between. The design was sawed out, and then a sharp knife blade inserted into the joint to separate the brass from the ebony. That gave two distinct designs. In one case it was a brass background with ebony inlay. In the other, an ebony background with brass inlay.

There will always be as many resulting combinations as there are original layers of material. A backing of cheap material is always necessary to support the finished work to which it must be securely glued. In polishing the finished surface, a steel scraper must first be used, followed by fine sand-paper; then polish.

Some of the newer forms of decoration, while lacking the richness of inlaid work, admit of greater freedom. Pyrography, for example, is closely akin to drawing, and in the hands of a careful worker may be made to produce very artistic effects. Like all arts, it also has its limitations. In woods of the pine family, it will not do at all, on account of the pitchy sap. In dark-coloured or very hard woods, it is equally unsatisfactory, so that it is used almost exclusively on basswood, because of the white colour, softness, even grain, and freedom from pitch.

Outfits for pyrography may be purchased quite reasonably. They consist of a glass bottle containing benzine; the vapour from this is forced through a rubber tube by means of a bulb held in the left hand out to a platinum point. This point is first heated in the flame of an alcohol lamp sufficiently to ignite the benzine vapour as it comes out through openings in the point.

While the left hand keeps pumping the vapour, the right hand guides the point along the lines of the design, which has been drawn or traced on the wood.

Many articles made and stamped with designs are to be had at the art stores; but the joy and satisfaction in achievement come from making the articles and originating the designs.

Basswood is very easily soiled by handling and a coat of white shellac should be applied after the burning is finished. Sometimes staining is used on certain parts of the design, as for flowers or fruit, and in that case the staining must be done before the shellac is applied.

XXXVII

THE CHECKER-BOARD

A favourite project among young woodworkers is the checker-board. While it is closely akin to inlaying, the method of making it to avoid unnecessary labour is here suggested. As the checker-board consists of sixty-four squares of equal size and divided equally between two kinds of wood, one dark and the other light, some way must be devised to insure their being exactly alike to make the board a success. Considerable care should be used in the selection of the woods, for while they must present a strong contrast in colour, they should be as nearly as possible of the same degree of hardness, to make the working uniform.

If soft woods are used, red gum and basswood make an agreeable contrast in colour. Basswood is not a very satisfactory wood to polish in its natural colour, however.

Among the hard woods, a combination of black walnut and rock maple, or mahogany and maple, or even cherry and maple, can be used. Any one of these combinations will be more satisfactory in the finished work than the soft woods mentioned. The work will be harder of course, but in woodwork as in other things, nothing really good is obtained without effort.

Assuming that the woods have been selected, four strips of dark and the same number in light coloured wood should be squared up to a width of $1\frac{1}{4}$ or $1\frac{1}{2}$ inches according to the size of the squares to be made.

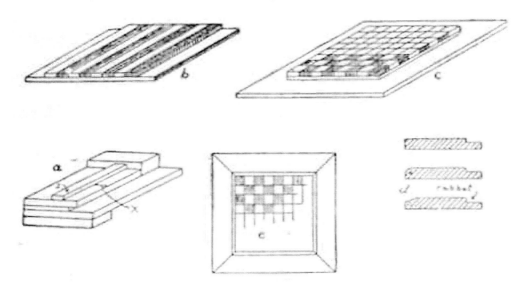

Fig. 187. Method of making a checker-board

As in other woodworking problems, have a full-sized or half-sized mechanical drawing ready before using a tool.

A checker-board built up of $1\frac{1}{4}$-inch squares will be ten inches square without the frame. (See Fig. 187.) With $1\frac{1}{2}$-inch squares, it will be twelve inches on each side. This is amply large and a satisfactory working size. The material should be either $\frac{1}{4}$ inch or $\frac{3}{8}$ inch thick. Plane the strips about sixteen inches long by one inch and a half wide.

Lay the four strips of dark wood on edge on the bench top and carefully fasten the four in the vise. Remove a light shaving to insure their width being all alike.

Treat the light strips the same way.

Next place all eight strips together and examine for inequalities. Too much care cannot be exercised at this point, as the success of the problem depends on it.

To make doubly sure, reverse every alternate strip end for end, and if inequalities appear place all eight strips in the vise and remove a light shaving. One of the best methods for making these strips of equal size and with perfectly square edges is to construct a shooting board, or arrange one already made, as shown at a.

The strip s is set to a gauge line made $1\frac{1}{2}$ inches from the edge. The strips are laid in this space and planed in the usual way, until the plane touches the stop. This makes the width of all pieces the same and gives true edges.

These eight strips placed alternately light and dark are now glued upon a backing of soft wood, $\frac{1}{4}$ inch or less in thickness. Gluing must be done thoroughly, each strip being rubbed back and forth until a good joint is made with its neighbour.

A piece of newspaper is spread over the top, heavy pieces of flat stock placed top and bottom, and the pressure from several hand screws applied while the glue is drying.

The best liquid glue obtainable should be used, and the paper on top prevents the hand screws being glued to the wood.

This combination must stand until the glue is thoroughly hard, if it takes forty-eight hours, which it does sometimes in damp weather.

When dry, remove hand screws and tear off paper. Square outside edges if backing projects or glue adheres. With a large try square or steel square lay out parallel lines across the combination $1\frac{3}{4}$ inches apart. Saw on the lines with cross cut saw, unless a mill is handy, when it can be done more accurately with a circular or band saw.

The new strips will be $1\frac{3}{4}$ inches wide, less the amount removed by the saw. Dress them down to a width of $1\frac{1}{2}$ inches on the shooting board. This should bring the eight pieces on each strip to squares $1\frac{1}{2}$ inches on a side.

Eight of these strips make the checker-board. The original pieces, being sixteen inches long, allow for two or three extra strips in case any are spoiled in sawing or planing.

173

These finished strips are now to be glued together on the permanent backing, which should be ¼ or ⅜ inch in thickness, of the same material as the frame is to be and about eight inches each way longer and wider than the checker-board proper.

This should be placed carefully in the centre of the backing, joints rubbed and fastened by cleats 1 × ½ inch tacked to the backing on all four sides.

While this is drying under pressure of the hand screws as in the first gluing, square up the moulding which is to act as a frame: *d* shows two styles. In both mouldings, a rabbet ½ inch or so wide and ⅛ inch deep should be made with rabbet plane. The outer edges may be square, rounded, or bevelled.

When the checker-board is removed from its final gluing, this moulding is to be mitred and fitted about it as in making a picture frame. Before doing this, remove all glue from edges with a chisel so that the frame will fit snugly to the checker-board.

The frame is to be glued to both backing and checker-board and again placed in hand screws. While this is drying, an inlaid border strip as wide as the rabbet, either plain or built up, should be prepared.

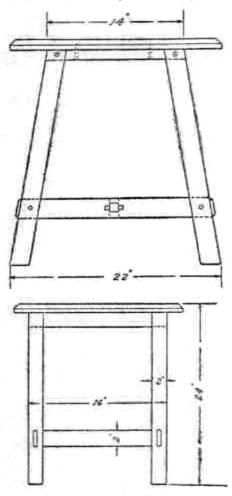

Fig. 188. Checker-board tables

This strip, as well as the rabbet, may be omitted entirely, but should the frame be of the same material as one of the woods used in the checker-board it is necessary, and in any case it adds a finish to the work that is very pleasing. Inlaid designs may be set into the frame and a very elaborate result obtained, if desired.

After this last gluing, set in the inlay, and when dry, plane, scrape, and sand-paper the whole surface flat, and square the edges of the frame.

This makes a very substantial and heavy board, worthy of any woodworker and worthy of being used as a table top. Such a table may be constructed as shown in Fig. 188. It calls for mortise and tenon joints cut at an angle, and if this style of work is considered too difficult vertical legs can be used. This under structure should be of the same kind of wood as the frame of the checker-board, and if oak is used the stain should be applied before placing the inlaid border. Bay wood is preferable to oak for inlaying but is more expensive.

On a small table of this size, where vertical legs are used, the base is so small that the structure is top-heavy and easily upset, so that the problem becomes a very interesting study in design.

When the entire table has been put together, polish it. If mahogany, finish in natural colour; if oak, any of the styles described in the chapter on staining may be used, with care taken to keep the checker-board itself in the natural colours.

XXXVIII

TOOL CASES AND CHESTS

After our boys had made several dovetailed and inlaid boxes, Ralph announced that his pupil was ready to attack the construction of a tool cabinet. It was to be fastened to the wall over the bench, designed to hold most of the small tools, and to be in such a position that it could be reached from the front of the bench.

The cabinet designed was really a dovetailed box 30 × 20 × 6 inches over all. It was made of ½-inch quartered oak except the back, which was ½-inch pine. The bill of material was:

1 piece pine 30 × 20 × ½   2 pieces oak 20 × 5½

1 piece oak 30 × 20 × ½   2 pieces oak 30 × 5½

The front and back, each 30 × 20 inches, were made of two pieces 30 × 10 inches, jointed and glued, placed in clamps over night and the joints planed down to take off the excess glue which had oozed out under pressure of the clamps. While these two parts were gluing, the sides and ends were dovetailed as in previous boxes.

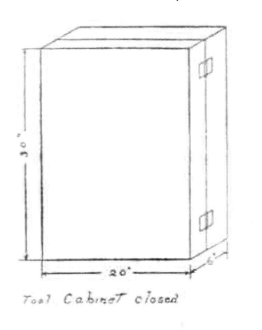
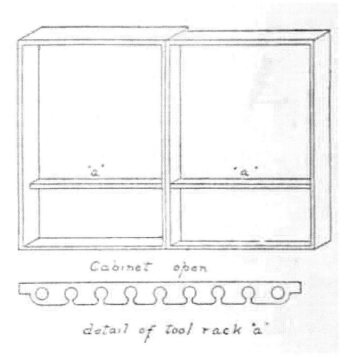

Fig. 189. A tool cabinet

When the front and back pieces were glued in place on the box, they were further fastened by 1-inch brads, set below the surface, and the holes filled with putty, coloured to correspond with the stain. The colour of the finish was a dark, handsome green. The box was sawed in two along a line 2½ inches from the front.

This divided the cabinet into two parts, the door or front section having a clear depth of 2 inches, and the back or wall section a depth of 3 inches.

After hinging the door section in position, the cabinet was stained inside and out, the outside polished and a hook for fastening the door shut was placed in position.

The cabinet was fastened to the studding of the shop by four strong screws 1½ inches long. The various nails, hooks, and tool racks were next added and the cabinet was ready to use.

Patent racks for holding chisels, gouges, etc., are sold in hardware stores, but our boys preferred to make their own. Their chisel rack is shown in Fig. 189.

After squaring up and cutting out the recesses at the ends, holes were bored, the opening from the front cut with back saw, and the sharp edges rounded with chisel and sand-paper.

Holes for the screws at the ends were bored and countersunk.

175

In locating a tool cabinet of this kind, while it should be very easily reached, and is usually open during work hours, it should be placed high enough so as to be easily opened or closed without striking tools and work on the bench. In other words, it should not be necessary to clear the bench top in order to open the cabinet. About 6 inches between under side of tool cabinet and bench top is about right.

An old-fashioned tool chest, suitable for shipping a whole kit of tools any distance, is shown in Fig. 190. These chests were usually fitted with trays divided into compartments for small tools and hardware. Such a chest may be made of either hard or soft wood and its construction is as follows:

After making out a list of material, square up sides and ends exactly as in making any box. Lay out, cut and fit the dovetails. The bottom, on account of its width, will have to be made of two pieces. These may be jointed, glued and placed in clamps or put together with a tongue and groove joint. The latter plan calls for a special plane. Having prepared the bottom by either of these methods, bore and countersink holes about 6 inches apart in the bottom and secure rigidly to sides and ends by $1\frac{1}{2}$ or $1\frac{3}{4}$ inch flat-head screws.

For the top, make a frame from $\frac{5}{8}$ to $\frac{3}{4}$ inch thick and 3 or 4 inches wide, putting the ends together with end lap or mortise and tenon joints.

Secure this frame to top of box by screws. These may be round-heads, or if it is desirable to hide them, the method shown in Fig. 190 can be used. This is accomplished by boring a $\frac{3}{16}$-inch hole through the top frame. At the same centre a $\frac{1}{2}$-inch hole is bored partly through. The screw is driven home and a round wooden plug glued into the $\frac{1}{2}$-inch hole. When dry, this plug is sawed off and planed smooth.

The top frame having been secured, two gauge lines are made for sawing the cover, as in previous boxes, and the two parts dressed to gauge lines, ready for hinging.

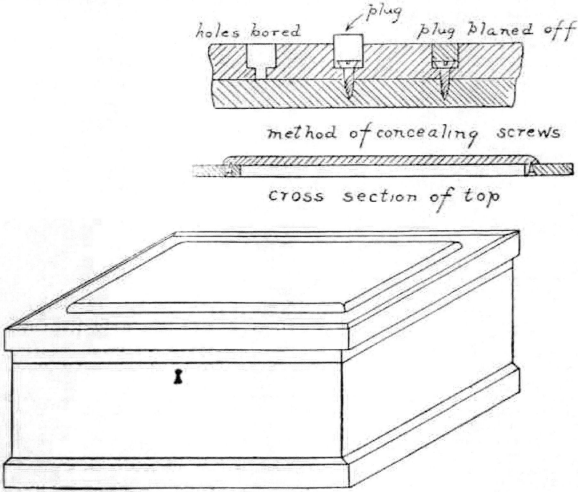

Fig. 190. The old-fashioned tool chest

Before putting on the hinges, the top is to be finished with a raised panel. Square up a piece of stock two inches longer and wider than the open space in the top frame. Round upper edges, and secure to frame by flat-head screws from the under side through holes bored and countersunk.

Next put on hinges, which should be large and strong, the variety known as strap hinges. Cut out space for lock, and fit. The holes for key are bored with a gimlet bit and cut out enough to allow the key to enter freely; or hasp, staple and padlock may be used.

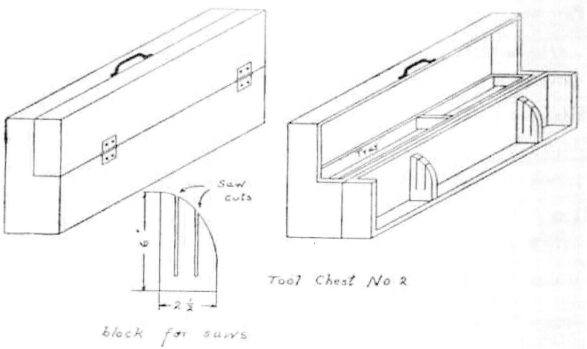

Fig. 191. Suit case tool chest

The bevelled base is mitred at corners, and brass corner plates to protect these lower corners are added.

The strip at the top corresponding to the base may be mitred and protected with corner plates, or the ordinary butt joint can be used. The bevel on this strip may be omitted. A chest of this variety, made of pine and painted, will stand a great deal of rough usage. Iron or brass handles at the ends are recommended for convenience in carrying. Our boys were not satisfied with this form of tool chest, as it required two people to carry it, and after some experimenting they evolved one in the form of a dress suit case, long, narrow, and high, that could be easily carried. It is shown in Fig. 191.

They first made a solid box 30 × 15 × 7 inches over all. It was put together with butt joints securely nailed, using ½-inch white wood.

One quarter of the box was sawed out, as shown on the end view, and hinged to the body by ornamental brass hinges. This quarter was fitted for two saws by making two blocks as shown in the drawing. The rip and cross cut saws were fitted into the saw kerfs cut in these two blocks, placed securely in the cover, and were held in place by a small piece of leather strap taken from a school book strap and nailed to inside of cover. A tray for small tools was made of ¼-inch stock the full length and width of the inside of the chest 1½ inches deep and made to rest flush with the top of lower section on little corner strips glued in the four corners.

For handle, two pieces of leather strap were secured, one to each top section, by screws. When the box was closed, these two straps came together and made a good handle. The objection to a solid handle is that it must be entirely on one section and that takes it out of the centre, so that the weight is not evenly distributed.

This is one of the most satisfactory styles of tool carrier devised. It will hold practically the whole kit and may be picked up like a dress suit case and transported just as readily. A hook and eye or hasp, staple and padlock should be used to hold the case securely closed.

For carrying bits of various kinds and sizes, a roll of ticking or denim divided into separate spaces is very desirable. These rolls with straps are sold in tool houses, but may be made at home by the sewing department. Besides protecting the cutting edges, they help to keep out dampness and rust.

XXXIX

BOOKCASES AND MAGAZINE RACKS
THE WALL RACK

In the modern home, the orderly arrangement of books and magazines calls for ample shelf space and the book shelf becomes a favourite piece of furniture among amateur woodworkers. The book rack for the books of the day has been taken up in Chapter XXVII. The book shelf for hanging on the wall is blocked out in Fig. 192.

The questions to be considered in the design are:

No. 1. Methods of fastening shelves to ends.

No. 2. The design of the ends.

No. 3. The back: is it necessary, and if so shall it be solid? Outline of back.

No. 4. Method of fastening to wall.

No. 1. The method of bringing shelves and ends together with plain butt joint and fastening with a round-head screw from the outside is the easiest and poorest. The whole weight on the shelves is carried by the screws. This method is shown at *a*. At *b*, a better method is indicated, the shelf being gained into the end and held in position by the screws. The weight in this case is carried by the ends. To hide the joint, the shelf may be slightly narrower than the end piece as shown in the top view at *c*, or the two parts may be of the same width as at *d*, the gained joint stopping half an inch or so short of the full width. These details apply to bookcases that stand on the floor as well as to smaller ones.

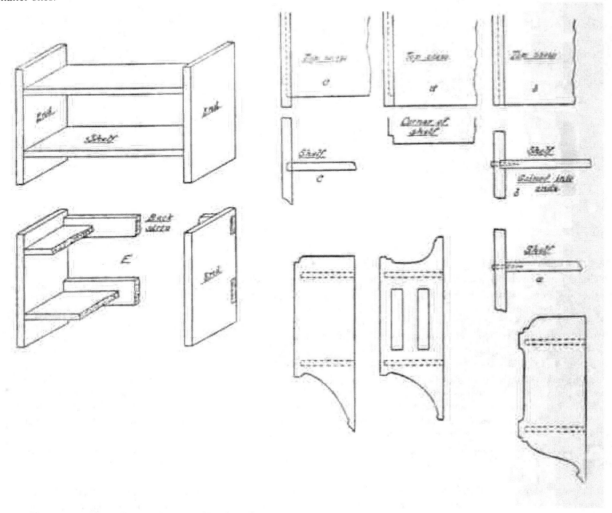

Fig. 192. The problem of designing a wall book rack

No. 2. The design of the ends is largely a matter of artistic taste, and where curves are used, the lower part is usually formed in such a way as to suggest a bracket.

No. 3. A back is only necessary to give the rack rigidity and to protect the wall. If made solid—*i. e.*, to cover the whole space between ends—it uses a good deal of wood and adds considerable weight. *E* shows a method of using only top and bottom strips. They will make the rack sufficiently rigid and the strip should be gained into the ends, bringing them flush with the back of end pieces.

No. 4. Find the location of wall studs by dropping a line with weight on it (plumb) from the nails on picture moulding, or by bringing the weight in front of nails on base board. Make fine pencil marks on the wall where the studs have been located. Find the horizontal distance between the marks and at this distance drill holes in back of book rack and secure to the studs by screws. This brings all the strain on the back strips. If the rack has no back, square up two hard wood strips about $\frac{3}{4}$ inch square and as long as the shelves. Drill screw holes in these strips and fasten to studs. Drill vertical holes at the back of each shelf $\frac{3}{8}$ inch in from edge, fit the shelves over cleats and screw down into them from upper side of shelves.

The cleats should be finished in the same colour as the book rack. This method makes a very solid and permanent fastening.

The length of a wall rack should be limited ordinarily to three feet, as the weight of three feet of books will give considerable sag to the shelves, and a greater length will call for a vertical partition and corresponding bracket underneath for its support.

THE BOOKCASE

This piece of furniture is seen in so many forms that a volume would be necessary simply to catalogue them. The essential features are strong ends or sides, usually a solid back, a base, shelves, often adjustable as to spacing, a top more or less ornamental, and often glass doors.

Perhaps the most important point in the construction is strength. A wobbly bookcase is an abomination, and the weight to be carried is frequently enormous.

A typical case without doors will be taken up and this may be modified, used as a unit and doubled or trebled at the will of the young carpenter. (Fig. 193.)

If it is made to occupy a certain space in a permanent home, it may be built in and made solid with the wall, but this is not often desirable, particularly in America, where people move frequently. As a general rule, two small bookcases are better than one large one. They may be easily shifted, changed from room to room, and are more apt to fit between windows.

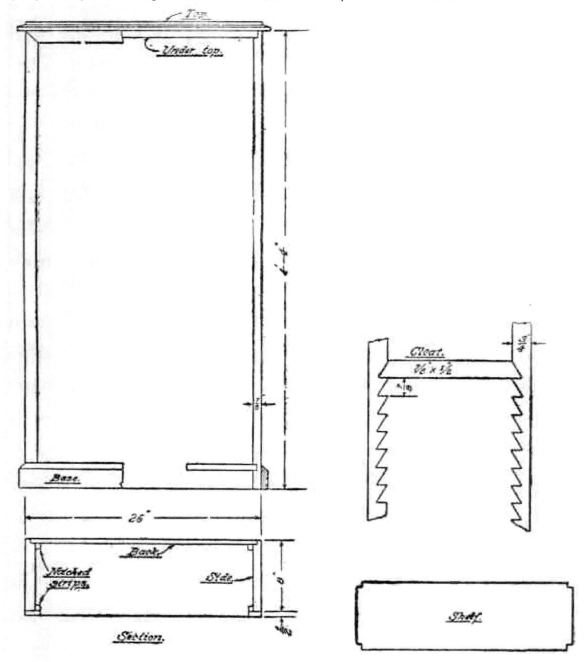

Fig. 193. The bookcase

The uprights 4 feet 4 inches long, 8 inches wide and $\frac{7}{8}$ inch thick, are rabbeted at the back so that the joint will not show from the side. The back is to be of $\frac{1}{2}$-inch white wood stained the same colour as the sides. The under top piece and bottom are gained into the sides, both joints being hidden by the later construction. The 3-inch bevelled base is mitred at the corners and cut off square at the back, covering only three sides, as the back is to be flush from top to bottom. The top is to have a moulded edge on three sides, and to be fastened to under top piece by flat-head screws from the under side through countersunk holes.

The four solid shelves are made adjustable in their spacing by the old-fashioned method of sawtoothed strips in each corner. Strips $\frac{7}{8} \times \frac{1}{2}$ inch are made to fit in the toothed spaces, and the shelves rest on these strips, of which two must be provided for each shelf.

The four toothed strips should be laid out and cut together to insure the shelves being level. The dimensions for all these pieces are given in the detailed drawings.

The front edges are covered by $\frac{1}{2}$-inch strips, beaded if desired, mitred at the top and cut to fit the bevelled base below. Nailed on with brads, these are set and the holes filled with putty, coloured to match the finish.

In the mission style, the shelves are frequently mortised through the sides and secured by pins or wedges. In this type of bookcase, a solid back is rarely used, and base and top are omitted. In a design of this kind, the top shelf becomes a book rack with ornamental ends. Often only the upper and lower shelves are mortised, the others being gained into the sides as described under wall racks. The lower part of the side is frequently modified to give a wider base and to make the case more stable. One objection to this is the amount of material wasted in cutting out, as the stock for the sides must be the full width of the base.

XL

THE MEDICINE CABINET

The wall cabinet for drugs and toilet articles, where the various household remedies may be found quickly, is illustrated in Fig. 194.

It calls for a panelled door, the construction and details of which are given in the drawing.

After squaring up the four pieces for styles and rails, plough a $\frac{1}{4}$-inch groove $\frac{3}{8}$ of an inch deep on the inner edge of all the pieces. This groove is to receive the panel which is planed down to fit. The two uprights are to be mortised at each end, as shown by dotted lines and edge view.

The tenons on the ends of the rails are cut with a shoulder. This closes the space made by the plough on the uprights, as shown in the top view.

The panel is squared up $\frac{3}{4}$ inch larger each way than the open space between rails and styles and a long bevel is planed on each of the four sides, leaving the thickness of the edges just great enough to fit the bottom of the grooves of rails and styles.

Another method of making a panel is to use thin wood which will just fit the grooves, and to fill the joints with a simple moulding mitred at the corners.

The raised panel is not difficult to make, however, and there is little difference in the time consumed by the two methods.

When the five parts are ready for assembling, the mortise joints are glued, the panel slipped into place and left free to shrink in the grooves. The door is placed in hand screws or clamps over night.

As it is to fit a definite space, always make a door slightly larger than its finished dimensions, to allow for planing off and fitting.

While it is drying, proceed with the building of the cabinet. The back inner edges of the sides are to be rabbeted to receive the back, which may be made of $\frac{1}{4}$ or $\frac{3}{8}$ inch white wood. Material for the cabinet proper may be any hard wood, or even white wood.

The shelves may be $\frac{1}{2}$ inch thick. Heavier material is not necessary, on account of the short span. They are to be gained into the sides to the depth of $\frac{3}{8}$ or $\frac{1}{2}$ inch. The spacing of the shelves should be adapted to the sizes of bottles to be accommodated, and the dimensions given in the drawing are merely suggestive.

The overhanging top may be made either with moulded edges on front and sides or be left square. It is secured by screws from the under side of the false top.

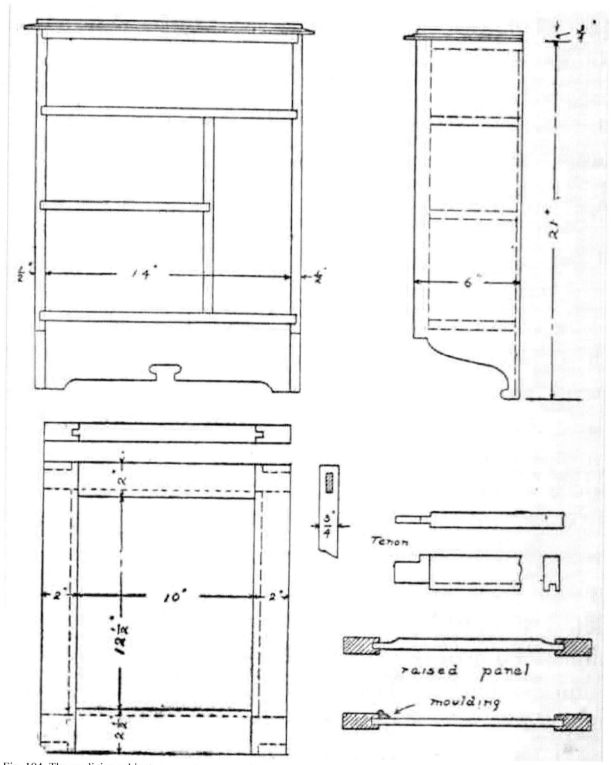

Fig. 194. The medicine cabinet

The sides are shown modified at the bottom to give a pleasing effect, and the back piece may either be brought down and cut to a curved outline, as indicated in the drawing, or stopped at the first shelf.

In assembling, first put the false top in place and nail it to the sides; next put the top on with screws, slip the shelves into their respective grooves, and glue. Put on the back, nailing securely to sides and shelves. To make the cabinet more rigid, drive 1-inch brads into the shelves from the outside set and fill the holes.

Last of all, fit the door, and fasten it with hinges and a catch. A lock may be used, but that is hardly advisable, as in case of an emergency the key may be lost at the critical moment. Stain and polish.

The method of fastening is by screws through the back into the wall studs.

Cabinets for various purposes can be designed along the lines just described, but in each case the method of construction is similar. A stronger cabinet would result if the top and bottom shelves were mortised through the sides in the mission style. The only objection to this is that if the horizontal space be limited, the projecting tenon may be in the way.

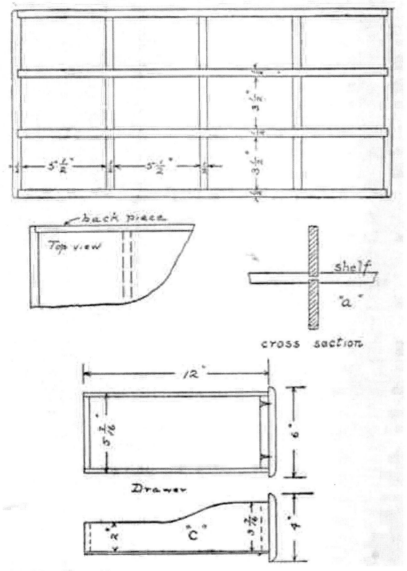

Fig. 195. A filing cabinet

The filing cabinet for papers shown in Fig. 195 is of radically different construction. As it is designed to stand on a desk, or independent shelf, the base may be very simple or omitted entirely, as in the drawing.

It is divided into twelve compartments, with a clear space in each of $12\frac{1}{2} \times 5\frac{1}{2} \times 3\frac{1}{2}$ inches, these being the outside dimensions of the drawers.

It is important in building up these compartments to use lumber that is well seasoned and free from warp. Gain the shelves into outside uprights, stopping the groove half an inch from the front.

Before sliding the shelves into the grooves, lay out on the four pieces the grooves for the three vertical partitions. It will be much easier to cut these grooves clear through from front to back, but a better appearance from the front can be obtained by stopping the grooves half an inch back, as on the sides.

Each vertical partition will then consist of three separate pieces slipped in from the back. A cross section of the cabinet will appear, as a. The quarter-inch back is to be gained into the sides as shown in the top view.

The construction of the drawer is shown at c, the sides being cut away toward the back. Otherwise the drawer is simply an open box made of $\frac{3}{8}$-inch pine or white wood, with $\frac{1}{4}$-inch bottom put together with brads.

The false front, made of the same material as top and sides, gives a suitable finish, and practically covers all joints; it is secured by flat-head screws from the inside.

In assembling the drawer, it should be made about $\frac{1}{16}$ inch smaller than the compartment it is to fit, to prevent binding in damp weather.

Bay wood, a light-coloured mahogany, is very appropriate for this piece of office furniture, the edges of partitions being stained to match. A brass drawer-pull, with a space left for a printed label, is to be put on after the polishing is done.

Filing cabinets made by this method may, of course, be made with drawers of different proportions and with any number of compartments, but this size is designed to hold long envelopes, letters, bills, etc.

XLI

MISSION FURNITURE

The library table (Fig. 196) is a good example of solid and permanent furniture construction. It represents the main principles of the mission style—solidity, strength, simplicity, straight lines, mortise and tenon joints, etc.

To a boy who has worked carefully up to this point it is entirely possible.

As the top is the only part to be glued up, this should be done first. Three boards of $\frac{7}{8}$-inch quartered oak 10 inches wide, or an equivalent that will aggregate a trifle over 30 inches, and 4 feet long, should be jointed and prepared for dowelling. The method of doing this is shown at a, where two jointed pieces are clamped together. The distance between dowels lengthwise should be measured, and lines squared across the edges with knife and try square. Two pencil lines, as at b, should be made across the joint. Set the marking gauge at $\frac{7}{16}$ inch. Remove the boards from vise or clamp, and from the faces touched by pencil lines, gauge lines cutting across the three knife lines on each edge.

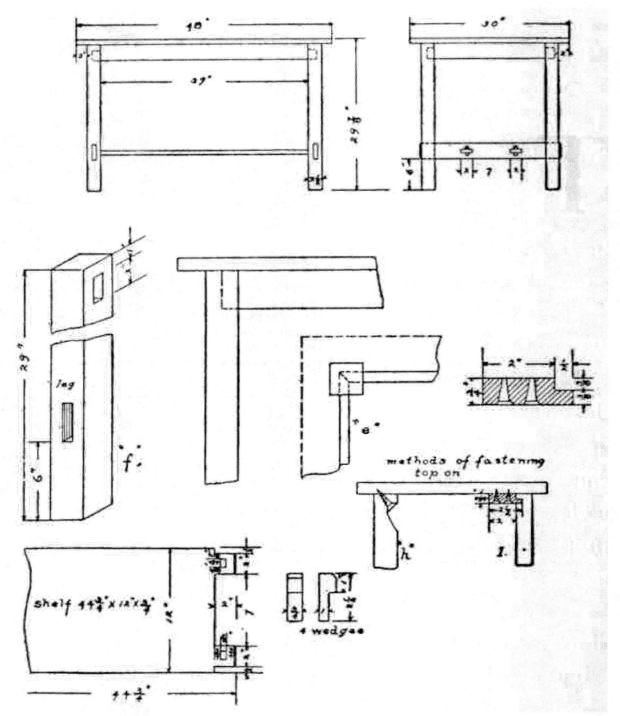

Fig. 196. A mission library table

Where these lines cross, bore $\frac{3}{8}$-inch holes with a dowel bit to the depth of at least 1 inch. Lay out the other dowelled joint in the same manner. Saw six pieces of $\frac{3}{8}$-inch dowel 2 inches long, and glue ends of each dowel in the holes prepared in the middle board, as shown at *c*.

Put a thin layer of glue on the joints with a brush and clamp the three pieces together. While the glue is hardening, proceed with the frame. This consists of four legs, four top rails, the lower cross rails, a shelf, and four wedges.

The sizes are as follows:

Top rails	$42 \times 3 \times \frac{7}{8}$
Top	$24 \times 3 \times \frac{7}{8}$

rails

Cross rails	$26\frac{1}{2} \times 3 \times \frac{7}{8}$
Shelf	$44\frac{3}{4} \times 12 \times \frac{3}{4}$ or $\frac{7}{8}$
Wedges	$2\frac{1}{2} \times \frac{7}{8} \times \frac{3}{4}$

The construction of the top rails is shown at *d* in the detail drawing. The only point calling for special attention is to see that the tenons are flush with outside of rail, being cut on only three sides, and the mitre at the end of each. The necessity for this mitre is shown in the drawing of the top of leg at *e*, where the two tenons are shown meeting in the blind mortises. The short rails are identical with those shown at *d*, except in length.

The detailed drawing of the legs is shown at *f*, and to make sure that the four are uniform, they should be laid out in pairs, the two at one end together, then the second pair; and finally the two pairs must be compared to discover any possible inaccuracies. The cutting of the mortises may be hastened by boring several holes inside the lines from each side.

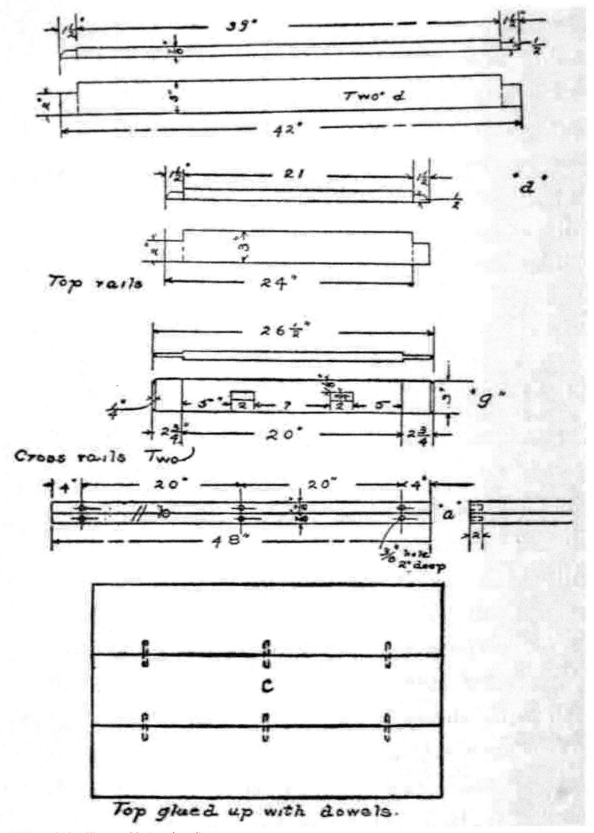

Fig. 196. A mission library table (continued)

The drawing at *g* shows the layout of the lower rails, with tenons at the ends, and mortises on flat sides to receive the tenons on ends of the shelf. As in previous cases, these two pieces should be laid out together.

The most difficult work up to this point is the cutting of the two blind mortises at the top of each leg to receive the mitred tenons. This operation could be simplified, by replacing the mortise and tenon at that point by a dowel joint, but it would no longer be genuine mission furniture, and a much weaker form of construction.

The drawing of the long shelf explains itself, two tenons being cut at each end and a rectangular hole cut through each tenon for the wedge. The tenons are shown with a slight bevel, which is cut with a chisel when all other work is finished.

Before proceeding further, it will be wise to try and fit all the joints. Number or letter the two parts of each joint, as it is finished, to assist in the final assembling. This process of fitting should take some time, for it cannot be hurried safely. When it is finished, the way to fasten the top to the frame should be considered.

Several methods are in use, and two are shown at *h* and *i*. At *h* a hole is bored at an angle in the rail. As it goes only part way through, it provides a shoulder for the screw head, and the screw is driven through a hole drilled for the purpose into the solid top.

If this method is used, at least ten screws would be needed for a table of this size, three on each side and two on each end.

The method shown at *i* is probably the better of the two. Blocks of wood of the shape and size given in the drawing are made and fitted into a groove ploughed in the rails.

This groove may be ploughed the full length of rail, or cut out for an inch or two with a chisel. The tongue and groove should fit snugly, and the block be securely fastened to the top with screws. Two blocks on each side and one on each end will be sufficient.

A simple method is to fasten top and frame by angle irons 2 inches long, on the inside.

This question having been decided, take the glued-up top from clamps and dress down to size. The under side should be trued up enough to fit neatly over tops of legs and rails, and the upper side should be planed, scraped, and sand-papered.

The final assembling should be done in this order:

Assemble the two ends separately. Each end consists of two legs, a top and a bottom rail. The mortise and tenon joints should be glued, and a clamp used at top and bottom. Test for squareness. When dry, remove clamps, insert shelf tenons and those of top rails in their mortises, and clamp lengthwise. Drive a wire brad through each tenon, from the side of leg least conspicuous, and set with nail punch.

Put on the top, and level bottom of legs where necessary. Remove all traces of glue, and fill brad holes with putty, coloured same as stain to be used.

Place wedges in mortises provided, and fasten each one with a small brad driven through the side of shelf tenons. Stain and polish.

THE TEA TABLE

This table is made low purposely, the legs being exactly two feet in length. The construction consists of four legs, two sets of cross rails, and a circular top two feet in diameter. As this top is too wide to be cut from one board, joint two pieces of $\frac{7}{8}$-inch stock, glue together, and place in clamp. The joint may be strengthened with dowels, as in previous cases. (Fig. 197.)

187

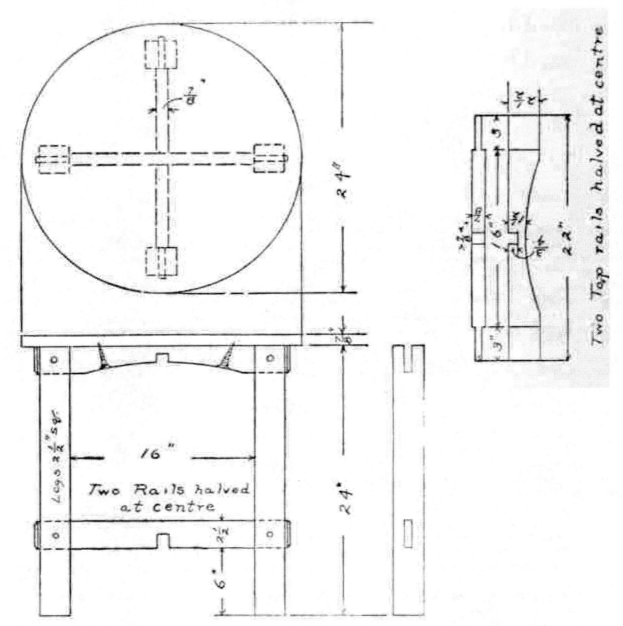

Fig. 197. A mission tea table

By proceeding in this order—gluing up first—no time need be lost in waiting. Square up the four legs and lay out the eight mortises, placing the four pieces in a vise or clamp to insure uniformity. Cut the mortises and lay the legs one side. The two sets of cross rails are to be halved at the centre, and may be straight or slightly curved, as shown. The curve improves the appearance without reducing the strength seriously, but if this form is decided on, the curve must be cut before laying out the halved joint.

After finishing the joint, the two rails of each set are clamped together and tenons laid out. Remove from clamp or vise and cut tenons. Test each set to make sure the halved joint at centre is satisfactory, and insert tenons in the mortises. Draw bore and fasten with round pins of the same material as the legs.

Before fastening the top rails in position, drill and countersink two holes in each piece for the screws, in the position shown in drawing. The bevels on end of tenons should be cut with the chisel before the final fastening.

The two boards composing the top when removed from clamps should be dressed flat on both sides, tested with a straight edge, and circle laid out with steel dividers set at a radius of twelve inches.

Saw close to this line with turning saw, chisel to line, and smooth with spokeshave and sand-paper block—a piece of pine 3 × 2 × 7/8 inches, with the sand-paper tacked on the 7/8-inch edge. Scrape and sand-paper top.

To fasten this top to the frame, lay the top upside down on the floor, and set the frame, inverted, on it. Measure carefully to locate the frame in proper position, and fasten with four 2½ or 2¾ inch flat head screws. Assuming that all parts of the frame have been scraped and sand-papered before assembling, the table is ready for polishing.

188

Oak is the wood commonly used for this piece of furniture, but if well seasoned, chestnut is lighter in weight and just as satisfactory as to grain and finish. (See staining and polishing.)

Sometimes in mission furniture the legs of the table are allowed to come up through the top. This design is shown at Fig. 198. The diameter of the top is 24 inches, but the height is increased, as this is designed as a centre or reading table. On account of the support furnished by the shoulder at the top of legs, the top set of rails is omitted, and the fastening made by four angle irons securely screwed to the top and legs.

This table, on account of the greater span between the legs, is as stable as the previous design. The cross rails are halved, and may be straight or curved on under side. If desired, a commodious shelf may be had by fastening a circular piece 19 inches or less in diameter to the top of cross rails. This will need to be glued up and cut like top piece.

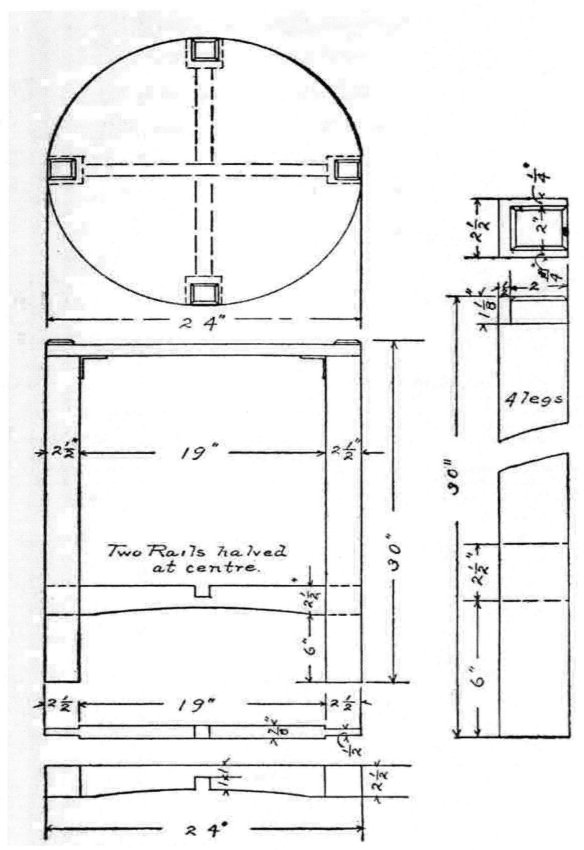

Fig. 198. A mission style centre table

The square tenon at the top of legs is shown in the detailed drawing, and care should be taken in laying out to insure the distance from the shoulder to bottom of leg being alike on all four, if the top is to be level.

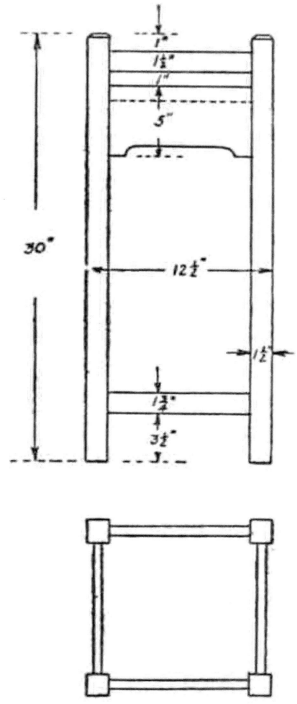

Fig. 199. Mission plant stand

After gluing up and dressing down the top, lay out circle and two-inch square openings for the tenons. Test these squares carefully before cutting, to make sure they are equally spaced, saw out circle, and finish as in previous table. Saw out the squares close to line and finish with chisel. In putting on angle irons, screw them to the top first and press it tightly down on the shoulders before fastening to legs. A strong cleat 18 or 20 inches long fastened to under side of top across the grain with four or five screws will help to prevent warping, but is not absolutely necessary. If the circular shelf is added, it is to be fastened to cross rails by screws from the under side through drilled holes.

DESIGNING MISSION FURNITURE

Boys who have followed the preceding instructions will be able to plan and construct the following designs without detailed explanations.

The two drawings for plant stands are in the nature of suggestions, and although taken from pieces actually made they show the great difference in form that is possible in meeting the same conditions.

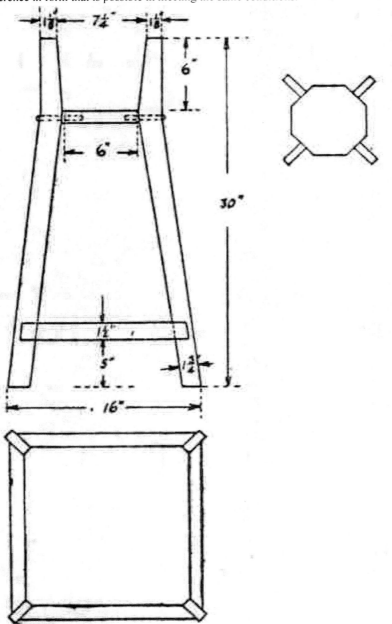

Fig. 200. Design for a plant stand

Fig. 199 is thoroughly representative of the so-called mission style with its mortise and tenon joints and straight square legs.

The shelf for holding the jardinière is indicated by dotted lines, and it is held by cleats fastened to the sides by flat-head screws.

A dark finish, antique or rich brown, is appropriate for either design. Fig. 200 shows a radically different form. The shelf is octagonal or square with the corners cut at 45 degrees to fit the legs.

The detail view shows the arrangement of lower rails meeting the legs at the same angle. The ends of rails are mitred and secured by wire nails set below the surface and holes filled. The fastening between upper shelf and legs may be either round-head blue screws or dowel pins of the same material as the legs, with the outer ends slightly rounded.

The shape of the legs makes this design weaker than Fig. 199, but their spread results in a more stable base and makes this stand less liable to upset.

The foot rest (Fig. 201) is to be provided with a cushion covered with leather nailed on with large-head craftsman nails.

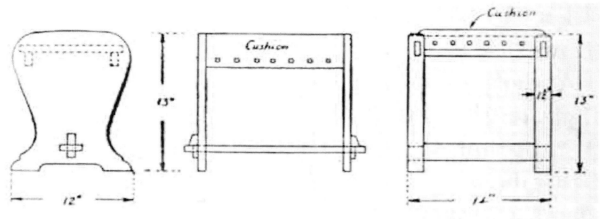

Fig. 201. Foot rest. Fig. 202. Footstool in mission style

The cushion may be filled with hair, excelsior, or even fine shavings, securely sewed in a cover of ticking and held in place by the leather cover. The leather must be brought down and nailed to the lower edge of the cross rails. Fasten the top to cleats screwed on inside of ends.

Fig. 202 shows the same problem worked out in straight lines, the leather being nailed to all four top rails.

Photograph by Helen W. Cooke
Assembling and Finishing.

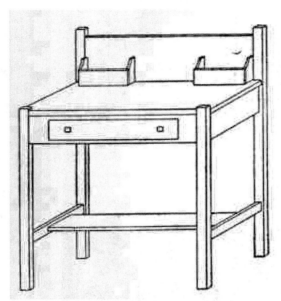 

Figs. 203 and 204. Mission desks. A study in design

Each of these pieces of furniture suggests a new one, and chairs, settees, umbrella stands, writing desks, etc., may be made along the same general lines.

The plant stand (Fig. 199) suggests the umbrella rack. The shelf is simply shifted from the top to bottom and provided with a brass tray to catch the water. Valuable suggestions for such furniture may be obtained by consulting catalogues of furniture, and by constant observations of well-made pieces.

These designs should never be copied, but used only as aids to the working out of original ideas.

The typical writing desk shown at Fig. 203 illustrates this point. While fairly well proportioned, the legs could well be heavier. The drawer is also faulty. Its position makes it necessary to move away from the desk in order to open it. The lower cross rail will be a nuisance when sitting close enough to write and other features might be criticised. Whether your design will be a success or not depends on the clearness with which all these details are thought out. Fig. 204 shows several of the above defects corrected.

XLII

THE CHEST

This is one of the most convenient and substantial pieces of furniture about the house. For the storage of linen, furs, or clothing it is invaluable. It may be placed in a corner, and with a liberal supply of sofa cushions makes an ideal cosey corner and seat.

The construction is purposely strong and heavy, and calls for good material like quartered oak, chestnut, walnut, or cedar. The latter wood, especially *red* cedar, is light in weight, but attractive in colour, and has the further advantage of being moth proof.

Fig. 205 *a* shows a well-proportioned chest of quartered oak. The horizontal rails are mortised into the heavy legs, and the panels may be arranged as shown in the detail.

A rabbet is cut on the inner edge of the rails, and a corresponding groove ploughed in the legs. The panel may be of one piece, set into the rabbet and grooves. Its large expanse may be carved, raised, or simply polished plain, allowing the natural grain to furnish the ornamentation.

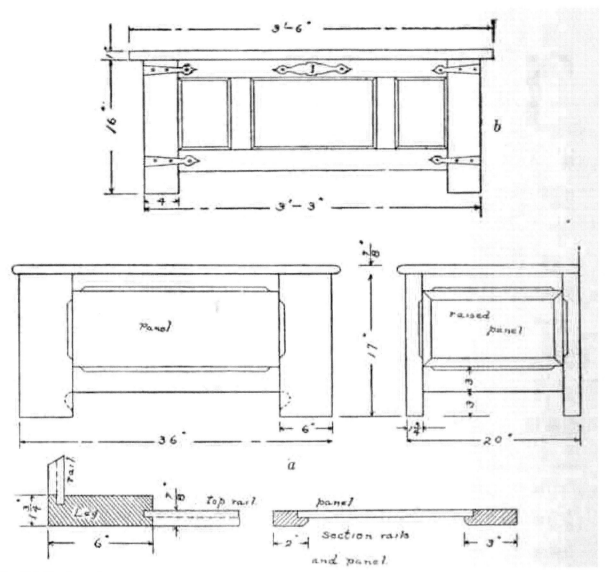

Fig. 205. The linen chest

The legs may be plain, as shown, or curved slightly at the bottom, as suggested in the detail. The top is too large to be made in one piece, and it should be built up like a table top, and hinged to upper back rail by strong iron or brass ornamental hinges.

If finished in a dark colour with dull surface, the metal corner plates and escutcheon will greatly enhance its appearance.

These may be made out of sheet brass. First lay out the design on paper. Cut out to the outline, and trace upon the surface of the sheet metal. A metal-cutting saw blade obtained from the hardware store can be fitted into the frame of the coping saw.

With this tool, saw on the lines exactly as in thin wood, and file the edges smooth. The holes for the heavy nails are drilled. If suitable big-headed nails cannot be found, brass screws may be used, and when in position, the heads filed to any desired shape.

An ancient green effect can be produced on such brass ornaments by painting with ammonia.

The cover of a large chest like this will need to be reinforced by strong cleats on the under side across the grain. They should be 3 × ⅞ inches, just long enough to allow the cover to close readily, and should be secured by five or six screws on each cleat.

The bottom may be pine or white wood, secured by nails or screws to ⅞-inch square cleats screwed on the inside of ends and sides. A chest of better proportion, but slightly more complicated in construction, is shown at b. Here the front is broken up into three panels, and a better space arrangement secured. The whole front in this case may be put together with mortise and tenon joints, as in panel door construction, or the simpler method just described may be used. The mortise and tenon form is the better way, and as usual takes more time.

Carved panels suggest a very rich and valuable piece of furniture, but they are not necessary, as a good flat polish showing the natural grain of the wood is very satisfactory.

XLIII

THE DRAWING OUTFIT

An equipment for mechanical drawing, except the instruments, can be easily made in the shop by any boy who has had some practice with tools.

The drawing board is the first thing needed, and several makes are in use, the object of all of them being to insure a true flat surface by overcoming the natural tendency of wood to warp.

Shrinkage will take place in spite of all precautions, but this is not a serious matter, and does not affect the usefulness of the board.

All boards, it is conceded, should be "built up," rather than consist of one piece. The idea is that the warping of one piece is somewhat counteracted by that of the adjoining pieces in other directions.

Fig. 206 shows three forms in common use. At *a* the ends are united to wide cleats by a tongue and groove joint.

In shrinking and expanding with weather changes, the board is free to slide along the joint, being glued only at the centre.

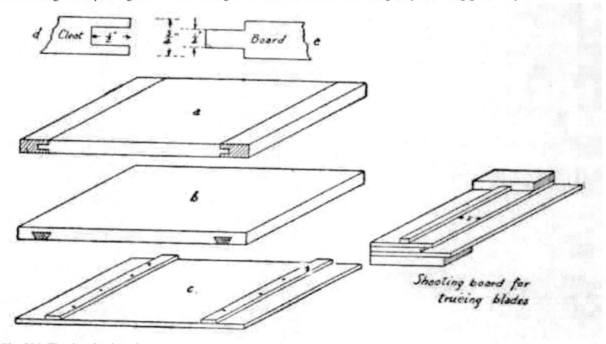

Fig. 206. The drawing board

At *b* two dovetail-shaped strips are inserted on the under side across the grain. This is more difficult cult to make on account of the shape of the groove, but it is otherwise satisfactory. At *c* two strong cleats are fastened across the under side by screws. This is the easiest and least satisfactory method, as the cleats are often in the way, making the board clumsy, and furthermore it does not allow for shrinkage, unless the screws are secured in grooves instead of in plain holes.

A good proportion for a small board is 24 × 18 inches. If the first method of construction is decided on, glue up four or five strips of well seasoned white pine, $\frac{7}{8}$ inch thick, of the width desired, and four inches shorter than the final length of board. Place in clamps for twenty-four hours, and when dry dress down perfectly true to a thickness of $\frac{3}{4}$ inch. Test for warp and wind, and square the ends.

Square up two pieces of stock $2\frac{1}{2}$ inches wide, with a length equal to width of board. For the tongue and groove joint, a set of tongue and grooving planes will be necessary. Two cutters for this purpose come with the modern universal plane, and if available this may be used. In either case, set the depth gauge at half an inch, and plow a groove on one edge of each strip $\frac{1}{4}$ inch wide to the full depth, as shown at *d*. On both ends of the board, plane the tongue same size as groove at *e*. Coat the tongue at each end of board with glue for a distance of six or eight inches at the centre, fit the end strips in position, and place in clamps over night. When dry, give the surface a final truing up, and also the ends, as the clamps may have made a slight change.

Go all over the surface with a sand-paper block, using 00 sand-paper, and shellac the board all over. When dry rub flat with the sand-paper block. Make a final test for any possible inaccuracy, and the board is ready for use.

T square and triangles may be made, but as rubber or celluloid triangles are better in some ways than wood, the former are recommended.

The T square is a very pretty little problem in woodwork, and may be made as follows:

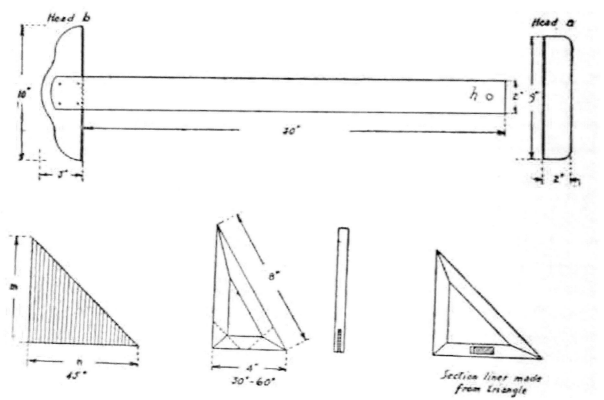

Fig. 207. T square and triangles

The design for the head may be either *a* or *b* (Fig. 207), *a* being simply a rectangular piece of hard wood, with two rounded corners: *b* is laid out as shown, sawed near the line and curved side finished with spokeshave. The straight side should be *perfectly* straight, as any variation will give horizontal lines out of parallel.

The blade may be of one piece, or built up. A very satisfactory combination is to make the head of black walnut, and the blade of hard maple, with black walnut edges. It will pay to make a special shooting board for this work, and to make several T squares at the same time. This shooting board should be slightly longer than the blade. (See Fig. 206.)

Gauge a line at a distance *x* from the edge, equal to the width of 2 inches, and tack a straight strip of wood up to this line as a guide. When the blade has been planed to its thickness of ⅛ inch, it is to be placed in space *x* and planed to width.

To plane a piece of hard wood down to an eighth of an inch, tack it to a pine board with three 1-inch brads. The location of these brads can be such that only one hole will be left in the blade to be filled up afterward. One should be in the position of the central screw over the head, the second at the point where hole *h* is to be bored, the third at about the centre of the blade. Set these brads slightly below the surface, and dress down smooth.

When tested and found true, lift the blade by inserting a knife blade under it, again fasten to the board with unfinished side up, and again dress down. Before removing from the board, lay out the curved end to correspond with the curve of the head, and cut to line with a chisel.

Remove from board, finish curved end with sand-paper block. Bore hole *h* for hanging up, locate holes for screws, and drill just large enough to allow ½-inch round-head brass or blued screws to pass through. In attaching the head, make sure that the two parts are at right angles, and use thin copper burrs or washers under the screw heads.

If the blade is to have edges of a different colour, joint the maple on shooting board, and glue the strips to it, before planing to thickness. This should be done on a flat board, with paper between it and the blade. Glue the three pieces together, and drive 1¼-inch brads up close to and touching the outside strips, at intervals of four inches. By bending these slightly over the blade, considerable pressure will be obtained, tending to keep the pieces together while glue is hardening.

Then proceed to dress down, and true up as before. When the process is once learned, considerable pin money may be made by disposing of the squares, and that will help to buy material for other things.

Triangles made from single pieces of wood are absolutely unreliable. Referring to Fig. 207, the 45-degree triangle shows the grain running up and down. As shrinkage takes place *m* will not change, but *n* will, and this will alter the angles; and besides a piece of thin wood this size will warp and make the triangle useless for mechanical drawing.

The 30-60 triangle illustrates the usual method of constructing a wooden triangle.

Aside from bisecting the 90, 60, and 30 degree angles to get the mitres, these joints, if simply glued, will be too weak for practical use. The edge view and dotted lines indicate a thin feather of wood glued into a saw cut made through the edge of each corner, the usual method of strengthening. It is a delicate operation, and is only recommended to boys who are fond of fine work.

197

A very serviceable section liner may be made from a wooden triangle by carefully cutting out of one side a rectangular opening, as shown in the detail. Make a piece of thin wood to fit this space, but ⅛-inch shorter, and fitted so as to move freely. By moving this block and the triangle, alternately, vertical or oblique lines can be drawn for sectioning, and they will be equally spaced. Other blocks varying in length will give a variety of spacings.

It is possibly one of the cheapest section liners, and the most satisfactory within the means of any one. Irregular or French curves may be made in thin wood. They should be drawn on the surface, sawed out with the coping saw, and sand-papered smooth. As their thickness should be but a trifle over 1/16 inch, they are very frail and easily broken. These curves can be easily made in sheet aluminum, and they will be much more satisfactory. This metal is handled similarly to thin wood, except that the saw must be a metal cutting blade.

Triangles may be made of the same material. Lay out the form with a sharp steel point or scriber, saw as close to lines as possible, and with a fine file finish to line. Then smooth the curves with fine emery paper wrapped around a lead pencil. To make straight edges, as on triangles, lay a sheet of emery cloth on bench, and rub triangle back and forth.

THE PANTAGRAPH

For copying designs, for reducing or enlarging, this old-fashioned instrument may be easily constructed. Fig. 208 shows it made of four strips of thin wood of equal length. Either pine or white wood will answer. The pieces have to be squared, twenty-five inches long, three quarters of an inch wide, and a quarter inch thick.

Bore or drill through the four pieces held in a vise, and space the holes shown in drawing three inches apart, ⅛ inch in size.

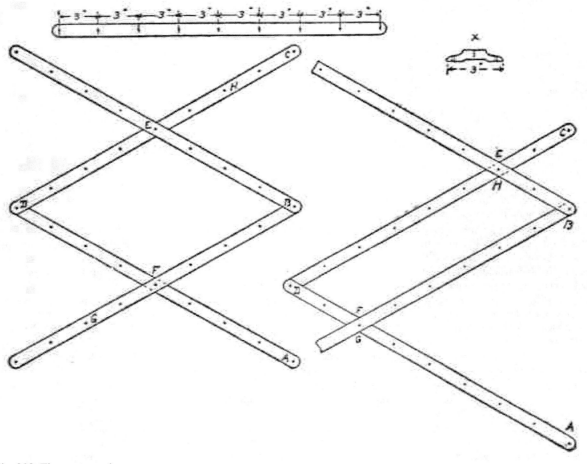

Fig. 208. The pantagraph

When put together, a, b and c should be in line. Point a is to remain fixed, the pantagraph being free to move around it as a pivot. To accomplish this, cut out a block, as shown at x, with a hole drilled at the centre for pivot, and two others for screwing to the drawing table or board.

The pin for this pivot may be a thick flat-head wire nail, screw, or even a screw eye. The joints d, e, and f are also pivots moving with the pantagraph. They may consist of thumb screws, and nuts, or screw eyes, and must move freely, yet without play.

Points b and c are to be interchangeable, one having a tracing point, the other a pencil.

The tracing point may be a wire nail, rivet, or screw, with the point filed sharp, and then slightly rounded. The pencil point should be a piece of lead pencil, whittled down to such a size as to pass through the hole at b and c, and make a snug fit.

To enlarge a design, place tracing point at b, and fasten original design under it to drawing board with thumb tacks.

Under *c* fasten a sheet of drawing paper. With the right hand at *b*, trace the design by carefully sliding tracing point along the lines. At the same time, with the left hand keep pencil point at *c* sufficiently in contact with the paper to make a clear line.

To reduce a drawing, reverse *b* and *c*, bringing pencil point and paper to *b*, and original to *c*. Pass tracer over design at *c*, and the reduced design will be traced at *b*. Different proportions between original and reproduction may be obtained by shifting the position of pivots *e* and *f*.

Fig. 208 shows pivot e shifted to position *h*. As distance *c e* should always equal distance *d f*, it now becomes necessary to move pivot *f* to point *g*. By remembering this rule, and placing pivots in various positions, a wide range of proportions is possible.

THE DRAWING TABLE

A table to hold the drawing board should be not less than 3 feet 2 inches high, as much of the work is performed standing up. A stool with revolving seat should be provided for the draughtsman to sit on occasionally.

The table top may be made slanting, but it is better practice to have a heavy flat top of pine, which may be used as a large drawing board itself, and to provide for the slant by using a triangular block under the farther end of drawing board. Two or three blocks may be made, about two feet long and of different sizes, to give different degrees of slant.

Tables for this purpose are often made with tops, which may be adjusted at different angles, and the young designer may try his inventive talent in this large field, but any arrangement which will bring an element of instability is to be studiously avoided. The drawing table should be as solid and rigid as possible.

The design in Fig. 209 was made by our boys, and has proved very satisfactory. It has much of the mission style about it, with its square legs and mortised joints.

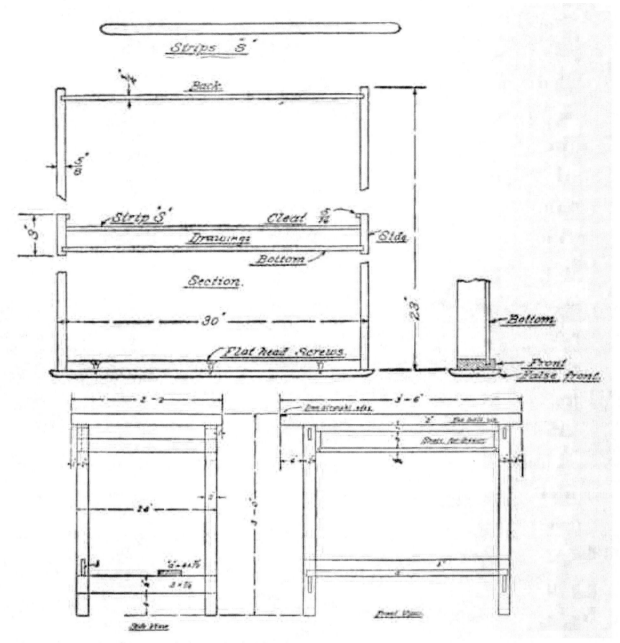

Fig. 209. Drawer for table and table for mechanical drawing

After the description of mission furniture construction in previous chapters, only a few points in the construction need be mentioned.

The board *a*, used as a foot rest, is necessary when sitting at the table on account of its height, and it also ties the frame together in the front. The cross rail *b* acts in the same capacity at the back.

The heavy pine top is "built up" like a drawing board of several pieces, and supported by two cleats 3 × ⅛ inches across the grain underneath. It may be attached to the frame by any one of the methods described under mission furniture, and its left-hand edge should be as true as that of the drawing board.

If an especially accurate edge is desired, a piece of iron 1 × ¼ inch, planed straight by a machinist, may be let into this edge, as shown in the drawing, and secured by flat-head screws through holes drilled and countersunk. This arrangement is seldom seen, but it is well worth the added cost.

The table shown is provided with a generous-sized drawer. This may be omitted, but is a great convenience for keeping plans and sketches. Its construction is shown in detail. The sides and front have a ¼-inch groove, ploughed to receive the bottom, and at the back end a vertical groove is cut to hold the back piece which is dadoed to fit.

At the top of each side is nailed a strip ⁵⁄₁₆ inch square. These cleats are to retain the strips *s*. Make these strips *s* of hard wood, preferably ash, and about ¹⁄₁₆ inch longer than the width of drawer, measured inside.

By placing the strips on top of drawings obliquely, and then straightening them across the drawer, they bind against the sides, and keep drawings down flat. The cleats at top of drawer prevent them from escaping at the top, especially when it becomes nearly full.

The extra front on the drawer with rounded edges covers up the joints around front of box, and is a purely ornamental feature. If this is used, secure to real front by flat-head screws from the inside.

The box which holds the drawers is to be secured to the legs by screws countersunk. Many modifications of this table will occur to the woodworker, such as additional drawers, but it must be kept in mind that comfortable knee room is essential, and the space on under side of the top is largely to be reserved for this important purpose.

A box for holding instruments has been described in another chapter, and triangles, rules, etc., may be kept in it.

The T square should be hung on a hook at either end of table, to overcome any tendency the thin blade may have to twist or warp, the weight of the head helping to draw it out straight.

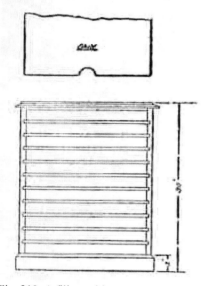

Fig. 210. A filing cabinet

All drawings should have a neat title, and a number. To work out a system of numbering so that any drawing may be found quickly is a good job for a rainy day.

A good filing cabinet for plans is suggested in Fig. 210. Dimensions are not given, as they will depend on the size of drawing paper used. A uniform-sized sheet should be adopted at the start, and the drawings scaled to accommodate this size of paper.

The shelves should be ¼ inch thick, and gained into sides as shown. A clear space of 1½ inches between the shelves will be ample, and a semicircular curve should be cut in the front. The depth of cabinet should not be over half an inch more than the width of the sheets.

A top and mitred base are shown, and the space between should be closed by a panelled door to keep out dust.

A cabinet of this style should not be less than thirty inches high, and if the whole space is not required for drawings, the lower part may be changed and fitted with drawers for models, specimens, and other treasures.

For boys who are interested in collecting, whether minerals, butterflies, or other things, such a cabinet may be made entirely of drawers, and the panelled door omitted.

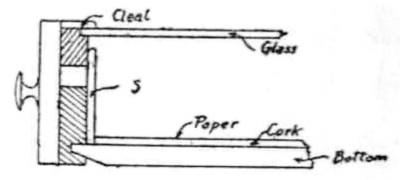

Fig. 211. Drawer construction

For the safe keeping of butterflies, moths, and other insects, an eminent scientist has recommended a drawer construction as shown at Fig. 211. This detail shows a section at the front, with the bottom piece gained into a groove. The bottom of the drawer is covered with a layer of sheet cork, and over it oiled paper. The upper part of box is not fastened, but is slipped down inside strips *s*, which have rounded tops, and extend around the four sides.

The upper half is grooved to receive a sheet of glass, which is held in place by a small cleat. By this method the drawer is covered while the specimens are visible, and dampness is kept out. The cork bottom is to receive the pins, and the specimens may be reached by simply taking out the top. The dimensions recommended for the drawer are 22 × 16 × 2 inches, outside measurements, and if a number are to be used, the spaces between the shelves of the cabinet should correspond with these figures.

A quaint conceit sometimes used by enthusiastic collectors is to make their boxes in the form of books, as shown at *a* (Fig. 212).

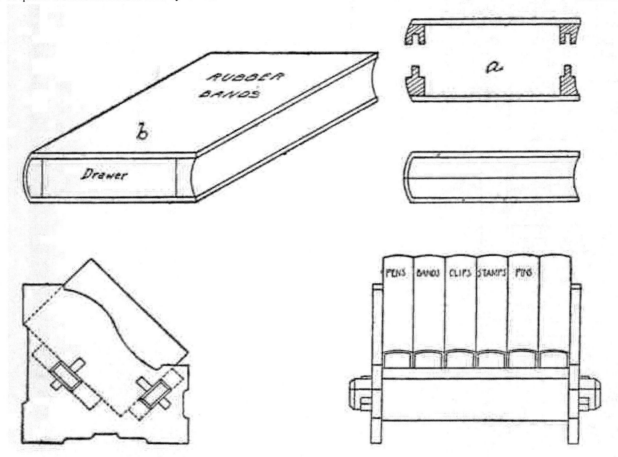

Fig. 212. Book shaped boxes

The outside has the shape of a book, the two halves being fitted by tongue and groove joint. This keeps out moisture, the great enemy of dried specimens, and when a number of these boxes, properly coloured and labelled, are piled on a shelf, they have the appearance of so many large volumes.

This unique idea may be used in other ways. A very pretty illustration is a stamp box for the writing desk, made up in the form of a book, which apparently has a silk ribbon for a book mark. This ribbon is the handle of a little drawer, which pulls out, disclosing the contents. The arrangement is shown at *b*. The idea may be carried still farther by having half a dozen of these small volumes in a book rack, the labels reading—"rubber bands," "pens," "stamps," etc. All should be stained a uniform colour, and the illusion may be carried still farther by gilding the parts which represent the edges of the leaves.

XLIV

WOODWORK FOR OUTDOOR SPORTS
THE TENNIS COURT

The young woodworker is especially well fitted for the preparation of a tennis court. He has learned the value of accurate measurements, and is accustomed to make a neat and finished job. While the making of a court seems a simple proposition, it may be a very expensive one, if help has to be hired, and all the equipment bought ready for use.

The first step is to select the exact location, which should either be level or practically so. Any discussion as to the merits of dirt or sod courts must be left to the reader. The court proper is 78 × 36 feet, the posts for the tennis net being three feet outside on either side, and the space at the ends between the court and stop nets fifteen to twenty feet more, making a total length of 118 feet.

The following method of laying out the court is recommended:

Make sure that the long way is exactly north and south, and drive in the ground a wooden stake at northeast corner A (Fig. 213). At B, directly west, drive stake 36 feet from A. A steel tape measure is by far the best thing to use for laying out, as cord stretches and leads to inaccuracies, and two tapes are better than one.

At the centre of each stake drive a strong nail. From B measure 78 feet south, and place a temporary stake. To insure the angle being 90 degrees, apply this test: From B along the line laid out last, measure 48 feet: slip the ring of the tape measure over the nail at A, and measure to this new point. If the angle is 90 degrees, this diagonal measurement should be 60 feet. If this measurement does not come right, shift the stake C, until this oblique line is exactly 60 feet, then lines A-B and B-C are at right angles. Having fixed this angle, again measure from B to C, and drive stake C at 78 feet from B.

Locate stake D 78 feet from A, and 36 feet from C. A final test should now be made by measuring the diagonals B-D and A-C. They should be exactly alike. These corner stakes may now be driven in flush with the surface, and they should be allowed to remain, to avoid the necessity of doing the work all over again later in the season when the lines become obscure. Measure in from each stake 4½ feet for the alleys and drive stakes in flush.

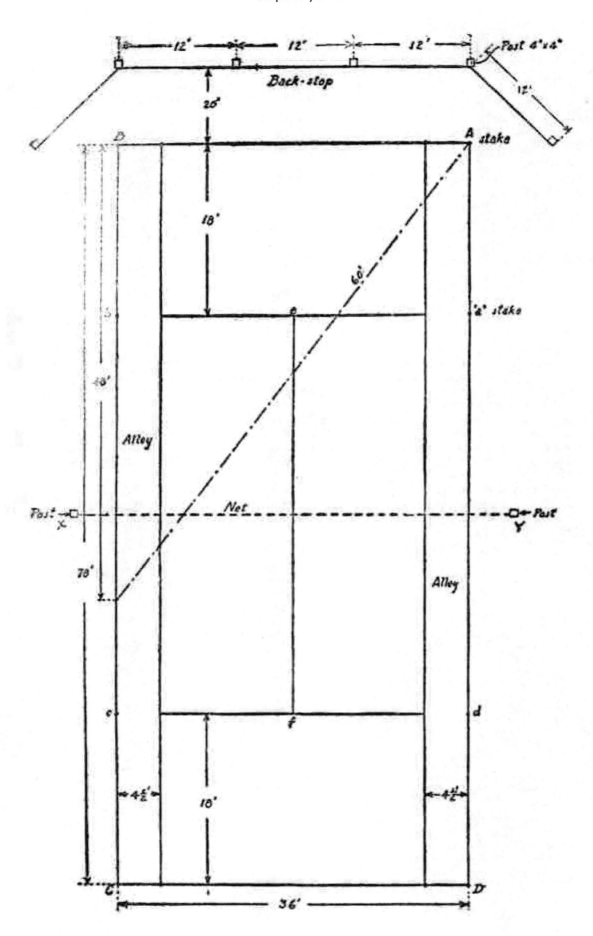

Fig. 213. The tennis court

Next measure from stakes *A*, *B*, *C*, *D* 18 feet along outside lines, and again drive in stakes *a*, *b*, *c*, *d*. By passing a cord from *a* to *b*, and from *c* to *d*, the service lines are laid out, omitting alleys. Find centre of service lines, and connect points *e* and *f*. The net crosses the centre of court from east to west, extending three feet beyond on each side. At these two points *x* and *y*, set the posts in the ground. By this method, the only stakes left in the ground are on the outside lines, and they must be driven in so that under no circumstances will a player stumble over them. They can always be found after a rain storm, and new lines laid out.

The posts for the net should be seven feet long and four inches square. Plane them off smooth, and coat the end which is to be in the ground with creosote or coal tar.

This coating should extend three feet six inches from the bottom, and as the post is to be three feet in the ground, this coating will extend six inches above. Decay takes place at the point of contact with the ground, and the creosote will prolong the life of the posts for many years, if the wood is well seasoned. Many posts for tennis nets are not sunk fully three feet in the ground, and consequently require guy ropes or wires to keep them upright. The time spent in digging the holes and tamping the dirt around posts is well spent, as the pull on them is severe, and they must stand upright.

Six inches from the top, bore a hole ¾ inch in diameter, east and west. The net must be three feet high at its centre, and three feet six inches at the posts. Pass the rope through these holes, and make fast to a cleat. These cleats may be of iron or wood, a sketch of a wooden cleat being shown at Fig. 215. They should be of oak or other hard wood, put on with two strong screws through holes which have been bored and countersunk. On the side of post toward the net, three strong screw eyes should be put about a foot apart, the lower one six inches from the ground. The net is to be fastened to these screw eyes to keep it in position. When everything is ready, paint the posts two coats of dark or bronze green.

The position of the tall poles for the back stop are shown in Fig. 213. Fifteen feet is none too far from the court for the stop net, and twenty would be better. Purchase twelve foot four by fours, and plane smooth, or have them dressed at the mill when ordering. This will reduce them to 3¾ × 3¾ inches. The method of enclosing the whole court by wire netting is seldom resorted to, unless the space available is very limited. The method here suggested of bringing the ends about at an angle of 45 degrees has been found very satisfactory in stopping swift service. Locate the post holes 12 feet apart, and dig them three feet deep. After treating the lower ends of posts for three and a half feet with creosote or tar, place in the ground, plumb each one while filling in, and tamp the earth about them firmly.

Strips 1 × 3 inches and 12 feet long must be used to join the posts at the top, else the pull necessary to straighten the wire will bring them out of plumb. These strips are to be nailed at the extreme top by eight-penny wire nails. When the structure is finished, except for the wire, paint with two coats of the same colour as the net posts.

The wire netting is chicken wire, inch and a half mesh, and three feet wide. Three of these strips will cover the space from the ground to the top. It is put on with staples nailed to the posts, stretched taut, and the joints where the strips touch wired together at intervals of three feet with soft iron wire.

If arranged as shown in the drawing, it will take six strips sixty feet long by three wide for the back stop, or 1080 square feet, and will cost $9 or $10.

Cheap cotton back stops are sold, but they are not very satisfactory, as they tighten in damp and sag in dry weather. For a permanent court belonging to a club the galvanized wire is well worth the difference in cost.

The size of the mesh is important, because although a tennis ball is 2½ inches in diameter, when driven hard it frequently goes through two-inch mesh.

There are many opportunities about the tennis court for the young woodworker to show his skill. Camp stools, settees, benches either plain or rustic, a chest to keep racquets and balls, fitted with a strong padlock, shelters for the spectators or club members, and even a small club house are among the possibilities.

Permanent structures, such as shelters and heavy benches, should generally be on the west side of the court, as spectators are usually present after the sun has passed the meridian, and it will then be at their back.

Tennis Court Accessories

THE CAMP-STOOL

Use hard wood such as maple, ash, or oak. The stock required for each stool will be four pieces 20½ × 1½ × 1 inches, two pieces 14 × 1⅛ × 1⅛ inches, and two pieces 10½ × ⅝ × ⅝ inches.

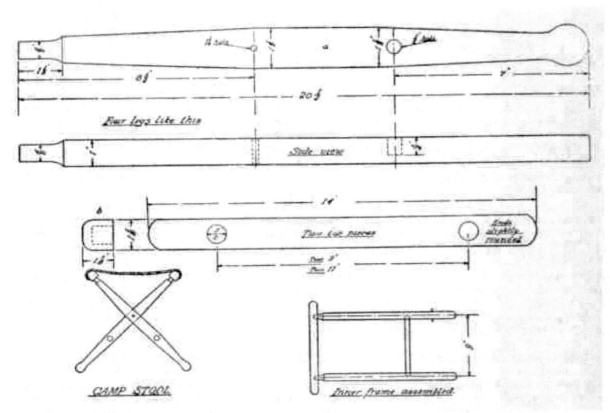

Fig. 214. The camp-stool

The four legs are made as shown at *a* (Fig. 214). The small end is to be rounded to a diameter of ⅝ inch; 8½ inches from this end a ³⁄₁₆-inch hole is bored for the rivet or bolt, which is to hold the legs together. Seven inches from the lower or foot end a ½-inch hole is bored ⅜ or ¾ inch deep. This is to receive the cross rod or dowel. The two top pieces 14 × 1⅛ × 1⅛ inches are rounded on two of their edges as shown at *b*. On the flat side of one of these bore two holes ⅝ inch diameter and ¾ inch deep, 9 inches apart, to receive the small end of the leg. On the other top piece, the holes are eleven inches apart.

The two cross pieces may be rounded, or pieces of ⅝-inch maple dowel used. In either case, the ends must be pared down to a diameter of ½ inch to fit the holes of this size. One is to be sawed nine inches long, the other eleven.

The camp-stool is composed of two frames pivoted together. Put together the inner frame, first gluing the legs into holes bored in top pieces, and at the same time gluing in the cross piece. These joints may be fastened by driving a brad through from the outside, or by wedges, as described in previous chapters. The outer frame is now put together, and the two pivoted. This is usually done with a rivet, a thin washer having been placed between the two sets of legs to relieve the friction. A small bolt and nut may be used, but as the nut is liable to come off, the bolt end should be riveted over the nut with the hammer.

Canvas or even a piece of carpet may be used for the seat. The size required is 15 by 12, the ends being tacked to the lower side of the top pieces. When canvas is used, it is usually turned under an inch on each side, and hemmed. In this case, its width must be at least fourteen inches. All articles which are to be handled much should have the edges slightly rounded; this rule applies to the camp-stool.

BENCHES

Folding settees for outdoor use are on the market at very cheap prices, but they are neither comfortable nor substantial. Fixed benches can be made of heavy but simple construction, as well as movable ones.

Fig. 215 shows the simplest possible form. Posts of locust, chestnut, or cedar are set in the ground to a depth of two feet or more. The diameter should be at least four inches.

A space one inch by three should be sawed out of each, as a rest for the cross pieces. These should be two by four stock, ten inches long, and must be securely nailed to the posts by eight or ten penny nails. The seat should be 16 inches or 18 inches above the ground, made of heavy plank at least two inches thick and 14 inches wide. Bore quarter-inch holes, countersink and fasten the top to cross pieces by three-inch flat-head screws. The span between cross pieces should not be over five feet, four would be better, so that a bench twelve feet long would call for six posts and three cross pieces, besides the top. Space the posts five feet apart between centres. This will allow an overhang of one foot at each end. The seat should be planed smooth, edges slightly rounded, and then two coats of boiled linseed oil applied. Painting seats is not advised, and varnish for outside work is seldom satisfactory. The wood for the top should be of some kind that is free from pitch, as the sun will draw it out, and a sticky seat result. Oak or maple will be very satisfactory.

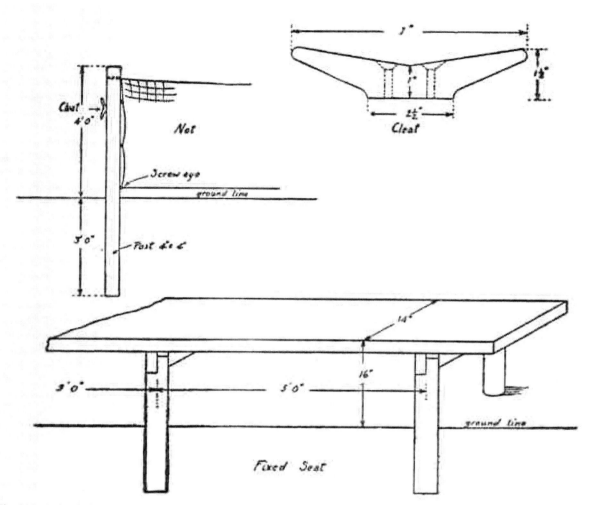

Fig. 215. A simple bench

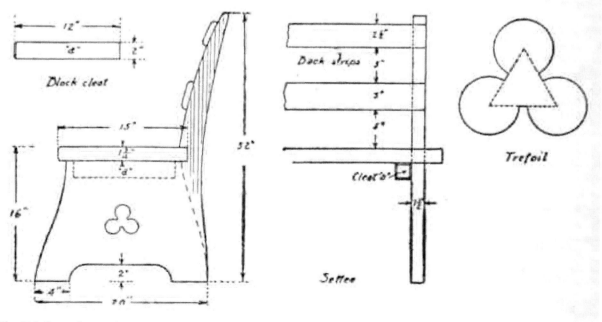

Fig. 216. Settee for tennis court

A movable settee of heavy construction is suggested in Fig. 216. The main dimensions for the standards supporting the seat and back strips are given, but the form may be modified to suit the young designer. There is considerable waste in making standards of this sort, and it is important to have the grain run in the direction indicated in the drawing. The two strips for the back, as well as the seat, should be put on with screws. The horizontal pieces on this settee will not give the necessary rigidity lengthwise, and it will be important to add braces under the seat. These may be in the form of heavy angle irons or square blocks, as shown at *a*. These blocks should be two inches square, and fastened with three-inch screws to both seat and standard. Everything about this settee is heavy and substantial, as all outdoor work should be. The camp-stool furnishes all the light furniture necessary.

The standards should never be more than four feet apart, so that a settee in this style, eight feet long, would require three standards.

This design can be changed to a simple bench by omitting the back and sawing the standard on its back edge to the same outline as the front, as suggested by the dotted line. The trefoil opening is made by boring three holes with a large bit at the points of a triangle.

The covered seat shown at Fig. 217 is one that may be constructed as shown, or modified in size, proportions, etc.

Small as it is, it will tax the skill of the young worker, and give him many of the problems of outdoor construction to figure out. It includes the setting and levelling of posts, framing, roofing, flooring, etc.

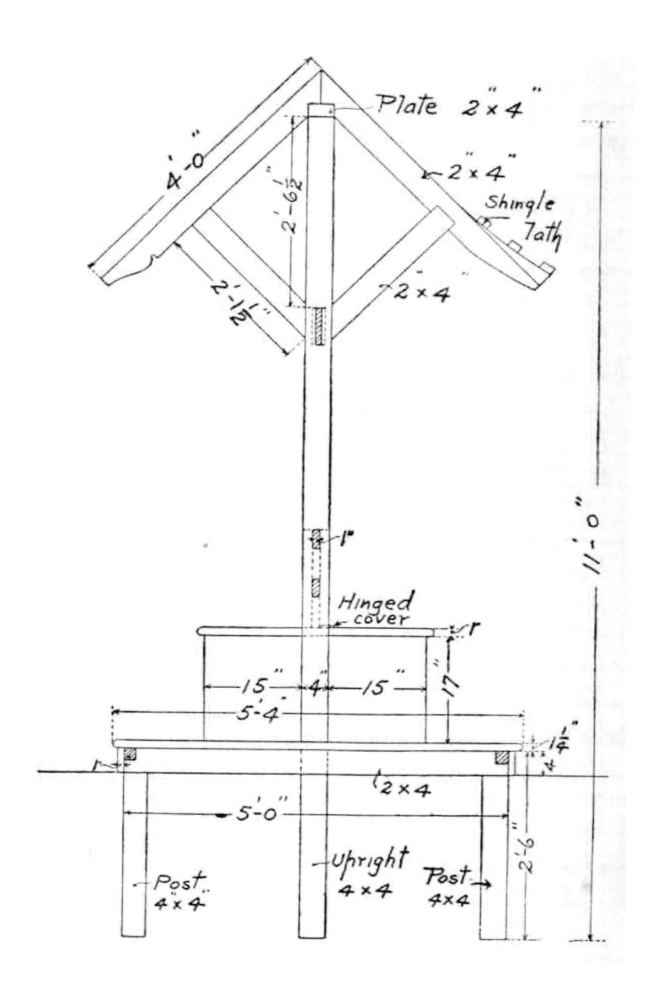

Plate 2"×4"

4'-0"

2"×4"

Shingle lath

2'-6½"

2-1½"

2"×4"

2"×4"

1"

Hinged cover

r

15" 4" 15"

17"

5-4"

1¼"

2×4"

5-0"

Upright 4×4

Post 4"×4"

Post 4×4

2-6"

Fig. 217. A covered seat

The material necessary should be first carefully estimated, with allowance made for waste. This is an item often forgotten by the amateur, and one especially to be provided for in framing. If the dimensions are to vary from those shown in our sketch, it would be wise to make a careful drawing first. In all outdoor structures, wind, rain, snow, and the effect of strong sunlight must be considered.

As this shelter is primarily for a tennis court, the timbers for the frame should be planed by hand or dressed at the mill, when purchased.

The 4×4 uprights should be bought 12 feet long, as this is a standard size, and set into the ground deep enough to bring the top nine feet above ground. The temptation to place posts only a little way in the ground must be overcome. The roof should be counted on to withstand a wind pressure of sixty miles an hour, and three feet in the ground is necessary in this case, as there are no braces to help support it.

Having cut the mortises for the horizontal tie piece a, place the first post in the hole dug for it, tamp the earth around it, and plumb with "level and plumb."

Another method would be to lay both uprights on the ground, place the tie piece in position, fasten with wooden pins driven through holes bored through the mortise and tenon joints, and nail the 2×4 plate on top of both posts. Then raise the structure, and place both posts in their respective holes at the same time.

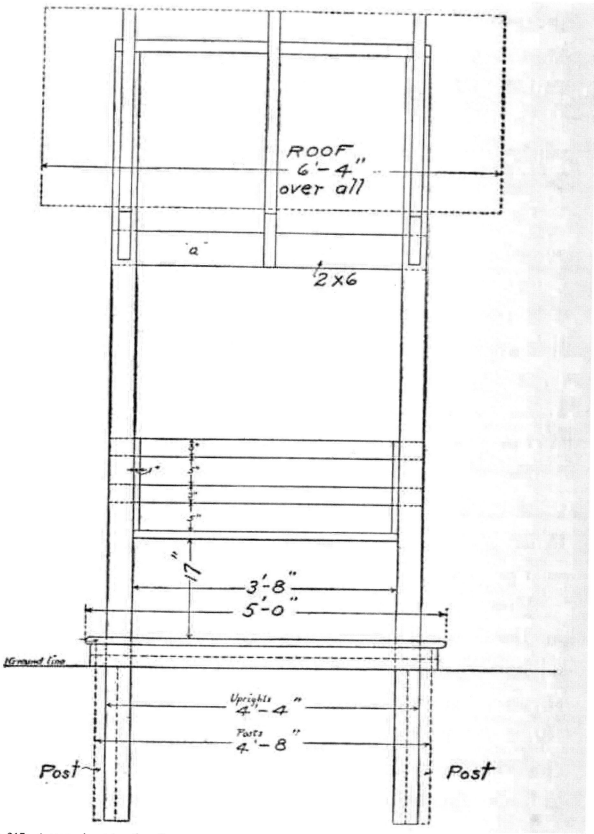

ROOF
6'-4"
over all

2 x 6

a

3'-8"
5'-0"

17"

Uprights
4'-4"

Posts
4'-8"

Ground line

Post

Post

Fig. 217a. A covered seat (continued)

211

In any work of this character, two boys should work together, and two trestles or saw horses will be a necessary part of their equipment. In mortise and tenon joints of this character a method called draw boring is frequently used. (See *b*, Fig. 217*b*.)

The hole for the pin or dowel is first bored across the centre of the mortise. The tenon is inserted snugly, and the bit again inserted until it makes a mark on the tenon. The tenon is withdrawn, and the centre of bit placed $\frac{1}{16}$ inch nearer the shoulder than the mark made, and the hole bored. This brings the distance *y* slightly less than *x*.

The three holes through which the pin is to pass are not in line when the tenon is again placed in mortise. The result is to draw the tenon tight, when the pin is driven home, and to make the joint a very snug one, as it should be.

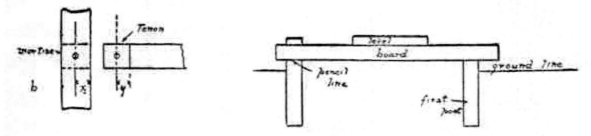

Fig. 217b. Draw boring a joint and method of levelling posts

If this method of constructing the frame on the ground is not used, the tie piece must be placed in position before the second post is set. Fasten the joints with the pins, and level the tie piece. If the two posts have been laid out together on the trestles, their tops must now come level and true.

This first step in making the structure is extremely important, as the success of the following work depends on it.

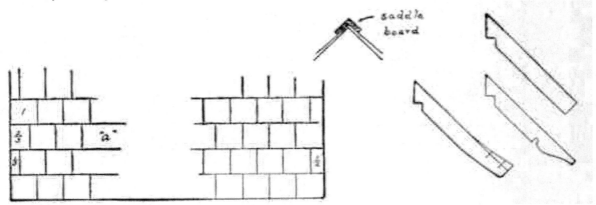

Fig. 218. Details of roof construction and forms of rafters

After tamping the uprights solidly, the corner posts for supporting the floor may be set in the ground. They should be of locust, cedar, or chestnut, and at least four inches in diameter. Set them in the ground not less than thirty inches, and flush with the ground line. It will be better to dig out three or four inches of top soil from the whole area, and afterward fill in with gravel, as this does not hold the moisture. This precaution will help to prevent decay, and, wherever possible, all the parts in contact with the earth should be painted with creosote. The outside of posts should be five feet one way and four feet eight inches the other. Their tops should be sawed off level. This may be done after setting. Saw one post at the desired height. To level the others with it, rest a straight board on first post, and while one boy holds the level on its upper edge, let the other make a pencil mark on the next post along under side of the board. Saw to this line, and level the remaining posts in the same manner. (Fig. 217*b*.)

The sill or frame for flooring must now be prepared. Use either 2 × 6 or 2 × 4 inch spruce. Cut two pieces five feet long, and two pieces four feet eight inches. Lay out half lap joints at the ends, and saw to the lines.

Spike this frame to the locust posts, and as it touches the outside of the uprights, nail to the latter, with ten-penny wire nails.

As additional support will be needed for the flooring, cut two 2 × 4, and fasten them across the frame either by half lap joint or spikes.

If this frame is planed on the outside, no finishing strip will be needed, but if it is rough sawed stock, a facing strip of 1 × 4 inch material should be placed on the outside, flush with the top of the frame.

The flooring may now be laid, using tongue and groove stock, and allowing it to project an inch beyond the frame on all four sides. The edges of this projection should be rounded with the plane. The flooring should be neatly fitted around the uprights, so that the latter may appear to come up through a solid floor 5 feet 4 inches by 5 feet 0 inches.

The roof should be made next, leaving the construction of the seat to the last. The roof timbers consist of six rafters four feet long, and six braces two feet one and a half inches long. Two methods are shown, and several combinations may be used. The rafters may have square ends, or some simple curved design may be sawed out, as suggested in the detailed drawing. (Fig. 218.)

The braces may meet the rafters in a plain butt joint, and be nailed, or they may be gained into the rafters, as shown in side view. This latter method makes a neat job, but it is not necessary, as far as strength is concerned. Nails are used in either case.

The straight rafter is of course the simpler and easier way, but the Japanese effect produced by a slight curve at the ends on the upper side is worth the little additional labour that it requires.

To secure this curve, saw out a template in white pine about fifteen inches long and 1½ inches wide, at one end, as shown in detail. The curve may be first drawn in pencil, and then sawed on the line.

From this template lay out six pieces of scrap, 2 × 4, and saw them all out the same size and shape. Nail them to the lower ends of the rafters on their top side.

The upper ends of the rafters are to be mitred, and the V-shaped notch cut as shown in detail drawing. (Fig. 219.)

The braces are square at one end, and mitred at the other.

Nail two rafters together at their mitred ends, using ten or twelve penny wire nails. Place in position over plate, and nail to it. Nail mitred end of braces to the upright, and then to rafter. The method of fastening two joints at right angles is called toe-nailing—nailing obliquely—as shown in detail.

The braces for middle rafters are fastened to the tie piece, and will need to be somewhat longer than the four fastened to the uprights. Their exact length should be determined by measurement, after the end rafters are secured. The end sawed off should be the square end, measurements being made from the extreme point of the mitred corner.

The roof is to be shingled. For this purpose, shingle lath, a standard commercial article, is to be nailed to the rafters at intervals of 5½ or 6 inches. For a steep roof like this, 6 inches will answer. This lath is to project beyond the outside rafters 9 inches or 1 foot. There must be a shingle lath at the top of each rafter, no matter how near the next one may come, and sometimes the whole roof is covered with boards as a support for the shingles, instead of lath.

Begin shingling at the lower end of the rafters, allowing the first course to project an inch beyond the first lath. To insure the end of the roof being straight, it is best to saw the lath after it is nailed to rafters.

The first course of shingles should be double—i. e., one over the other, joints broken.

On good and permanent roofs, where the pitch is not as great as in this case, the method shown at a (Fig. 218) is frequently used. After the first course is laid, the second is begun with a third of a shingle, the next with two thirds, the next with a whole one. It makes a tighter roof than that in which each joint comes over the centre of the one below. The carpenter marks the courses after the first with a chalk line. Measure up six inches from the lower edge, at each end of the roof. Take a piece of mason's line or strong cord, rub it with a piece of chalk, hold it taut at the two pencil marks, pull it up in the centre, and allow it to snap back to the roof. It will leave a straight chalk line from end to end, and the lower edge of the next course of shingles is laid to this line. Two shingle nails are to be used on each shingle, driven into the shingle lath high enough up to be covered by the next course.

On very fine work, the edges of shingles where they touch are first planed, but for ordinary purposes this is not necessary.

Shingle one side of the roof clear up to the ridge, allowing the last course to present six inches or so to the weather. Saw off carefully all that part which projects, close to the ridge. This will allow the shingles from the second side to project over those of the first, and when the second side is finished it is to be sawed off at the ridge as before.

To protect the ridge from leaks, saddle boards are sometimes added. These are strips of pine lapped over the top and nailed, as shown in detailed drawing.

If the curved rafters are used, the pull of the nails will make the shingles conform to the curve, unless it is excessive.

Many methods are used by carpenters in finishing roofs, and considerable time and material are used in constructing cornices. In this simple structure, if the timbers have been planed as suggested, it will be well to leave it as it is, with the rafters exposed, especially if the ornamental curves have been sawed before erection. If the roof has been made with boards, instead of shingle laths, the whole construction is honestly and frankly visible. The old-fashioned method of putting on "gingerbread" work, ornaments sawed on a hand or jig-saw, is to be condemned. Let all your construction be strong, simple, and straightforward.

Shingles are sometimes stained or painted. Staining is by far the better treatment, but the shingles should be dipped into the stain and dried before they are put on. The stains sold by most paint stores come in a variety of colours. Some shade of green, red, or brown should be selected, according to the colour of the body of the structure. A red roof on a white structure looks well, as it is usually seen against a background of blue sky and green foliage. A light gray building with white trimmings and red roof makes a pleasing combination.

It only remains to construct the seat. This is made double, with a back between the uprights, and the seat cover is hinged to make a chest below for racquets, etc. This double seat is designed to give the greatest possible seating accommodation for this size of shelter. It has the disadvantage of one seat facing the wrong way, and if the structure is made longer it is suggested that the back seat be omitted.

Construct a box without top or bottom 34 inches by 3 feet 8 inches. The material may be the same as the floor, but in any case it must be tongue and groove matched boards. This box will just slip in between the uprights and must be securely nailed to them. To fasten to the floor, nail cleats to the latter just inside the box, and nail the sides and ends of the box to these cleats. Further to strengthen the box, square cleats should be nailed upright in each corner of the inside.

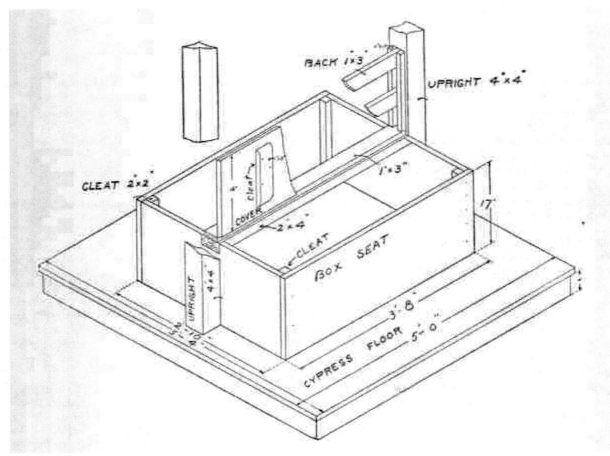

Fig. 218a. Box seat

The backbone of the box is a piece of 2 × 4 spruce. Its length will be the distance between the uprights or the length of the box. Saw down through the box ends exactly 2 inches, with the saw against the uprights, and remove the piece 4 × 2 from each end. Into these two spaces slip the 2 × 4 and toenail to uprights. Nail to the top of this 2 × 4 along its centre a piece of 1 × 3 pine, the same length as the 2 × 4. The box covers are to be hinged to this pine strip and will rest on the edge of the 2 × 4 which will carry the weight.

Seat covers are to be the same length as the box, with just enough clearance to let them move freely between the uprights. As they are 16 inches wide, it is doubtful whether a single board that width will be available. They may be made of tongue and groove boards, with cleats 3 × ⅞ inches screwed on the under side, just long enough to allow the cover to close. Outside edges should be rounded and three strong hinges used on each cover. As it has a bearing surface on front and ends of the box, no extra support will be needed.

If a support for the back is desired, two strips 3 × 1¼ with rounded edges may be fastened to the uprights, and as the pressure may be both ways, they should be nailed between two upright cleats at each end. The cleats ⅞ × 1¼ are nailed to uprights, or the strips may be mortised through.

The sharp edges of the uprights may be bevelled or chamfered where people are likely to come in contact with them.

The structure is now ready for painting. Set all nails with nail punch, and give the first or priming coat to the whole structure, shingles excepted. This should be done when the wood is dry, not directly after a rain. When this coat is dry, fill all nail holes with putty and give second coat of paint. If the priming coat was thin a third coat may be necessary to give the desired result. Use a little drier in the paint and when necessary to thin it use boiled linseed oil. As white would not be suitable for the seats and floor, a light gray for the seats and a darker shade for the floor may be used.

XLV

THE PERGOLA

Among the many structures used to beautify the grounds of a suburban or country place, the pergola is seen less than it should be. It is a luxury, but so is a couch hammock, and many other details of our modern life might be placed under the same heading. As an arbour for the training of the vines, the pergola adds more dignity to a place than any other structure, always assuming that it is well built and in good proportion. Its length must of course depend on the local circumstances. It should lead somewhere, as from the house to the flower garden, or from house to stable. It should, in other words, not be placed on the grounds simply as an ornament. Its purpose should be to give a certain amount of privacy to a walk.

The oldest recognized style of architecture is known as post and beam construction, as suggested in Fig. 219, where two vertical members support a horizontal one. This style was used by the Egyptians and Greeks, and was a large factor in deciding the form of the old Greek temples. The pergola consists of two parallel rows of columns connected by longitudinal beams and cross beams.

A very artistic one may be built by two boys with the assistance of a third person in the heavy work of lifting and placing the columns. If a small-sized structure with 6-inch columns is built, two boys can handle the whole construction alone.

This small size is not recommended, however, as one of the first requisites of the pergola is a massive appearance of solidity and permanence.

The proportions for two sizes are given in the drawing, and they may be modified to suit the size of the ground, buildings, etc. (Fig. 220.)

Wooden columns in many styles, sizes, and proportions are on the market and may be bought from any lumber dealer. The bases and caps are separate and should be ordered to fit the columns.

The construction of the pergola brings the young carpenter in contact with several new problems. The first is the subject of foundations. These may be in the form of concrete, which is permanent and solid, and will not decay, as any form of wooden post will do in time. The ground should be as nearly level as possible, and should be staked out with eight stakes, as shown in the drawing. (Fig. 221.)

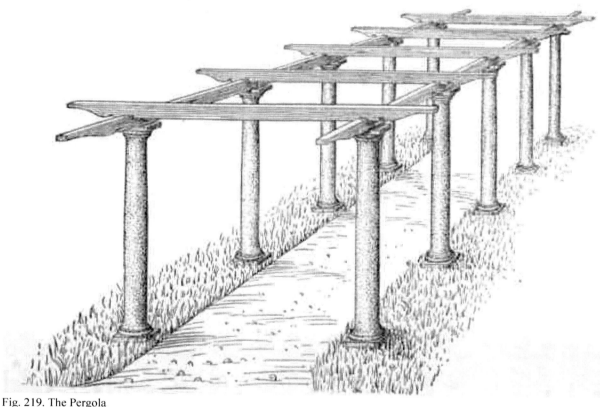

Fig. 219. The Pergola

The stakes are three feet from the centre of the columns in each case, and angle *a c d* should be made square at the beginning. Measure distance *a b* equal to *c d*. From *a* measure along a line stretched from *a* to *b* three feet, and then three spaces of twelve feet each. Measure the same distance from *c* along *c d*, and place stakes at each point. A line stretched from *e* to *f* should pass over the centre of the stakes marking the centre of each column, as these latter stakes will be dug out in the process of excavating for the foundation, while stakes *e* and *f* are necessary for the proper location of the holes.

After digging the first two holes, test their accuracy by again stretching a cord or masons' line from *e* to *f*. Proceed with the next set of holes in the same way, placing new stakes three feet out from centres to correspond with *e* and *f*. When the eight holes have been dug, the arrangement will appear as shown at *g*, twelve stakes being left in the ground. Should the pergola be longer or narrower, the same method would be used, the dimensions only being altered. The size of the holes will depend on the following considerations:

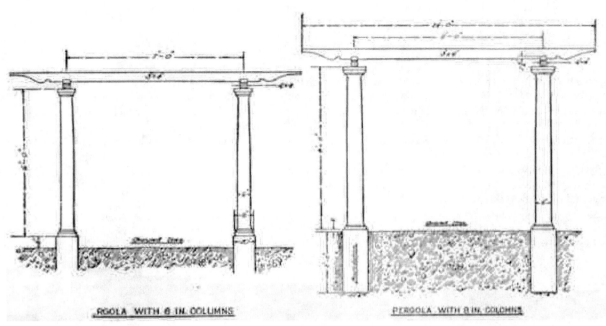

Fig. 220. The pergola

Assuming that we are building the large pergola with eight-inch columns, the base will be about twelve inches square. Measure the base and add two inches to it, making, say, a fourteen-inch square, the size of the foundation. A box in the form shown at *a*, 14 inches square inside, must be made. No nails are used on the box. It is held together by cleats *c c*. They must be made to fit snugly, and are to be knocked off when the cement has hardened—*i. e.*, about four days after making.

These boxes may be full depth of the hole, three feet, or, as is sometimes done, the hole is made just the right size and the box, about eighteen inches in length, wedged into the top as shown at *i*. This method calls for considerable care in levelling the top of the box and securing the proper projection above ground, as well as in pouring in the cement without dislodging it, but the box is removed more easily than is the case with a full-length one. The decision about this point determines the size of the hole. In case the short box is used, the hole must be fifteen inches square and just enough shaved from the sides at top to receive the box.

If the full length box is used, the hole should be about twenty inches square, to allow the cleats to be knocked off and boards withdrawn.

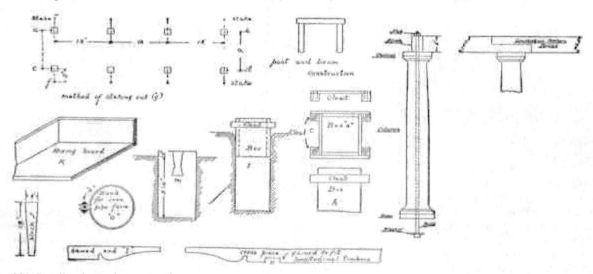

Fig. 221. Details of pergola construction

This weighty question having been decided, prepare to mix concrete. Make a mixing board about five or six feet square of flooring boards fastened to heavy cleats on the under side. It should have two or three sides nailed on, as shown at *k*. Also prepare eight wooden blocks, as shown in drawing. These may be fifteen to eighteen inches long, sawed from 4 × 4 timber, planed smooth and with a slight taper toward the lower end. The purpose of these blocks will be apparent later on. The concrete is composed of four parts clean gravel to one of Portland cement, and the best is always the cheapest in the long run. Use a pail for mixing and place four pailfuls of gravel on the mixing board. Pour over this one pailful of dry cement and mix thoroughly, turning the whole mass several times. When thoroughly mixed, pour on water, half a pailful at a time, and turn again with the shovel until the whole mass is wet. Shovel this into the first box. It will probably take two such mixings to fill it. Now place in the top of the concrete one of the tapering blocks, allowing it to project about three or four inches above the surface of the concrete. The block should be rubbed with grease or oil before insertion to make it withdraw easily. As soon as the block is placed, pass the line from stakes *e* to *f* and make sure that the block is exactly at the centre.

In every case it is to be withdrawn in about an hour, or as soon as the concrete has set, but before it has gripped the block too tightly; otherwise withdrawal will be a difficult matter. The object of this performance is to leave in the centre of the foundation a hole about a foot deep and four inches across. Level the top of concrete with a trowel and test with the level.

All the foundations are made alike and no effort should be spared to see that the boxes are level and in line with each other. Test from end stakes *a b c d* and from across stakes with the masons' line. This work will be easier if the four end foundations are made first.

To do the work thoroughly, two boys may count on the process, from the staking out to the finishing of foundations, occupying about three days. It is the most important and laborious part of the work and when finished represents about one third of the labour on the pergola.

The concrete should stand at least four days before it is touched again, and during that time the timber may be prepared. Besides the eight columns, there will be needed:

6 pcs. 4×6 ins.—16 ft. long

15 pcs. 3×6 ins.—14 ft. long

144 ft. (running) 1×2 ins.

8 pcs. of $\frac{5}{8}$-in. round iron

The iron should be 18 inches longer than the total height of the wooden columns, including base and cap. This should be determined by actual measurement. The rods can be obtained from a blacksmith. Have him cut a thread at each end and provide two nuts for each rod. They are to extend clear through each column from the bottom of the hole in the foundation, through the longitudinal timbers that rest on the cap, to bolt the whole structure together securely.

Columns come either built up or solid. The solid ones have a core bored out through the centre, so that in either case the rod can easily pass through from top to bottom. A hole should be bored $\frac{3}{4}$ inch diameter through the centre of both cap and base to allow the bolt to pass easily.

In ordering timbers, have them dressed on all sides at the mill. Have the fifteen 3×6 inch pieces sawed on both ends as shown at *l*, and have one end on four of the 4×6 inch pieces sawed the same shape. The two remaining 4×6 inch pieces are to be square on the ends.

A week after making the concrete foundations, the boxes having been removed and the holes filled in with earth well tamped down, the openings in the top may be cut out with a long cold chisel, as shown at *m*. This need not be a very particular job. The object is to dovetail the cement, to be used in filling up the opening to the foundation, and it can be done roughly. The setting of the columns on their foundations is performed as follows:

Nail base and cap to each column and slip a long bolt clear through. At the bottom the bolt will be allowed to project. At the top pass it through a piece of wood 6 inches high, a $\frac{3}{4}$-inch hole being bored for the purpose.

Fill the opening in the foundation with clear cement mixed with enough water to bring it to the consistency of paint. Set the column on its foundation, with the end of the bolt and its nut and a large washer immersed in the cement. This will harden quickly, making a strong bond with the foundation and holding the bolt rigid. Plumb the column, and if it shows a tendency to lean, place thin wedges under it until it stands true when tested by the plumb and level on all sides.

Treat all the posts alike and when one row has been set, run the masons' line along the bolts on top and see that they are in line. Everything should be ready before starting this job, as clear cement hardens quickly and any moving of the columns that may be necessary in lining them up must be done before it sets. A good method is to place the end posts first, tie the masons' line to the bolts and line the other two posts as they are set.

When they are all on their foundations at last you will begin to realize for the first time the value and beauty of the task you have undertaken. Our boys were so excited that every member of the family, and some of the neighbours, were dragged out as spectators. It did not seem possible that two boys could handle such a large proposition, but there it stood as if it were intended to stand for a century. Harry was for putting on the superstructure at once, but Ralph had to warn him not to touch it until the cement had thoroughly hardened.

They allowed it to stand two days before they removed the 6-inch blocks from the bolts at the top and began the work of placing the long 4×6 inch timbers. These members were lapped as shown in the drawing, $\frac{3}{4}$-inch holes being bored to receive the bolts.

When all the timbers on one side were in place, the nuts were screwed down snug on each bolt with a monkey wrench. The work, with the cutting, fitting, and boring, consumed a whole day, and a second day was used up on the second row. It was not necessary to call the family out again. The boys had all the help that could be desired in lifting, and were also blessed with a continuous audience.

The cross timbers were gained out to a depth of $1\frac{1}{2}$ inches, and fitted over the long 4×6 inch pieces, as shown at *n*. There was one over the centre of each column, and an additional piece was removed to provide for the nut, which was thereby entirely concealed. The remaining cross pieces were spaced three feet apart on centres, and all spiked securely to the 4×6's. It was found advisable to bore $\frac{1}{4}$-inch holes for the spikes, and to sink their heads below the surface with a nail set.

It only remained to nail on to the cross pieces five rows of 1×2 in the position shown.

All nail holes and cracks were puttied, and the entire structure down to the cement foundation was given three coats of white paint. Built in this manner, the pergola will stand for many years, and already the boys have planted wistaria, honeysuckles, crimson rambler, trumpet, and other vines to cover it.

217

The columns themselves may be easily made of concrete. The form may be made of six or eight inch iron pipe. When this is bought, have it split in half lengthwise at a machine shop. Six-inch pipe cut in this way will cost about a dollar a foot, but it will last a lifetime if protected from rust, and very often the concrete posts may be sold, so that the form will soon pay for itself.

Have a blacksmith make two iron bands, as shown at *o*. Have a $\frac{5}{16}$-inch hole drilled at *a* through both ends. These bands are used to hold the two halves of the iron form together, and are tightened by a bolt and nut at *a*.

Dig a pit for the form to stand in, so that the cement may be easily poured in. This pit may be about three feet deep by two feet square, and the sides supported by a box without a bottom.

To make a column, clamp the two bands about the form, and place in the bottom end a circular piece of wood, with a hole in the centre to insure the iron rod being in the middle. Place the form upright in the pit, and secure it firmly by nailing strips of wood across the top of the box. Place the iron rod in the centre, passing it through the hole in the bottom. Pour in the cement quite wet, and tamp it down occasionally until full. It will settle a little, and will need to be filled to the top. A circular piece of wood, similar to the one at the bottom, may be used to centre the rod at the top. This must be done as soon as the form is filled, before the concrete has had a chance to set.

Use four parts of fine, clean sifted gravel to one of cement. Allow the form to stand four days. Remove the clamps, and draw the form out on the ground. Tap it gently, and remove one half of the iron pipe. Roll it over upon two pieces of board, and remove the other half. The concrete will be very heavy, and the assistance of a full-grown man may be needed to draw the form out of the pit.

The inside of the form should be cleaned and thoroughly oiled. This should always be done before making a column to insure its coming out easily, as concrete forms a strong bond with iron, and otherwise the column may be broken in trying to get it out. The result will be a perfectly round but not perfectly smooth column. It should be coated with a wash of clear cement and water, using a wide brush. The colour may be made white by adding a lump of lime to the cement and water, and two coats of this solution about the consistency of milk will be necessary. The last coat may be put on after the columns are on their foundations. The placing of the posts on the square foundations is heavy work and the help of a labourer should be secured.

These plain posts are not as ornamental as wooden columns, with their bases and capitals, but they make a very substantial structure that cannot decay and will last a century.

XLVI

POULTRY HOUSES

There are a hundred ways of raising chickens, and ninety of them are wrong.

This is not a treatise on poultry raising, for there are many elements which enter into the problem—incubation, brooding, feeding, etc. But assuming that one of the main points aimed at is the production of eggs in winter, when they are scarce and expensive, the *housing* of chickens is admitted by poultry raisers to be one of the first considerations.

The house should be sixteen feet deep, should face south, and no glass should be used in its construction. A window nine or ten feet long by two and a half feet high placed four feet above the ground is recommended, and it should be covered with netting or chicken wire on the outside, but left open all day, even in zero weather. It is closed at night, by a screen of canvas or duck fastened to a light wooden frame. The frame is hinged at the top, and hooked up to the ceiling during the day.

The following description is taken from the experience of several poultry men who have been successful, and have made money by selling eggs.

The principle of this construction is that ventilation is a prime necessity, and that dampness is the one thing to be avoided. With these objects attained, chickens will stand almost any amount of cold, and with proper feeding and the strictest cleanliness, egg production will continue throughout the winter.

Some successful men insist on a wooden floor, others recommend one of gravel ten inches deep. The construction given here calls for the gravel floor on the ground level.

Many recommend a litter of straw ten inches or more deep on the gravel. The morning meal is thrown on this litter so that the chickens are forced to scratch for their breakfast, getting the blood in circulation by this early morning exercise.

As the method of building this house is typical of many outdoor structures, it will be taken up in detail. It would make an excellent work shop or cabin, with a few modifications, such as a floor of boards, and the addition of a few windows. Before it is finished the builders will probably regret, as our boys did, that it was to be used by their chickens instead of for themselves. (See Fig. 222.)

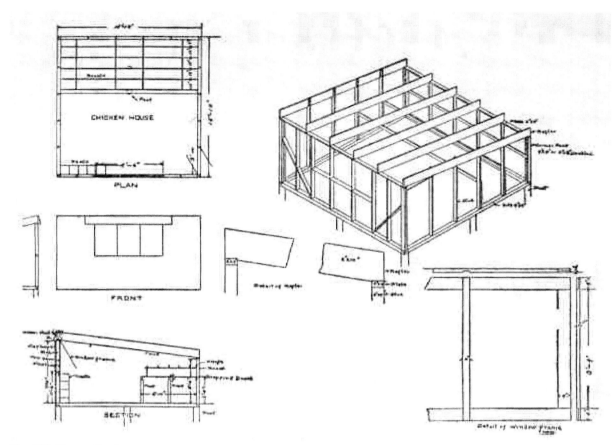

Fig. 222. The poultry house

Set eight locust or chestnut posts in the ground and saw off six inches above the lowest point. Level in the same manner as for the sheltered seat described for the tennis court, and see that the outsides of posts measure 15 feet 10 inches over all measurements.

Square the corners by the 3-4-5 method, laying the 4 × 4 inch sill pieces on top of posts while doing this. The sill is put together with halved joint, and spiked to the posts with twelve-penny wire nails. The corner posts are 4 × 4 inch spruce, with square ends toenailed to the sill.

Plumb these posts, and tie in position by temporary braces, using for this purpose shingle lath or strips of boards.

The plates along front and back are 2 × 4 inches, nailed to posts from the top.

The frame may now be finished by placing the 2 × 4-inch studding, toenailing to sill and plates on the ends, and sill and rafters on the sides.

The frames for door and window are shown in the illustration.

The rafters spaced three feet apart are 2 × 8 or 2 × 10 inches. This large size is due to the long span of sixteen feet, with no middle support from underneath.

The ends of rafters are cut to fit snugly over the plates, as shown, and sawed straight up and down to correspond with vertical walls front and back. No overhang is provided for the roof, as commercial roofing paper is to cover the whole outside of the house. In case it is to be used for other purposes than poultry raising, this feature should be modified, and the rafters allowed to project both front and back.

With the rafters nailed in position, permanent braces may be put in at the corners, as shown in the drawing, and temporary braces removed.

If the building is to be used as a shop, a second door directly opposite the one shown is recommended. For this purpose the position of the work bench would be on the front directly under the long window, and the two doors would then be in the proper place to permit the planing of long boards.

When the frame is finished, the question of siding must be taken up. If the original purpose of the building is to be carried out, poultry experts claim that a double wall is very desirable as a barrier against dampness, which arises primarily from the exhalations of the birds. If the walls are cold, this dampness will condense on them, while with a double wall this does not take place, as the dampness escapes with the air. The outside casing may be of ship-lap boards or tongued and grooved material. For a cabin or shop, novelty siding, clapboards or even shingles may be used. Bring the square ends of the boards flush with the openings for door and window, and nail to corner posts and studding with eight or ten penny wire nails.

Finish the two sides, sawing off the sheathing along the top of rafters. Cover front and back clear up to top of rafters, and bring ends of boards flush with outside of the side sheathing.

219

Several methods of finishing corners of frame buildings are shown in Fig. 223. At *a* is shown the corner of this chicken house. No corner boards are used over the outer sheathing, as the whole structure is to be covered with roofing paper.

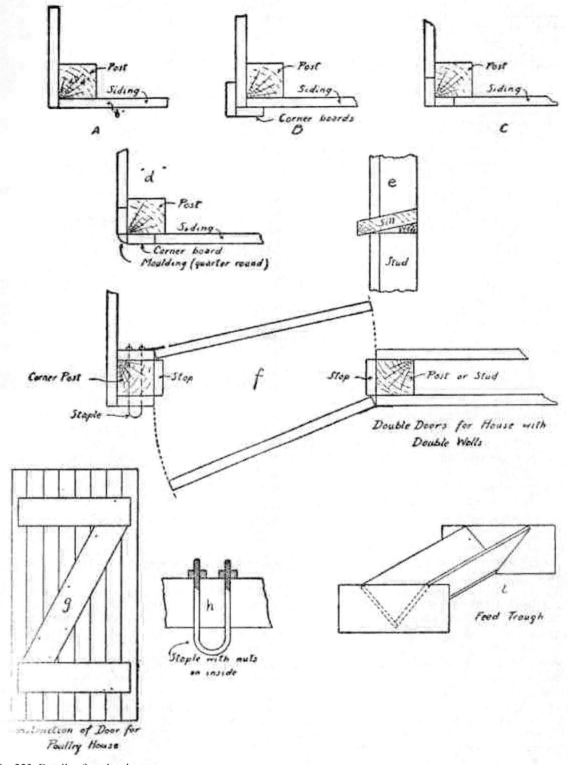

Fig. 223. Details of poultry house

At *b* is shown the finish for a stable or cheap cottage, with outside trim nailed over the sheathing. This is the cheapest, easiest, and poorest method of corner finish for ordinary outhouses. At *c* a better method is shown, with trim nailed to the posts, and clapboards fitted up close to it and nailed to corner posts. A still better finish is shown at *d*, where the trim is nailed to posts but not lapped. The angles between corner trim filled with a quarter round moulding make a good joint and a neat finish. If the double wall is to be used, a second boarding is made on the inside of studding and under side of rafters, first covering the space with building paper tacked to the inside of studding, and nailing the boards—either ship-lap or tongue and groove—to the frame work.

Door and window sills are made with an outward slant to provide a water table. A cross section of window sill is shown in the detail drawing at e. As there is no window in this building except the canvas screen, the construction of a window frame is not necessary. If the double wall is made, a double door, one opening in and the other out, will be in order. The outside door, flush with outer sheathing, and the same arrangement inside are shown at f.

A door sill will not be necessary, and the construction of the doors is shown at g. The material is tongue and groove boards fitted to the opening, so as to close easily, yet to provide for expansion in wet weather, and held together by heavy cleats $3 \times \frac{7}{8}$ inches on the inside, as shown. The inner door is fastened by a hook and eye, and the outer one with hasp, staple, and padlock.

As the window opening is covered with wire, the only way a thief can get in is by cutting the wire and canvas or by drawing the staple. The latter method can be prevented by the use of special staples, with threads cut on each end, and fastened on the inside by nuts, as shown at h. These staples are sold at all hardware stores.

The construction of the frame for the canvas screen is shown in Fig. 222. The lap joint is used throughout, and the outside dimensions are two inches greater than the window opening. Tack the canvas or duck to the side of the frame next the window, and provide two hooks and eyes to fasten it down at night. Strong iron butt hinges should be used on this frame, and heavy T or strap hinges on the doors.

The outside of the house is finished, except for a water-shed over the window, and the cover for the entire outside of strong roofing paper. This is sold usually with a special cement for making tight joints and with tin washers for the nails. The water table is simply a board projecting at an angle and fastened to triangular brackets, as shown at a (Fig. 222). The roofing paper brought down over this board, and tacked to the under side or edge, makes a watertight joint.

The inside woodwork consists of roosts, dropping platform, and nests.

The dropping platform is a floor of tongue and groove boards, placed three feet from the ground on posts, and extending the full length of the house.

The roosts are fastened to a strong frame, as shown in drawing, and the frame—in sections—is hinged at the back. Each morning this frame is raised, hooked to the ceiling, and the dropping platform cleaned.

The construction of the nests is a subject on which poultry experts differ widely, but whatever form is adopted, the material may usually be obtained from old boxes or packing cases.

The outdoor runs for summer consist of wire netting fastened to chestnut, cedar, or locust posts. If other woods are used, the lower parts should be coated with creosote. This is also a good disinfectant, to be used for cleaning the roosts occasionally.

Many accessories for the poultry house may be made of wood, but opinions of specialists are so antagonistic that it is hardly safe to advocate any one type. A feed trough is shown at i (Fig. 223). It may be made from box material, and consists of two boards nailed together at right angles, supported at the ends by two horizontal pieces nailed on. Brooder houses, feed, and incubator houses, and the many other details of poultry raising are well within the power of any careful boy, and the designs should be selected from the expert whose system he has decided to follow.

XLVII

HOUSING OF OUTDOOR PETS

The care of rabbits, guinea pigs, and other pets becomes of absorbing interest to every boy at some time, and he is fortunate indeed if he has room outdoors to engage in this pastime properly.

The comfort of the little animals, and their protection from their natural enemies, the cat, dog, weasel, etc., should be well looked after. Fig. 224 shows a very simple and convenient house for animals which do not gnaw through wood, as the rabbit and guinea pig.

These two animals will usually live together peaceably, except when breeding. The mothers become sensitive and jealous of all strangers when raising a family. The house proper has a sloping roof, which is hinged to provide a convenient method of reaching any part of the inside.

The large space covered on all sides by wire netting is the yard, or runway.

The front of the house should face south, and be covered with netting, except the door, which slides up in the grooves provided, as shown in the detail.

The northern end of yard is boarded clear up to the top. This shuts off the cold north winds, and in that kind of a house rabbits will live the year round.

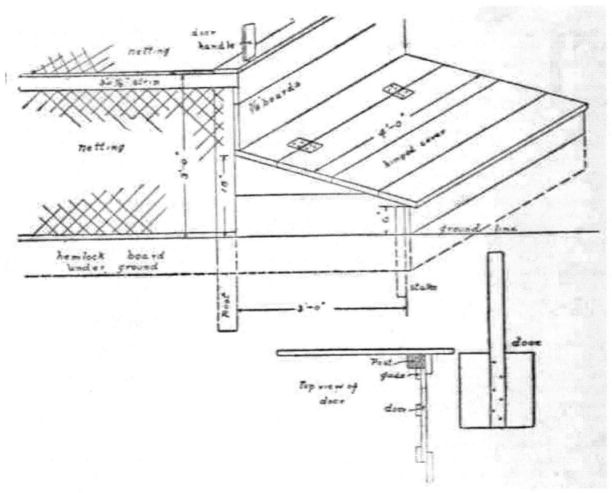

Fig. 224. Rabbit house

Guinea pigs will thrive in such a structure until the thermometer reaches zero.

These interesting and harmless creatures come from Brazil, and when the temperature reaches that point, it is better to take them indoors, as they catch cold and die of pneumonia, like human beings.

The runway is covered at the top with two-inch wire netting to keep out cats, who seem to take delight in killing both pigs and rabbits.

The upright corner posts should be set at least two feet in the ground, braced along the top by strips, to which the netting is fastened with staples, or double-pointed tacks.

A hemlock board should be set in the ground all around the yard, with a projection of an inch or two for securing the netting at the ground line.

Hemlock is cheap and will last longer in the ground than spruce. If the rabbits start to burrow, they become discouraged by finding this board in the way on every side. These planks or boards may be rough-sawed lumber.

The inside of the house should be coated with creosote and painted outside a bronze green. A dark-coloured house is warmer than a white one, as may be easily proved by placing a thermometer, first under a black hat, then under a white one. This is probably the reason why people in the tropics wear white clothing.

A door the full height of the yard should be provided at the far end, as it is sometimes necessary to get in for cleaning or other purposes.

The hinged roof should be made water tight by covering with some form of commercial roofing paper, or by using tongue and grooved boards well painted.

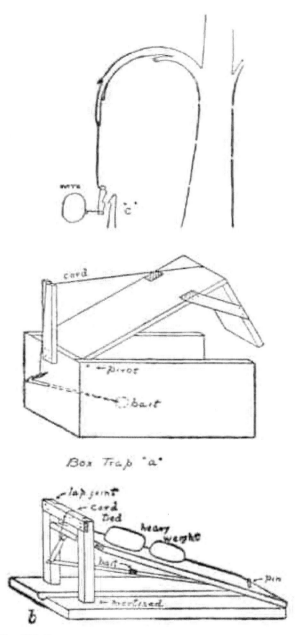

Fig. 225. Traps

The door sliding in grooves, as shown, has a long handle, which projects up through the top of the runway, so that it may be opened or closed from the outside. It can be made from box material.

A number of these houses may be placed in a row and allowed to open into a large yard, or there may be individual runs. The latter method is more satisfactory, as a large run can easily be obtained by providing doors between the yards.

In the country, where weasels, mink or other wild enemies bother the rabbits, they can be caught in traps. The ordinary box trap at *a*, Fig. 225, is designed to catch the animals alive. Its construction is clearly shown in the drawing, one end covered with wire netting, or made solid, and the other provided with a door, arranged to drop easily in the groove when the trigger has been disturbed. The simple construction of the trigger is shown in the detail, while the bait is attached to a string. As soon as this is disturbed the door drops.

A typical dead-fall trap is shown at *b*. The weights placed on the sloping board should be heavy, as this trap is designed to kill its victim. For this reason it should never be used where there is any possibility of a pet cat or dog being caught. The trigger is very sensitive, and the slightest pull at the bait is sufficient to bring the weight down on the unfortunate animal.

The uprights should be mortised through the base board, and the cross piece at top halved to the uprights. The sloping board with weights fastened to it has a generous-sized hole fitted loosely over a dowel at the right-hand end of bottom board. A groove cut in the latter allows the weighted board to fit tightly when it falls, the dowel with bait dropping into the groove.

223

Fig. 225 at *c* shows a snare frequently used. It should be placed in front of a hollow log, box, or barrel, so that the animal must put his head through the loop of wire in order to reach the bait.

The first pull at the end of the trigger releases the spindle, and the bent sapling does the rest. The loop of wire should be held open and in position by twigs conveniently placed.

The killing of our few remaining wild creatures, however, should never be done for sport. It is excusable only when they become destructive or troublesome. Squirrels, rabbits, and chipmunks are much more interesting as friends than as caged or killed victims.

XLVIII

OUTDOOR CARPENTRY

Outdoor construction or carpentry, as distinguished from the indoor work of the cabinet maker, calls for a general acquaintance with tools, some mathematics, an elementary knowledge of the strength of materials, and a good supply of common sense. It demands also some knowledge of the effects of frost on foundations, and requires judgment in providing for the elements, wind, rain, snow, and sun.

Every building may be resolved into certain parts, such as foundations, framing, roof, door, and window frames, outside covering or siding, flooring, partitions, doors and windows, wall covering or ceiling, interior finish, hardware, etc. These will be taken up in their order.

FOUNDATIONS

These, like all details, depend on the size and purpose of the building. The method of setting a small building on posts has been explained under poultry house, and sheltered seat for tennis court. It should be used only for small structures, such as camp buildings, sea-shore cottages, and out-buildings. Brick, stone, and concrete all have their advantages, but for young builders, concrete is perhaps the best and easiest to handle. The woodwork necessary for concrete work is extremely important, and its possibilities have hardly been touched, even to-day. The box or form should present the smooth side of the boards to the concrete, and should be so constructed that the form may be readily removed after the concrete has hardened. This sounds like a simple matter, but it becomes complicated in many cases. The method of fastening the wooden frame to a concrete foundation is suggested in the chapter on the making of a pergola. In some houses the frame is simply laid on the concrete, and the weight of the building is trusted to keep it in place.

In the case of small structures this would not be sufficient, and a better way would be to imbed bolts in the cement before it hardens. Pass these bolts through holes bored in the sill, and fasten them with nut and washer on top, after the concrete has hardened.

Any foundation should be sunk at least three feet in the ground, otherwise it will be "heaved" by the frost. Where a cellar is to be built, the foundation should be of sufficient depth to leave at least 6 feet 6 inches in the clear between floor of cellar and under side of floor beams, and seven feet would be better. If the foundation extends two feet above the ground, its bottom would be 5 feet 6 inches below the ground level.

The thickness of the concrete wall must depend on the size and weight of the building, and for a small cottage it should not be less than ten inches. The columns described for the pergola make an excellent foundation for a small building to be placed on posts, as they do not decay and are permanent. They may be used to advantage for porches in place of wooden posts.

After a building is completed, some of the top soil removed in digging the cellar should be graded up to the foundation at a slight slope, to shed the rain and carry it away from the building. The box for a concrete wall should be well supported and braced, as the weight is sufficient to force the boards out of position. The method shown at Fig. 226 is frequently used, the ⅞ or 1 inch plank being supported by 2 × 4 inch studs, which in turn are braced as shown. On cheap work the outside boarding is omitted, the earth being shaved with the shovel as near the position of outer casing as possible. Of course, this earth wall is only useful within a foot or so from the surface. At this point the outer boarding must commence, and be continued to top of foundation. In order to have the foundation level on top, it is best to level the wooden form all around the four sides. If the concrete is brought exactly to the top, and a straight edge is run along the edges of the form, the resulting wall must be level, provided the box has been made so. Concrete does not flow enough to level itself.

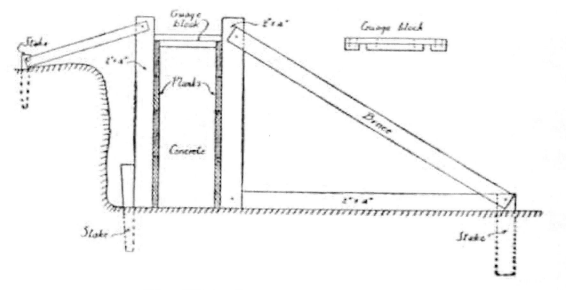

Fig. 226. Concrete foundations

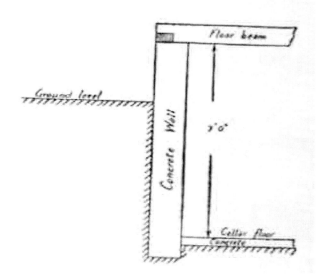

Fig. 226. Concrete foundations

FRAMING

This is a subject on which volumes have been written. The general arrangement with the names and sizes of the various members is shown in the drawing, a design for a small cottage, or bungalow. (Fig. 227.)

The heavy timbers forming the sill are cut to the outside dimensions of foundation and halved at the corners. Fasten the joints with ten or twelve penny nails. Cut all corner posts exactly the same length, toenail at corners to sill, and hold in position by temporary braces. Plumb the posts as the braces are nailed. Two boys must work at this job, one holding the plumb and the other nailing the braces. Cut and halve the ends of plate the same length as sill, and nail to corner posts. Cut 2 × 4 studs same length as posts, then nail to sill and plate 16 inches apart on centres. The openings to be left for doors and windows will break up the even spacing of the studs, but it should be made as uniform as possible. The spaces for door and window frames are to be enclosed with double studs to give the necessary strength. Corner braces are very desirable and in the old-fashioned braced frame were mortised into plate and post, and sill and post. (Fig. 227a.)

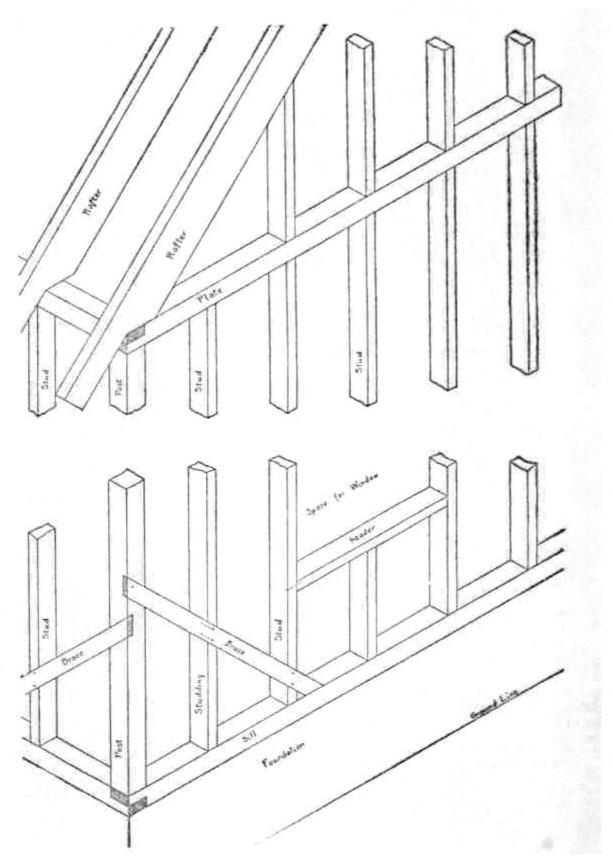

Fig. 227. Corner framing

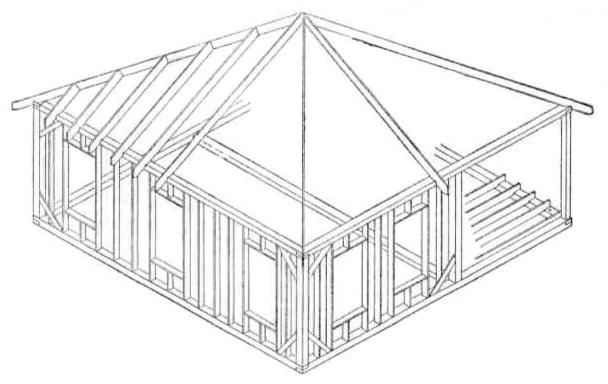

Fig. 227a. Frame of bungalow

For a simple structure the necessary bracing may be obtained by "letting into" the studding 3 × 1 inch strips, as shown in drawing. To do this hold the brace in the position it is to occupy, and make a pencil mark on both sides of it on each timber, sawing on the inside of these lines to a depth equal to thickness of brace. Remove the wood between saw cuts with a chisel. Test to see that brace comes flush with outside of studs, and nail securely in position.

When the frame is finished up to the roof the putting on of the siding may begin at any time.

SIDING

The outside of the building, siding or weather boarding, is an important item, as it is designed to protect the interior from sun, cold, and storms. It should be watertight, and may be made of various materials, put on in several ways.

In a house to be used in winter, the first layer should be of wide ship-lap boards. If put on diagonally it will act as a permanent bracing, and while this is the better way, it takes more time than horizontal siding. In either case nail to every stud and timber the board touches. Begin at the bottom of sill, break joints as the work progresses upward, and saw ends even with outside of posts.

At all door and window openings bring edges of siding flush with openings.

This inner siding is to be covered with building paper, door and window frames set, tin flashing nailed over doors and windows, and outer covering put on.

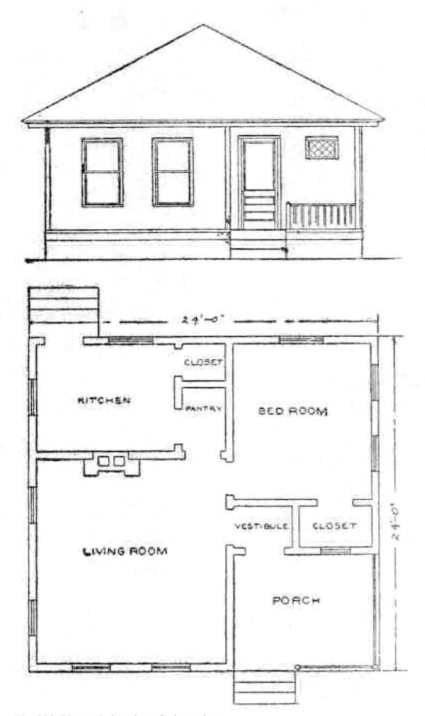

Fig. 228. Plan and elevation of a bungalow

Before proceeding with outside sheathing, however, the roof should be framed and covered.

ROOFING

It is a difficult matter to say that one part of a house is more important than another, as all parts are important, but a building with an unstable or leaky roof is an abomination. The framing of the roof must be strong enough to withstand gales, blizzards, drenching rains, and the weight of tons of wet snow.

As the method of shingling has been described under tennis court shelter, it is only necessary to take up the subject of the frame. Boys will do well to confine their early efforts to plain sloping, or possibly hipped roofs.

These two styles are illustrated in Fig. 229.

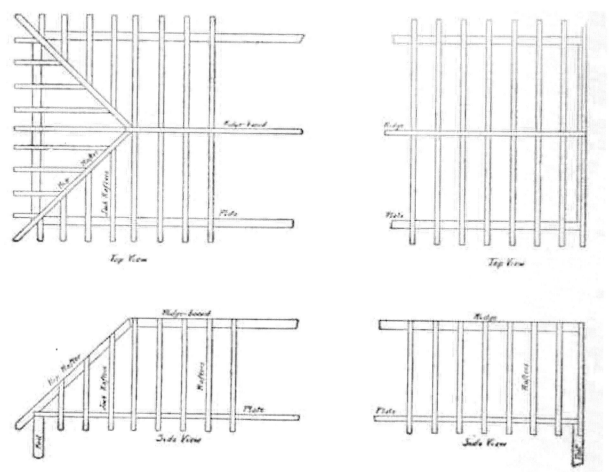

Fig. 229. Roof framing

The hip roof is the more pleasing and the more difficult to make. It reduces the attic space, if that is a consideration, and is harder to cover, or rather it consumes more time, as the question of whether a piece of work is difficult or not is really a question of whether or not you know how to do it.

The method of fitting the rafters is shown at Fig. 230. To find length of rafters, make a drawing to scale, in which *a-b* is the height above plate level and *c-b* half the width of the building measured on the plate or sill. The angle for cutting the mitre at the ridge may be obtained from the drawing, also the angles where the fit occurs at the plate. The length should be distance *a-c* plus about two feet for the overhang.

A ridge board is usually inserted between the top ends of the rafters, and if made from a ⅞-inch board, half an inch should be deducted from the length of rafters to allow for the difference.

The shape of lower end of rafters will depend on the kind of finish or cornice to be used. Two kinds are shown, the first and simpler being suitable for a barn or rough building.

On account of the high price of lumber, most boys will be obliged to use the most inexpensive style of finish.

Cut all the rafters the same size, and in erecting space them as nearly two feet apart as possible.

229

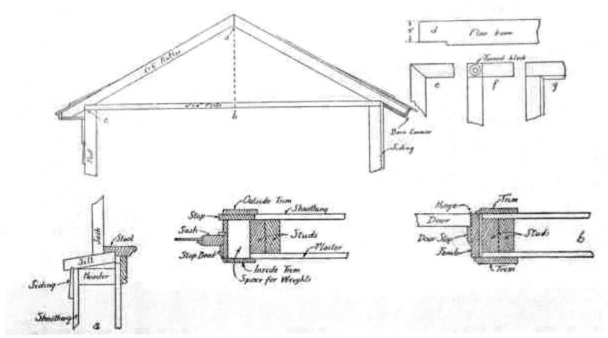

Fig. 230. Building details

The first pair should be flush with the edge of plate and temporarily held in position by braces of shingle lath. It will be necessary in erecting the roof to place timbers and floor boards across the top of plate as a temporary floor to work on. Nail rafters to ridge board, and plate with ten-penny wire nails. Two boys must work together on this job, as every part of the work must be plumb.

When all the rafters are in place, cut and fit the short studs between plate and rafters, being careful to leave the openings for windows in the places called for on the plan.

The ship-lap siding may now be continued up to top edge of rafters, and sawed off even with upper edge.

If novelty siding is used without any under sheathing, it may be treated in the same way.

Shingling may now be done as described under tennis court accessories.

WINDOW AND DOOR FRAMES

These may be bought at the mill ready made. Very few carpenters make their own, as they are staple articles coming in standard sizes. Second-hand sashes and frames may often be bought at very reasonable rates, and it never pays to make either.

Set the frames in the openings left for them, and nail to studs. To make sure that the fit between frames and openings shall be right, it is best to take the plans to the mill, and explain to the mill man just what is desired.

FLOORING

The floor beams may be set at any time after the frame has been erected up to the plate. As it will be necessary to work around inside more or less, the sooner they are in position the better. As these beams, supposed to be 10 × 2 inches, often vary in width, the floor is liable to be uneven, unless they are cut to fit the sill.

The amount cut out need not be very much, but a certain distance, say nine inches, should be marked from the top edge, and the lower corner cut out as shown at *d* (Fig. 230). This will bring all the top edges level, when they are in position.

The span of the floor beams—the distance from the sill to the next support—is important, as a floor is called upon sometimes to support great weight, as when a number of people are present, or a heavy piece of furniture such as a piano rests on it.

For floor beams 2 × 8, a span of not over twelve feet should be allowed; for 2 × 10 a slightly greater span may be used; but in either case the supporting beam in the centre of the floor should be halved into the sill with upper edge flush, and should be supported at intervals of ten feet by posts set in the floor of cellar, or to a depth of three feet in the ground in case there is no cellar. This supporting beam should be placed when the sill is set on foundation. Nail floor beams to sill, and where the two beams from opposite sides of the building lap or pass each other over the beam in centre, nail them to each other and to the beam.

The flooring of tongue and groove stuff may now be laid, cutting ends square and fitting them up close to studding, or, what is still better, clear out to the sheathing.

The outside weather boards may now be put on, after deciding on one of the corner finishes described under poultry house. A flashing of tin—painted—must be placed over door and window frames, before the clapboarding or siding reaches these points. This siding is sawed off square, and makes a butt joint with the outer casing of door and window frames.

Some form of building paper is nailed to the first siding in good buildings, and pays for itself in the long run, by reducing the amount of fuel necessary to heat the building in winter.

If the house is a sea-shore cottage or camp only to be used in summer, both the paper and inner sheathing may be omitted, and the expense account materially reduced.

The finishing of the interior may be left to the last, or done on stormy days. In the meanwhile, several important questions must be settled. One is the style of flue or chimney to be provided for the stove.

If the building is to be permanent, a brick chimney should be built by a mason. The danger of fire originating from defective bricklaying makes it advisable to have this work done by a tradesman.

For summer cottages or camp buildings a simple stove pipe can be used, but in any event it should be put up before the final roof covering is on, and "flashed," that is protected by tin laid over the roof timbers, and made watertight. This does away with leaks around the chimney, and the tin should be put on in such a way as to prevent the shingles from coming in direct contact with the hot chimney.

In these days of oil stoves, which are often used for summer cooking, the chimney may be omitted entirely. At the same time it must be remembered that there are cold, damp nights, when a stove is very comfortable at the shore or in the woods.

In regard to interior finish, if the walls are to be plastered, three coats will need to be put on by a skilled plasterer. Thin yellow pine ceiling stuff, often used for camp buildings, is easily put on, and quite satisfactory. Laid on diagonally it is very pleasing, but the beads catch more dust than the vertical strips do. The latter method calls for horizontal strips laid between the studs for nailing, while a simple quarter round moulding laid in all corners gives the finish. A common practice in camps is to have no interior wall covering, but to leave the timbers exposed. For a dwelling, the frame should be of dressed lumber, which may be stained to conform with the general colour scheme.

The inside trim around doors and windows may now be put on. Three methods of finishing around windows are shown at e, f, g (Fig. 230), and one of these types should be adopted before ordering the trim from the mill. This work should be simplified as much as possible, not only to save time, but because decoration may well be left to pictures, artistic metal work, trophies, and things which are of interest from their history or association.

DOORS AND WINDOWS

If second-hand material is not used it is advisable to purchase these staple articles from a mill where they are made in standard sizes.

When ordered for certain size spaces they come a little too large. This allowance is for material to be removed in fitting. Inside doors are usually the last things to be hung. The windows should be hung as soon as the construction will allow it, in order to keep out rain.

Secure the pulleys for upper and lower sash into the window frame on both sides of parting strip about four inches from top of window frame.

Attach the sash cord and find its proper length by experiment. Tie securely to sash weights. See that the two sashes make a good, tight joint where they meet, and tack the window stop to frame with brads. The stop is to be ordered with the trim, and mitred at the top. The construction at the sill is shown at a (Fig. 230).

The arrangement of door frames is shown at b. After mitring the door stop, nail to door frame at a distance from its edge equal to thickness of door. Fit the door by planing to the space inside frame. The hinges are put on as shown, being sunk flush with edge of both door and door frame. When hanging the door, it is a good plan to place small wedges under it, to allow for the sag which will result as soon as its weight is thrown on the hinges.

Saddles are usually placed under doors to allow them to swing clear of carpet and rugs. To allow for the thickness of these saddles, $\frac{3}{4}$ inch should be allowed between floor and bottom of door. The saddles are to be fitted around edges of door frame, making a neat finish.

For plastered walls a six-inch base board is necessary. This may be put on with butt joints and nailed to studding with small head finishing nails, as for all trim.

The base is usually topped by a base moulding mitred in the corners.

This style of construction is for a permanent house. For rough or temporary buildings, many modifications may be adopted. Batten doors, as described for the poultry house, may be cheaply and readily made.

Batten blinds made by the same method are very desirable for buildings like summer camps, which are to be vacant for long periods. This does away with the temptation some people find to break windows in unoccupied houses.

The siding for a small building may be of tongue and groove boards put on vertically, and now that lumber is so expensive these items are all important.

The lumber from packing cases may be used for making very many of the pieces of furniture in a camp, such as stools, benches, tables, shelves, cupboards, bookcases, etc. Many of these useful articles can be made without tearing the boxes apart.

A very useful chest and seat combined may be made by fitting a box with a strong cover, strengthened by cleats on its under side and hinged with strap hinges to the back.

A cushion of burlap filled with shavings, straw, seaweed, or sweet grass will make this a very satisfactory settee, and the storage space inside will always be available. The outside of the box should be smoothed, all nail holes filled with putty, and the whole thing stained.

Very interesting panelling effects may be obtained by tacking on strips of the same thickness as the outside cleats.

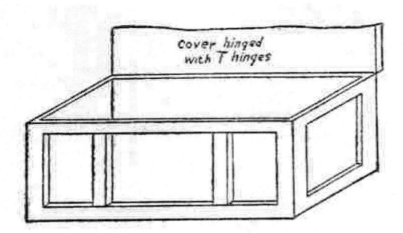

Fig. 231. Chest made from packing case

Where the supply of wood is limited, many similar articles will suggest themselves to the young carpenter. The chair shown at Fig. 231a can all be made of wood from packing boxes, except the square legs. These may be obtained by sawing 2 × 4 inch spruce in half and planing smooth. The rails can be put on with mortise and tenon, or they may be gained into the legs and fastened with nails or screws. The seat is built up of several pieces fastened to cleats on under side, with front edges rounded. To make this hard bottomed chair more comfortable, have a thin cushion of canvas or burlap fastened by a canvas cover and tacked to edges. The wide strip across the back may be treated in the same way. One coat of stain, or two of Japalac or some similarly prepared varnish will make a very serviceable finish for camp purposes.

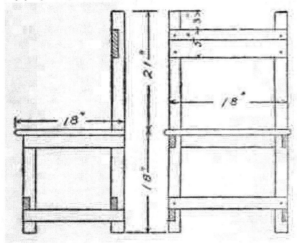

Fig. 231a. Chair

The proportions of a porch settee of the same general character are given at Fig. 231b. The legs may be cut out of pieces of spruce studding, and all but the long rails obtained from box material. These long pieces may be cut from ⅞-inch siding left over when putting up the cabin. Floor boards with tongue and groove planed off will answer very well.

The long back strip will be more rigid if mortised into the ends, and the upright strips will be needed to give it the necessary strength.

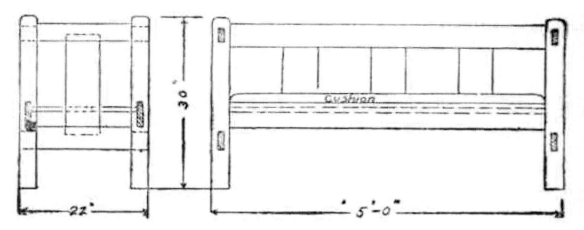

Fig. 231b. Settee made from box material

One of the most comfortable articles for a camp in the woods is the couch hammock. The materials required are:

A cot.

Four yards of strong canvas a yard wide.

Forty feet of clothesline.

Two chains or strong pieces of rope about 4 or 5 feet long.

A grommet set and some grommets.

Remove the legs from the cot. They are usually attached by bolts or rivets. If the latter, cut with a cold chisel.

Lay the canvas in one piece on the floor and place the cot at its centre. Make pencil marks at the ends to indicate where the fold begins as at B B (Fig. 232). Lap the canvas as shown and sew securely, leaving a space at the fold for the clothesline to pass through.

The square ends are to be hemmed and folded over pieces of broomstick.

With the grommet punch make holes through the canvas just below the broomstick and secure with the grommets. Make these holes about 5 inches apart. They are to hold the line which is to pass from iron fitting C through first grommet hole and back until it has passed once through each grommet.

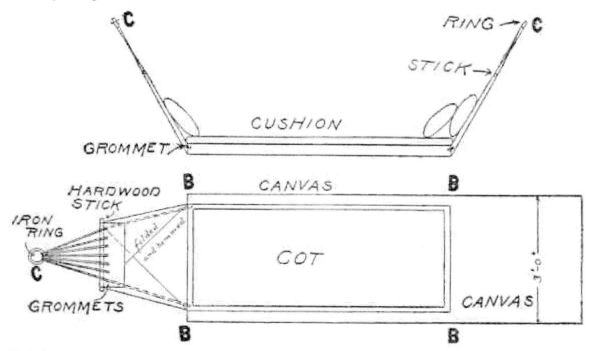

Fig. 232. Couch hammock made from a cot

The fitting is found on all hammocks and can be taken from an old one, or an iron ring may be substituted. Before beginning to weave the rope through the grommets, pass its end down to B and make fast to a stout screw eye fastened to under side of frame of cot. This brings the weight on the rope instead of on the canvas, an important item when five or six people sit on the couch at one time. Treat both ends

233

alike. The canvas will be wide enough to fold up and entirely cover the edges of cot. When everything has been adjusted, fasten the chains or heavy rope to the iron rings, and secure to the trees or veranda columns by heavy hooks. A light mattress covered with blankets, or a specially made cushion to cover the whole cot, and several sofa pillows will add the finishing touches to a very serviceable and satisfactory article.

The cost will be about one third of those on sale, and this may be reduced 50 per cent. if a grommet set can be borrowed, as this is the chief item of expense, assuming that an old cot is used.

This hammock should not be left out in the rain, as its steel springs will rust.

XLIX

STAINING, POLISHING, AND FINISHING

This branch of woodwork is a trade by itself and under modern methods of specialization the men who do this work do nothing else. The methods of finishing are legion and every polisher has a few little "kinks" of his own which he regards as trade secrets.

The personal equation enters very largely into the work, and if twenty boys have a given method explained to them and they all polish, say, a box of the same size and material, there will result twenty different kinds of polished surfaces.

This is due to difference in temperament. Some boys are patient and painstaking. Others are nervously anxious to get through and see how it looks. It is a fact particularly true of finishing that it cannot be hurried without endangering the result. Every coat must be thoroughly dry and hard before the next one is put on. Different woods require different treatment, and the elements of good taste, colour, and harmony all enter into the problem.

These statements are not made to discourage the young woodworker, because finishing can be done well by any boy who will use reasonable care, but to emphasize the fact that it is poor policy to make a fine piece of woodwork and then spoil it at the last moment by hurry.

Staining is something on which opinions differ greatly. Some artists claim that only the natural colour of the wood should be used, but a great deal of staining is done, and we must leave artistic arguments to others.

The extent to which staining is carried may be illustrated by the following finishes used on one kind of wood—oak:

Golden oak	Antwerp oak	Rotterdam
English oak	Ox blood	Antique
Forest green	Weathered oak	Cathedral oak
Austrian	Flemish brown	Flemish green
Silver gray	Sumatra brown	Filipino
Mission oak	Malachite	Fumed oak
	Bog oak	

The writer believes that staining to make imitations is wrong, such as staining cherry or birch to give the impression of mahogany.

The list of materials for staining is very bewildering, and it is advisable to reduce the list to a few reliable ones and learn to use them well. They may be divided roughly into three classes: oil stains, water stains, and stains produced from drugs or chemicals.

Oil stains are dry colours ground in oil such as chrome yellow, Prussian blue, burnt umber, burnt sienna, etc. When preparing one of these for use, thin with turpentine and linseed oil and apply with a brush. After it has stood for a few moments rub off with a piece of cotton waste or rag.

Water stains are colours dissolved in water.

After applying this kind allow it to dry. Sand-paper the surface flat and apply a second coat of half the strength.

Stains produced from drugs and chemicals include such materials as logwood, bichromate of potash, ammonia, iron sulphate, acetate of iron, etc.

The preparation of the surfaces to be finished is very important and means the removing of any defects, such as scratches, by means of plane, scraper, and fine sand-paper.

These defects always show much more prominently after polishing than before, so that too great pains cannot be taken in preparation. Assuming that the surface is ready, the first question to be considered is whether the wood is open or close grained. If an open grained wood, a coat of filler may be used; if close grained this may be dispensed with. The following list will enable the beginner to decide:

Open grained woods requiring filler:

Oak, ash, chestnut, mahogany, walnut, butternut.

Close grained woods; no filler required:

White wood, pine, cherry, birch, beech, gum, sycamore or buttonball; maple, cedar, cypress, red wood.

Filler may be made at home, but it is a staple article to be found in paint stores and it is advisable to buy it ready made. It comes in paste and liquid forms, and the paste is recommended. It must be thinned with turpentine to the consistency of cream and applied with a brush. As soon as it begins to dry, rub off the excess across the grain with a handful of excelsior, waste, burlap, or rags and allow it to stand over night to dry.

When the wood is to be stained the colour is frequently mixed with the filler.

The object of all this is to fill up the pores of the wood to give a flat, solid surface for the polishing. Sometimes even on open grained woods filler is omitted entirely.

Suppose that the work in hand is a footstool or tabourette made of oak and we wish to give it a forest green finish.

Photograph by Helen W. Cooke
Staining and Polishing.

The process would be as follows:

Prepare the stain by mixing a small quantity of chrome yellow and Prussian blue on a piece of wood. Mix thoroughly with a putty knife or old chisel and thin with boiled linseed oil and turpentine; add blue or yellow until a beautiful dark green is obtained. Add this to the filler, using turpentine for thinning, until the whole mass of liquid is the desired colour and as thick as cream. Paint the footstool all over with this filler. As soon as it starts to dry, rub off as explained.

The next day sand-paper smooth and give a coat of shellac. When hard, sand-paper flat and give a second coat of shellac.

From this point on the process depends on whether a glossy polish is desired or a dead flat surface. For an article of furniture like a footstool a highly polished surface would be a mistake, as it would soon be scratched, and while furniture is not to be abused, it is to be used, and shoe nails make scratches.

A dead flat surface may be obtained by rubbing down the third coat of shellac with fine ground pumice stone or rotten stone and water. If too flat, rub the surface with raw linseed oil and wipe dry.

Some boys will obtain a better finish with two coats of shellac than others will with four.

After the first coat of shellac, varnish is often used for the remaining coats, but it takes much longer to harden and requires careful handling.

Shellac is a product obtained from certain trees in the Orient. It may be bought in the dry state at paint stores and dissolved in alcohol. Grain alcohol is the best and most expensive, but wood alcohol is cheaper and will answer all ordinary purposes. The shellac may be bought in cans all ready for use, and there are two distinct kinds—orange and white.

White shellac is the more expensive, but should be used on light-coloured woods, such as maple, to avoid spoiling the colour.

Varnish comes in so many grades and kinds that it is best to go to a reliable dealer and tell him just for what purpose you expect to use it. There are outside varnishes, rubbing varnishes, light flowing varnishes, etc.

When by exposure it becomes thick so that the brush drags, it should be thinned with a little turpentine.

There is a great difference in the methods of using shellac and varnish. The former being dissolved in alcohol evaporates quickly, so that it must be put on thinly and as rapidly as possible. Varnish, on the other hand, may take forty-eight hours or more to dry, so that the brush can be drawn over the surface several times to remove air bubbles. It is not possible to do this with shellac. The brush used in shellac should never be laid on the top of the jar or can, as it will harden in a very short time. The care of brushes is an important item. Varnish brushes should be cleaned with turpentine, shellac brushes with alcohol, and when cleaned it is better to keep all brushes in a pail of water than to allow them to become dry.

The jar or wide mouthed bottle used for shellac should be kept covered else a great deal will be lost by evaporation. A jam jar makes a convenient receptacle for this, as it has an opening wide enough to allow the use of a flat brush. Evaporation may be prevented by inverting another jar of the same size over it. The shellac on the rim will hold them together practically airtight with the brush inside.

RELATIVE ADVANTAGES OF OIL AND WATER STAINS

The merits of these two classes of stains may be stated briefly. Water stains enter more deeply into the pores of the wood because of their lighter body. The hard parts of the surface hold practically none of the stain and constitute the high lights of the finished surface. But water stains raise the grain and make sand-papering necessary to bring the surface flat again. For this reason, some polishers first give a coat of water to raise the grain and when dry sand-paper flat before staining.

Oil stains do not raise the grain, but owing to their heavier body do not penetrate so deeply and more of the stain is lost in rubbing off. Oil has a tendency to darken wood, so that wood stained with oil colours has a tendency to become clouded or muddy with age.

For staining old work, oil stains should be used rather than water stains. Old work has the pores already filled and water has little chance to penetrate.

Some chemicals and aniline dyes are very satisfactory. Bismarck brown, which may be bought at the chemist's as a powder, is soluble in alcohol and gives a rich reddish brown. It is very powerful and a very small quantity is necessary. Bichromate of potash comes in the form of lumps and crystals. It is soluble in water. Put half a dozen crystals in a quart milk bottle of water and allow it to stand over night. Warm or hot water will dissolve the crystals more quickly. It is to be put on with a brush and gives rich brown tints, the shade depending on its strength, the kind of wood and the number of coats. It gives excellent results on oak and chestnut, and is used to "age" bay wood to a dark mahogany, while several coats of it will bring white wood to the colour of natural black walnut.

Each coat must be allowed to dry and then be rubbed flat with fine sand-paper.

This treatment may be followed by two or three coats of orange shellac, rubbed down.

For "antique" finish on oak or chestnut, dissolve lampblack in turpentine, mix with filler and proceed with polishing as explained.

A decoction of logwood is often used to produce dark and even black effects. The logwood extract is cheap and comes in the form of gum or resin. Several lumps of this are boiled in a gallon of water and applied as any water stain.

Acetate of iron, made from iron filings and vinegar, is used for dark browns occasionally. The filings should be allowed to stand for several days in the vinegar. The acid present is acetic. It unites with the iron forming the acetate of iron.

POLISHING

The method given above is for a substantial solid finish, but sometimes a boy will have some difficulty in obtaining the desired finish through lack of patience or some other cause.

A French polish may help to give the finishing touch. For this a piece of cheese cloth about 6 inches square, a piece of cotton waste about the size of a walnut, a little shellac and raw linseed oil are necessary.

Dip the waste lightly in shellac; fold the cheese cloth around it, making a soft pad, dip the pad in the oil and rub quickly and constantly in circles, gradually covering the whole surface. As the shellac hardens or sticks, use a little more oil and squeeze the pad slightly to bring the shellac through the cheese cloth. The oil prevents the shellac from sticking and a little experience will give the right balance between the two. When the polish becomes so bright that it shows the slightest finger mark, wipe dry with a piece of soft flannel.

WAX POLISH

This is used where a dull or flat finish is required. It can be applied directly after staining or filling.

Dissolve beeswax in turpentine to the consistency of filler. Heat hastens this part of the process, but is not necessary unless time is a consideration. The wax is applied with a soft rag or waste and rubbed and rubbed. The turpentine evaporates, leaving the wax. Several rubbings at intervals of a week will give the desired effect, and the surface may be brightened at any time by an additional application.

It should be remembered in all forms of polishing that dust is the great enemy. Wherever possible a piece of furniture after receiving a coat of shellac or varnish should be placed in a room or closet where no dust can settle on it. It should also be kept out of the sun to avoid blistering. The action of some stains like bichromate of potash is affected by the sun and should be either kept out of direct sunlight entirely or so placed that all parts receive the same amount, else the parts in shadow will be of a different shade from the rest of the surface.

L

DURABILITY, DECAY, AND PRESERVATION OF WOOD

It is now known that decay in wood is caused by fungi or low forms of plant life which cannot live without a certain amount of water, food, heat and air.

A fence post decays first at the place where it enters the ground, because at that point the conditions are most favourable. If wood can be kept entirely under water, one item—air—is lacking, so the fungous growths cannot exist and the wood will last indefinitely. This has been proved in many instances. One of the old Viking ships was raised from the bottom of the Christiania Fjord, Norway, after having been under water for a thousand years and it was found to be in a perfect state of preservation. Even the rudder oar or steerboard and wooden shields were intact.

As soon as it was brought into the air the process of decay began, and it became necessary to coat it with preservative. It stands today, 103 feet long, in the museum at Christiania.

Many other instances of under-water preservation might be mentioned.

The other extreme is also true. Wood which is kept perfectly dry will last indefinitely, as in the case of woodwork taken from the pyramids of Egypt, 3,000 years old, which is found to be perfectly preserved.

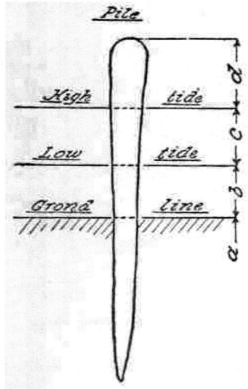

Fig. 233. A pile

But when wood is alternately wet and dry it decays rapidly. A pile driven into the bottom of a tidal river is a good illustration. If such a pile be divided into four sections (see Fig. 233), *a* is always in the ground, *b* is always in the water, *c* is alternately in air and water, *d* is always in the air. Sections *a* and *b* may be considered to be under the same conditions and should last the longest; *c* should decay first: *d* would last indefinitely if the atmosphere were always perfectly dry; but humidity and rain, air and heat combined finally bring about decay, and although this part of the pile will last longer than *c* it will in time decay. Section *c* should be coated with a preservative.

Various woods under the same conditions act very differently and according to no well understood law. For example, in contact with the soil black locust is our most durable wood. It is very hard, and its life under these conditions is estimated at from ninety to a hundred years. Red cedar comes next, though it is soft wood. Oak decays in a few years; chestnut, much softer, lasts two or three times as long. Our approaching timber famine has induced a study of this subject, since the preservation of wood is becoming an absolute necessity.

It has been found that certain materials put on the wood before it is placed in the ground prolong its life. Coal tar, wood tar, paint, and creosote all help, but creosote has so far proved to be the best. It is one of the by-products of coal tar and is being used extensively by the railroad companies for prolonging the life of ties.

Experiments with creosote have brought out some very interesting facts. It has been found that after being treated with the hot creosote all woods resist decay alike, regardless of their hardness or softness. Consequently, a treated cheap wood will last as long as an originally valuable one. This is a great gain, as it allows us to make use of wood like the poplar which would otherwise be practically of no value.

The various coatings we put on wood, such as paint, varnish, oil, etc., are intended not only to beautify but to preserve it, which they do by filling up the pores and excluding moisture, preventing fungous growths, etc. All of these coatings should be put only on dry wood, else they prevent evaporation of the sap and may hasten decay.

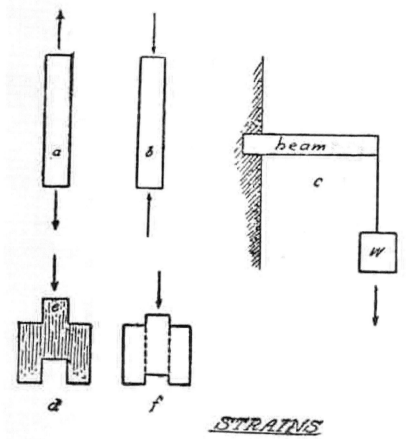

Fig. 234. Strains

Drying lumber increases its strength, as it has been found by experiment, even as much as 400 per cent. if no checking occurs. When this happens it counteracts much of the gain, and if the wood absorbs moisture once more the strength will decrease. The strength of the various timbers varies greatly, and sap wood is usually weaker than heart wood.

The strains that may be brought to bear on timbers are illustrated in Fig. 234, the arrows indicating the directions in which the forces operate. At *a* the wood is under tension, the forces at work on it tending to pull it apart. At *b* the piece is under compression, the forces tending to reduce its length by forcing its fibres together. A pillar supporting a weight is under compression. At *c* the weight tends to bend the beam. The upper part is under tension, the lower part under compression. This is known as beam action, and depends on whether the beam is supported at one end, as shown, or on both ends. Also it is important to know whether the beam has a uniformly distributed load or whether the weight is at one point only. The problems relative to beam action are largely of an engineering character and involve considerable mathematics.

Shearing is the sliding of one part of the timber along the grain. If a piece of wood is cut to the form shown at *d* and a weight applied at *e*, the tendency will be for this upper part to slide down as shown at *f*. When this occurs, shearing has taken place.

The strength of wood differs in resisting these various strains, the tensile strength being greater than the crushing or compressive strength. Ash, for example, has a tensile strength of 16,000 pounds to the square inch, but its crushing strength is only 6800 for the same size. The tensile strength of dry white pine is 10,000 pounds, its crushing strength 5400 pounds, and its shearing strength varies from 250 pounds to 500 pounds, showing that its weakest point is along the grain. If the young woodworker becomes ambitious enough to think of designing a bridge or large building he can find these figures in any engineers' hand-book. There are so many important factors to be considered that the amateur will do well to go ahead with great caution. Knots and other defects reduce the proportionate strength of large beams greatly, so that it would not be safe to assume that a beam 6 inches square would be 36 times as strong as a piece 1 inch square.

In upright posts of considerable length, not alone the crushing strength must be considered, but a bending action enters into the problem. Wherever the question of danger to life enters, as in a bridge or a house, it is wise to leave a large margin for safety. We realize this fully when we read of a grand stand holding hundreds or thousands of people collapsing under the weight. The architect has also to reckon with still other elements, such as wind pressure and vibration.

LI

MATHEMATICS OF WOODWORK

The woodworker soon discovers that arithmetic is a very practical and necessary subject. He will meet many problems both in drawing and in actual construction which test his ability and call for some knowledge even of elementary geometry. It is important to be able to estimate from his drawing just how much lumber will be needed. He will soon discover through intercourse with dealers in lumber that there are certain standard sizes, and he should make his designs as far as possible conform at least to standard thicknesses.

Common boards are sawed 1 inch thick. When dressed on two sides the thickness is reduced to $\frac{7}{8}$. In planning some part of a structure to be 1 inch thick it is better to make the dimension $\frac{7}{8}$ inch, else it will be necessary to have heavier material planed to 1 inch and the cost will be that of the heavier lumber, plus the expense of planing. In buying $\frac{1}{2}$-inch dressed lumber, very often inch boards are dressed down to the required thickness, and the purchaser pays for 1-inch wood, in addition to the dressing. The boy is surprised to find that it costs more for $\frac{1}{2}$-inch than for inch material. Standard lengths are 10, 12, 14, 16, etc., feet. Widths vary, and as wood shrinks only across the grain—with one or two exceptions—this dimension cannot be depended on, as the amount of shrinkage depends somewhat on the age after cutting. Whenever possible, it is wise to go to the lumber yard and select your own material, choosing boards that are free from knots, shakes, etc. Clear lumber—free from knots—costs more, but is worth the difference.

MEASUREMENTS

A measurement is a comparison. We measure the length of a lot by comparing it with the standard of length, the yard or foot. We measure a farm by comparing its area with the standard unit of surface measure, the acre, square rod, or square yard.

In every measurement we must first have an accepted standard unit. The history of units of measurement is a very interesting one, and its difficulty arises from the fact that no two things in nature are the same. One of the ancient units of length was the cubit, supposed to be the length of a man's forearm, from the elbow to the end of the middle finger. This, like other natural units, varied and was therefore unreliable. As civilization progressed it became necessary for the various governments to take up the question of units of measurements and to define just what they should be.

Our own standards are copied from those of Great Britain, and although congress is empowered to prescribe what shall be our units, little has been changed, so that with few exceptions we are still using English measurements.

The almost hopeless confusion and unnecessary complication of figures is shown in the following tables as compared with the metric system:

12 inches	= 1 foot	0 = 01	millimetre
3 feet	= 1 yard (standard)	0 = 1	centimetre
5½ yards or 16½ feet	} = 1 rod	1 = decimetre	
		1 = metre	
320 rods or 1760 yards or 5280 feet	} = 1 mile	10 = dekametre	
		10 0 = hectometre	
		10 00 = kilometre	

The original English definition of an inch was "three barley corns" with rounded ends. The meter is 1/10,000,000 (one ten-millionth) of a quadrant of the earth's circumference, i. e., the distance from the pole to the equator measured along one of the meridians of longitude. The length of three barley corns might be different from the next three, so here was the original difficulty again. The designers of the metric system went back to the earth itself as the only unchangeable thing—and—are we sure there is no change in the earth's circumference? The great advantage of the metric is that it is a decimal system and includes weights as well as surfaces and solids. Our weights are even more distracting than our long measure. We have in fact two kinds of weight measure—troy and avoirdupois.

TROY	AVOIRDUPOIS	METRIC
24 gr. = 1 pwt.	16 oz. = 1 lb.	0.01 milligram
20 pwt. = 1 oz.	112 lb. = 1 cwt.	0.1 centigram
12 oz. = 1 lb.	20 cwt. = 1 ton	1 decigram
5760 gr. = 1 lb.	2240 lb. = 1 long ton	1 gram
	2000 lb. = 1 short ton	10 dekigram
	100 lb. = 1 short cwt.	100 hectogram
	7000 gr. = 1 lb.	1000 kilogram

In surface measurements, the same differences are seen:

AMERICAN OR ENGLISH	METRIC
9 sq. ft. = 1 sq. yd.	0.01 sq. centimetre
30 1/4 sq. yds. = 1 sq. rod	0.1 sq. decimetre
16 0 sq. rods } = 1 acre	1 sq. metre
48 40 sq. yds. }	100 are
64 0 acres = 1 sq. mile	10,000 hectare
	1,000,000 sq. kilometre

In measures of volumes we are as badly off:

DRY	LIQUID	METRIC
2 pints = 1 quart	2 pints = 1 quart	0.01 millilitre
8 quarts = 1 peck	4 qts. = 1 gallon	0.1 centilitre
4 pecks = 1 bushel	1 gal. = 231 cu. ins.	1 decilitre
4 quarts = 268.8 cu. ins.		1 litre or cu. decim.
1 heaped bushel = 1¼ struck bushels.		100 dekalitre
		1000 hectolitre

The cone in a heaped bushel must be not less than 6 ins. high.

As if this were not enough, when we go to sea we use another system. The depth of water is measured in fathoms (6 feet = 1 fathom), the mile is 6086.07 feet long = 1.152664 land miles, and 3 sea miles = 1 league. In our cubic measure:

1728 cubic inches = 1 cubic foot

27 cubic feet = 1 cubic yard

A cord of wood is 4 ft. × 4 ft. × 8 ft. = 128 cubic feet.

A perch of masonry is 16½ × 1½ × 1 = 24.75 cubic feet

Isn't it about time we used the metric system? The reader will not mind one more standard unit. Lumber is measured by the board foot. Its dimensions are $12 \times 12 \times 1$ inches; it contains 144 cubic inches and is $1\frac{1}{12}$ of a cubic foot. A board 10 feet long, 1 foot wide and 1 inch thick contains 10 board feet. One of the same length and width but only $\frac{1}{2}$ inch thick contains 5 board feet.

The contents of any piece of timber reduced to cubic inches can be found in board feet by dividing by 144, or from cubic feet by multiplying by 12. As simple examples: How many board feet in a piece of lumber containing 2,880 cubic inches? $\frac{2880}{144} = 20$ board feet. How much wood in a joist 16 feet long, 12 inches wide and 6 inches thick? $16 \times 1 \times \frac{1}{2} = 8$ cubic feet: $8 \times 12 = 96$ board feet. A simpler method may be used in most cases. How much wood in a beam 9 inches $\times$ 6 inches, 14 feet long? Imagine this timber built up of 1-inch boards. As there are nine of them, and each 14 ft. $\times \frac{1}{2}$ foot $\times$ 1 inch and contains 7 board feet (Fig. 235), $7 \times 9 = 63$ board feet. Again, how much wood in a timber 8 inches $\times$ 4 inches, 18 feet long? This is equivalent to 4 boards 1 inch thick and 8 inches or $\frac{2}{3}$ foot wide. Each board is $18 \times \frac{2}{3} \times 1 = 12$ board feet, and $12 \times 4 = 48$, answer. (See b, Fig. 235).

To take a theoretical case: How much wood in a solid circular log of uniform diameter, 16 inches in diameter, 13 feet and 9 inches long? Find the area of a 16-inch circle in square inches, multiply by length in inches and divide by 144.

$16 \times 16 \times .7854 = 201$ 13 ft. 9 in. = 165 inches

$\frac{(201 \times 165)}{144} = 130\frac{45}{144}$ board feet

It is not likely that a boy would often need to figure such an example, but if the approximate weight of such a timber were desired, this method could be used, reducing the answer to cubic feet and multiplying by the weight per cubic foot.

A knowledge of square root is often of great value to the woodworker for estimating diagonals or squaring foundations. The latter is usually based on the known relation of an hypothenuse to its base and altitude. It is the carpenters' 3-4-5 rule. The square of the base added to the square of the altitude = square of the hypothenuse. $3^2 = 9$, $4^2 = 16$; $9 + 16 = 25$. The square root of 25 is 5. (See Fig. 235). To square the corner of his foundation the carpenter measures 6 feet one way and 8 the other. If his 10-foot pole just touches the two marks, the corner is square. $6^2 = 36$, $8^2 = 64$; $36 + 64 = 100$. $\sqrt{100} = 10$. This method was used in laying out the tennis court, the figures being 36, 48, 60—3, 4, and 5 multiplied by 12.

To take a more practical case, suppose we are called upon to estimate exactly, without any allowance for waste, the amount of lumber in a packing case built of one-inch stock, whose outside dimensions are 4 feet 8 inches $\times$ 3 feet 2 inches $\times$ 2 feet 8 inches. Referring to the drawing (Fig. 235, d), we draw up the following bill of material:

pieces	(top and bottom)	4 ft. 8 in. $\times$ 3 ft. 2 in.
	(sides)	4 ft. 8 in. $\times$ 2 ft. 6 in.
"	(ends)	3 ft. 0 in. $\times$ 2 ft. 6 in.

The top and bottom, extending full length and width, are the full dimensions of the box, while the sides, although full length, are not the full height, on account of the thickness of the top and bottom pieces—hence the dimensions, 2 feet 6 inches. From the ends must be deducted two inches from each dimension, for the same reason. In multiplying, simplify as much as possible. There are four pieces 2 feet 6 inches wide; as their combined length is 15 feet 4 inches, we have $15\frac{1}{3}$ feet $\times 2\frac{1}{2}$ feet $= 38\frac{1}{3}$ square feet. The combined length of top and bottom is 9 feet 4 inches $= 9\frac{1}{3} \times 3\frac{1}{6} = 29\frac{5}{9}$, and $38\frac{1}{3} + 29\frac{5}{9} = 67\frac{8}{9}$ or 68 board feet, ignoring such a small amount as $\frac{1}{5}$ of a foot. This is close figuring, too close for practical work, but it is better to figure the exact amount, and then make allowances for waste, than to depend on loose methods of figuring, such as dropping fractions, to take care of the waste.

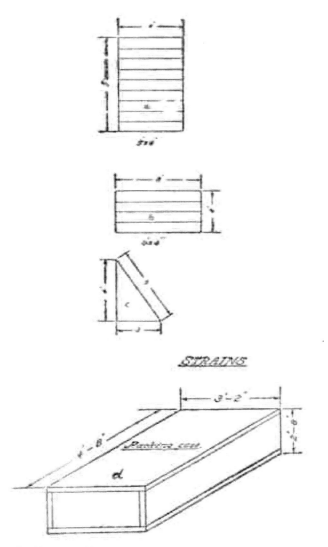

STRAINS

Fig. 235. A packing case

As a good example of estimation, take the hexagonal tabourette shown in Fig. 178; the five pieces, aside from the hexagon under and supporting the top, which may be made from scrap lumber, are shown laid out in Fig. 236. The board must be at least twelve inches wide in order to get out of it the large hexagon. The legs may be laid out as shown with space left between for sawing, yet even by this method considerable waste will result, and it should be kept constantly in mind that as far as possible waste is to be reduced to a minimum. "Wood butcher" is the common shop name for the workman who spoils more material than he uses.

The great advantage of making out a bill of material before starting is that it not only makes you study your drawing, but causes you to consider the best method of laying out the blank pieces.

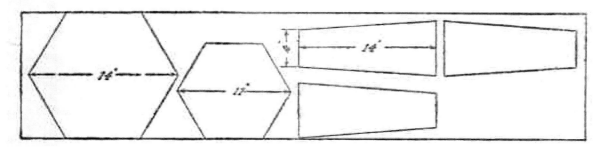

Fig. 236. Laying out the pieces for a tabourette

It is often necessary to find the areas of figures other than the square or parallelogram. Assume that we are to floor a room in an octagonal tower or summer house. If the distance across the flat sides of the octagon is sixteen feet, leaving out the item of waste, how many square feet will be required?

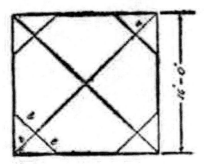

Fig. 237. Finding the area of an octagon

The octagon may be drawn in a square and its area will be that of the square, less the four triangles in the corners. (Fig. 237). So the problem resolves itself into finding the area of one of these triangles. If we knew the length of one of the sides of the octagon, the solution would be simple, but we only know that the eight sides are equal. The following method may be worked out: Find the diagonal of the sixteen foot square. It is 22.6+. Deduct the distance across the flats, 16, leaving 6.6 feet equally divided between a and b; $a = 3.3$ and it may be proved that $c = a = d$. So in each corner we have a triangle whose base is 6.6×3.3. The area of a triangle equals half its base by the altitude. Therefore the area of each triangle is 3.3×3.3 and $3.3 \times 3.3 \times 4$ equals 43.56 square feet, the combined area of the four corners. This deducted from the area of the square leaves the area of the octagon, or $256 - 43.56 = 212.44$ square feet.

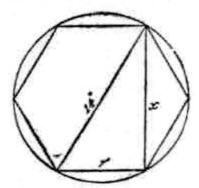

Fig. 238. Problem of the hexagon

Assume that our problem is to find the narrowest board we can use to cut out a hexagon whose diameter is fourteen inches. As shown in Chapter IV, the hexagon is drawn in a circle. One of the sides is equal to the radius or half the diameter. This gives us the arrangement shown in Fig. 238, in which our problem is confined to the right-angled triangle whose base is seven and hypothenuse fourteen. From our knowledge of triangles, we deduct the square of seven (49) from the square of 14 (196), leaving $196 - 49 = 147$, which is the square of the altitude. Then $\sqrt{147} = 12.12$, which is the narrowest board from which we can obtain a hexagon 14 inches in diameter.

These examples are given to show the close connection between woodwork and arithmetic.

LII

LUMBER: NO. 1

It is hardly possible for a boy to select and purchase wood for his various purposes without some knowledge of the different woods and their peculiar characteristics. No two are exactly alike, and in fact two trees of the same kind growing in different parts of the country under different conditions will produce timber of very different qualities. This is specially noticeable in the tulip or white wood, for example. A tree of this species, growing in a swamp in the South, will yield a very different wood from one grown on high ground in the North.

Again, the same wood is known in different localities by different names, so in order to have a sound knowledge of lumber, it is really necessary to know something about the trees. White wood, just mentioned, is called, in many localities, yellow poplar. As a matter of fact, it is not a poplar, nor is it related to the poplars, being a member of the magnolia family.

The following pages, devoted to this subject, are the cream of many talks between our boys, boiled down to the important facts and arranged in some order. It was a hobby of Ralph's, and Harry became so enthusiastic over it that they frequently laid aside their work and took long walks through the country studying trees.

Harry started a small nursery in the garden and is raising young trees from seeds and cuttings. As he remarked to Ralph one day: "It's astonishing how little people know about trees! Why they are the most interesting things that grow. Just think how many things we get from them besides wood; maple sugar, rubber, turpentine, wood alcohol, tannin for making leather, shellac, Canada balsam, spruce gum, and nuts! All of our nuts except peanuts come from trees—hickory, walnuts, butternuts, beechnuts, chestnuts, pecans, almonds, etc."

Ralph noticed that as Harry's interest in the trees grew he became less wasteful of his wood in the shop. The fact that a tree had to be cut, and in most cases killed, in order to furnish him with lumber, seemed to worry him. One day when he was thoughtfully at work in the shop, he blurted out, "It's a shame that so many trees have to be cut down for lumber!"

"Yes," said Ralph, "it seems so; yet if no lumber was wasted, it would not be so bad. It is estimated that 75 per cent. of the wood cut down is wasted."

"How?" asked the boy.

"Well, in the first place, many lumbermen after cutting the tree down, take just the log or lower part and leave the top to decay. It often happens that they leave the tops and branches as a great mass of litter, which soon becomes as dry as tinder, an invitation to the smallest spark to start a fire, and more woodland is destroyed by fire each year than I care to tell you."

"How much?" asked Harry.

"Every year, between twelve and fifteen million acres, and some years three times as much."

"How much is a million acres?"

"You can get some idea from this: Long Island, N. Y., is a hundred miles long and about twenty across in the widest part. It contains about a million acres. Imagine this covered by solid woods, multiply by fifteen and you would have a good idea of the amount of woodland burned over every year."

"Gracious!" exclaimed the boy. "I should think every tree would have been burned years ago."

"Well, this is a big country," said Ralph. "I figured it out once. The United States is large enough to make six hundred states the size of Connecticut, and have room for twenty-five or thirty more. The state of Texas alone could be cut up into a hundred pieces as large as Connecticut.

"The forest fire is one of our worst enemies. It is far worse than the lumberman, because when he cuts down trees it gives hundreds of young seedlings which are struggling to live in the shade a chance to grow and cover the ground with a new forest; but the fire kills these young seedlings and even burns the seeds that are lying in the leaves waiting to grow. That is one of the worst things to be said against the forest fire."

"Does it kill every tree?"

"Oh, no! Trees like the oak sprout from the old roots, but most evergreen trees are killed outright."

"What happens then?"

"Why, it depends. If the forest is mixed, hard woods and conifers, the hard woods, or some of them, will in time send up sprouts, and where you formerly had a mixed stand, you will in a few years have only hard woods, unless some of the evergreens were not touched. In that case, their seeds will in time replace the old evergreens."

"How long does it take?"

"From forty to a hundred years to have a large forest. Some evergreens, like the spruce, increase in diameter very slowly."

"What happens when the forest that is burned is all evergreens, and they are all killed?" asked the irrepressible boy.

"The process of reforesting in that case is very slow. Trees of little value, like the poplar or birch, appear first, because their seeds are light and are carried a considerable distance by the wind. If fires pass over the same area every few years, the forest will never come back unless seeds are planted. There are large areas in this country thus denuded, and instead of a forest we have a scrubby growth of bushes that are of little value to anybody.

"Huckleberries grow in burned-over land luxuriantly, and in some sections it is suspected that the people who make money by gathering the berries burn the brush purposely.

"The forest cover is valuable for other things besides timber. The snow melts slowly in an evergreen forest, because the rays of the sun cannot penetrate with full strength. This allows the water to sink into the ground slowly, and to come out lower down in the form of springs.

"Where there is no forest the snow melts much more quickly, the water rushes down the hills in streams, carrying with it the top soil, which is of so much value to the farmer, cutting the hillsides into gullies, causing floods in the valleys, and filling up the rivers with silt or mud.

"This spoils the streams, ruins the land, and causes millions of dollars' worth of damage to property. If you doubt it, read the newspaper accounts of floods in the valleys of the Ohio, Missouri, and Mississippi every spring."

"But I should think by this time all the soil would be washed away."

"It will be in time. There are large areas in China where the soil is washed away to the bare rock. The population has been obliged to emigrate because when the soil goes, the population can no longer live."

"Well, what are we going to do about it?" asked Harry in amazement.

"Wait a minute," said Ralph, warming up to his subject. "The Mississippi carries into the Gulf of Mexico every year seven and a half billion cubic feet of soil; enough to cover Long Island two inches deep every year."

"What are we going to do?" repeated the boy.

"We can do one of two things," said Ralph sagely, "We can follow in the footsteps of China and let the land go to ruin; or we can follow the example of Germany, take care of our forests—or what is left of them—and plant new ones. It is one of the greatest questions in this country to-day, and you are going to hear a lot about it before you are twenty-one."

LIII

LUMBER: NO. 2

The lumber business ranks fourth in the great industries of the United States. The Department of Forestry at Washington estimates that we are using three times as much wood yearly as the annual growth of the forest.

A grand total of 150,000,000,000 board feet of lumber for all purposes, including firewood, is the estimated amount, a figure the mind can hardly grasp.

The railroads of our country rest on 1,200,000,000 ties. The average life of a tie is about ten years, so that we must replace one tenth, or 120,000,000, each year. As the average forest produces two hundred ties to the acre, this item alone calls for half a million acres of woods every year.

The tie is only one item in the great business of railroading, immense quantities of lumber being required for trestles, platforms, stations, bridges, etc., so that a full million of acres must be cut annually to keep our railroads operating.

Place this item against the fifteen million burned, and the statement may be made that we burn enough each year to supply the railroads for fifteen years. To offset this loss several railroad companies are now planting trees for a future supply, as the many attempts to supplant the wooden tie with a manufactured one have not been very successful.

The six thousand mines of various kinds within our border use up 5,000,000,000 board feet every year, and so on through the list of wood-consuming industries. As our population doubles, the consumption of lumber quadruples. To-day, five hundred feet of wood is used annually for every man, woman, and child, as compared with the sixty feet used in Europe. Already our many industries are beginning to feel the shortage, and prices constantly go up.

Turpentine, which is made from the Southern yellow pine, requires a new "orchard" of 800,000 acres yearly to keep up the demand; and when we realize that one third of the lumber cut is yellow pine, it is little wonder that the price of turpentine and other naval stores keeps moving upward.

Where and when will it stop? We read a great deal about the transformation of water power into electrical energy, but the flow of streams is dependent on forests, and the spring floods are followed by drought. While the Ohio River rises forty feet in the spring, it is possible to walk over the river bed almost dry shod the following summer.

We hear much about irrigation, but irrigation is dependent largely on mountain forests.

So a burning question has arisen in these United States, called conservation, or the husbanding of the great resources that have made our country what it is.

The forest resources are different from those of the mines. There is a definite end to the supply of coal, iron, gold, and silver, but by proper care the forest may be made to yield a continuous crop of lumber.

Forestry does not mean the fencing in of the woods, but the handling of them in such a way that no more is cut than the annual growth. This has been practised in Germany on scientific principles with such success that the production has been increased 300 per cent., and where seventy-five years ago they obtained twenty cubic feet from each acre a year, they now cut sixty, and the forest continues to grow luxuriantly.

What Germany has done we can do, and millions of acres now useless can be made to yield large quantities of wood while continually clothed with growing forests.

The cutting of lumber is usually done when the sap is dormant, preferably in the winter. The logs are gotten to the mill by the cheapest method, which usually consists in floating them down a stream or river; but now that most of the remaining forest is remote, it is quite common to have portable mills transported into the woods where the trees are cut and sawed into planks or the larger sizes of timber and from there loaded on the cars.

The old-fashioned method was more picturesque, and the "drive" started with the breaking up of the ice in the spring. Thousands and hundreds of thousands of logs were guided down stream, pulled off shore when they became stranded, and the jams were broken up until the smooth water below made sorting possible.

As several companies might be driving down the same stream, each log was marked by an axe with the private mark of the one to which it belonged. After many vicissitudes, the drive would reach the sorting boom, where the lumber of the various companies would be separated and made up into rafts.

A boom is a chain of logs fastened together by iron chains, and extending into the river. It may reach clear across, or one end can be anchored in the stream to allow a passage for boats. In that case the river end has to be anchored up stream to catch the logs.

One of the most serious things encountered on a drive is the log jam. It may be caused in many ways but usually by some obstruction, as a shoal, rocks, a narrowing of the river, etc.

The lumberman has a vocabulary of his own, and he recognizes several kinds of jams, such as wing jams, solid jams, etc.

No matter how caused, it is the business of the lumber jack to break up the jam, and sometimes before it can be done a late freeze will occur and the whole mass become solid ice and logs. It is sometimes necessary to use dynamite to break it up. The breaking up is a dangerous time for the driver, who must sometimes run for his life across the moving mass of logs to the shore.

After they are made into rafts, steamers are used to tow the logs to the various mills. It is slow work, but when the destination is reached, the real process of converting the tree into lumber begins. Often the rafts stay in the water for months before being broken up, and the logs guided to the endless chain which drags them up into the mill.

From this time on the action is very rapid. The modern mill is a mass of rapidly moving machinery, guided and controlled by comparatively few men. Three distinct classes of saws are used—circular, band, and gang saws, and different mills in the same neighborhood use different methods.

Band saws are continuous bands of steel, often 48 feet long, and as wide as 8 inches, which pass over two large wheels like a belt. Gang saws are straight and move up and down rapidly. A number of them are fastened to horizontal pieces, the distance apart being adjustable to the thickness of timber desired.

Before passing through the gang saw, the logs are usually edged, i. e., a slab is cut from two opposite sides. The log is then turned over on one of these flat sides, so that as it passes through the gang saw the planks are all the same width.

The slabs or edgings are passed through other saws and cut to the width and length of a lath, all the waste possible being made into lath or other by-products.

As we use four billions of lath a year, this is an important item.

The process varies with the kind of lumber and its future purpose, but a great deal is wasted in many mills. The refuse is used for fuel, and in some cases burned in stacks built specially for the purpose of getting rid of it. This is one of the forms of waste which will undoubtedly be done away with in the future, and already many lumbermen are at work on the problem. The sawdust is conveyed directly to the furnaces under the boiler and used in the generation of steam.

LIV

LUMBER: NO. 3

Having finally reached the commercial stage, the lumber is shipped away from the mill either by water or by rail to the lumber yards of the country.

Here it should be seasoned. In the past this process consisted of piling the planks in the open air in such a way that air could circulate freely through the pile, allowing the sap to evaporate and the wood to dry evenly. This was a sure but slow process, and in the hurry of modern life quicker methods have been tried.

One of these is known as kiln drying, by which the time is reduced to a few weeks. It consists of piling the wood in a room like a kiln and drying it by artificial heat. The result is not so satisfactory as the natural method, because the sap near the surface hardens and prevents the inner moisture from escaping, so that kiln-dried lumber while dry at the surface is "green" inside. When planed till part of the surface is removed the green wood is brought near to the air again, and warping is liable to occur.

Other methods have been tried, such as steaming to vaporize the sap, and soaking in hot water for the same purpose. Of course these processes all add to the cost of lumber, yet so valuable is time that it is difficult to obtain good old-fashioned seasoned wood unless it has lain for some time in a local yard.

In order to understand the phenomena of warping, shrinkage, checking, shakes, etc., it is necessary to know something of how the tree grows. Like all living organisms, it is made up of minute cells. The new cells are formed on the outside of the tree under the bark, and here the sap is most active. The cause of the flow of sap is not very clearly understood, but it corresponds to blood in the human body, in that it carries the nourishment that forms the cells. As a new mass or layer of soft new cells forms each season, the layers may be distinctly seen and counted, but the line of separation is not a sharply drawn one, as we find by examining a cross section of wood with the microscope. However, the layers or annual rings are distinct enough to be counted, so that the age of the tree at the time it was cut down may be readily discovered.

The new or sap wood, then, is further from the centre each year, and while the old cells may not be dead, they contain less and less sap, are therefore drier, and after a few years change colour, becoming darker.

There is often a very great contrast between the colour of the heart wood and that of the sap wood, although the latter may be represented by several years of growth.

These annual rings are not actually circular, but very irregular, and often wider in some parts than in others. The study of these rings is very interesting, and it shows that the tree usually increases in diameter more rapidly during the first few years than later. Very often, after growing slowly for several years, the tree will apparently grow rapidly again. The cause of this cannot be determined without a knowledge of the tree's history.

It has been proved by experiment that thinning the forest increases the growth of the remaining trees 18 per cent., and these peculiarities in the rings may have been due to some like cause. The bearing of this fact on the peculiarities of warping and shrinkage is that when cut down the log is drier at the heart and more sappy at the outside, so that evaporation occurs near the surface.

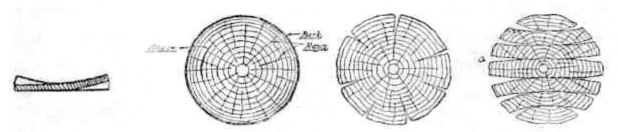

Fig. 239. Warping, wind, and shrinkage.

The effect of it is shown in Fig. 239. The outside drawing together has opened the wood, or "checked" it, most at the outside, diminishing toward the centre. The evaporation would have occurred just the same had the log been cut into planks, causing them to curl as shown at *a*. This is known as warping, and it is one of the troubles of the woodworker. In construction it must be constantly guarded against, and overcome as far as possible. It cannot be entirely prevented, but if the wood has been well seasoned before it is used a large part of the warp will be taken out in the planing mill, or in the squaring up.

Twisting, winding, and warping are also caused by the two sides of a board having been subjected to different degrees of heat, moisture, etc. If a plank is laid on the floor, the upper part is more exposed to the air and to changes of temperature and humidity; therefore it curls.

If a board is stood on end or placed in a rack where there is a free circulation of air, the curling will be much less. Even in a rack, if several boards are piled one on another, the top one will have different conditions from the others and be apt to curl or wind.

Shrinkage is a term applied to the decrease in diameter of the tree, due to sap evaporation.

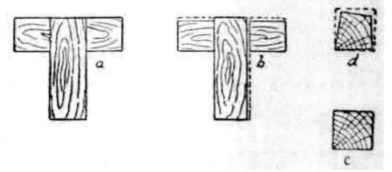

Fig. 240. Effect of shrinkage on lumber

In the case of the board it means a decrease in width, and it varies greatly in different trees and their woods. As shrinkage is always across the grain, its effect on a common joint may be illustrated in Fig. 240. At *a* is shown a middle lap joint just put together. If the wood is not well seasoned, shrinkage will in time change it to the form shown at *b*, which is exaggerated to make the meaning clear.

A square piece of timber, one corner of which is the centre of the tree, will change from *c* to *d*. Shrinkage as well as warping must be taken into consideration in construction.

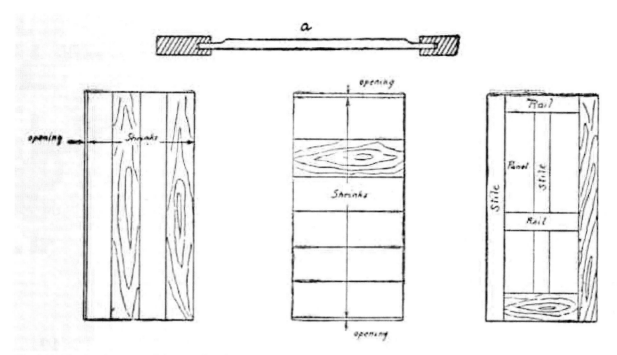

Fig. 241. The development of the panelled door

The development of the panelled door is a good illustration. Suppose we wish to close a space with a door, knowing little about shrinkage. Let us construct it by the simplest method, say four vertical boards. If the width of these boards equals the opening when the door is built (Fig. 241) there will soon be an opening wide enough for the fingers to enter and lift up a latch on the inside. The door is very much of a failure. We notice, however, that there is no opening at top or bottom. An idea! We construct a door with planks placed horizontally. Now although we find after a while no opening at the sides we do find openings at top and bottom. The panelled door is not constructed solely for beauty but to overcome shrinkage as far as possible. Fig. 241 shows the various parts. The rails maintain the width, the only shrinkage being in the cross grain of the stiles, and they preserve the height except for the small amount in the rails. The remaining spaces are panelled, the construction being shown at a. Both stiles and rails have a groove plowed out to receive the edges of the panel. This should be free to shrink in the grooves, where it is invisible, but if the mistake is made of fastening the panel edges rigidly in these grooves the panel will shrink anyway and frequently split from top to bottom.

Many other forms of construction which we have seen daily as long as we can remember have equally sound reasons for their form. No piece of woodwork should be designed without considering how it will be affected by shrinkage and warping.

In selecting lumber always look out for "shakes." This is a defect caused by the separation of the annual rings. A tree may be considered as a series of irregular cylinders of diminishing diameters. The forest-grown tree is much more spindling, tall, and straight than the low-crowned, heavy-branched specimen grown in the open, where there is no crowding.

The swaying of the forest tree in the wind, especially when its neighbours have been cut down, is sometimes sufficient to make the rings separate and slide one within the other. This is more noticeable in some species than others and it gives the wood a serious fault. (Fig. 239).

"Winding" is the result when the ends and sides are no longer parallel. Like all peculiar characteristics of wood, this varies greatly in lumber of various kinds, and may be largely avoided by exposing both sides to the same conditions, or keeping equally distributed weight on it until used. When winding becomes excessive, the board is useless for any kind of work.

LV

LUMBER: NO. 4

The woods of the United States are classified roughly as hard and soft; and trees as broad-leaved or deciduous, and evergreen or coniferous.

In a general way, the trees which drop their leaves in the fall—the broad-leaved—produce hard woods and the evergreens soft woods. There are so many exceptions, however, that the rule is a very rough guide.

Several of the coniferous trees drop their leaves or needles in the fall, like the larch or tamarack, and some woods from evergreens are harder than some woods from broad-leaved trees. Yellow pine is harder than basswood, which, according to the rule, should be a hard wood. As a matter of fact, it is softer than the majority of woods cut from evergreens. The only way to gain a comprehensive knowledge of this interesting subject is by experience and study. Making a collection of woods, leaves, and seeds is one of the most fascinating studies a boy can take up. He will soon discover that not only is every wood different from every other wood in grain, colour, odour, and hardness, but some woods are strong and elastic, others strong and brittle, weak, etc., and that every tree has a different leaf, bark, flower, and seed from its neighbour. He will find groups or families, such as the oaks, the maples, the pines, spruces, cedars, etc., with several members of each group, all different, yet having family characteristics. He will be surprised at the endless extent of the subject; the willow for instance has a hundred and fifty known varieties. He will find himself, like our boys, dipping into botany and geology to discover perhaps, as Harry did, that the oak was once an evergreen, and that it still holds a good proportion of its leaves all winter.

He will learn that there are broad-leaved evergreens like the laurel and rhododendron; that some trees are evergreen in the South, and lose their leaves in the North; that some shrubs of the Northern states become trees farther south. He may even wrestle with the problem "What is a tree?" or, "Where does the shrub leave off and the tree begin?"

The study of the many methods nature has devised for distributing seeds has evolved whole volumes; so has the question of how the buds on the trees are protected in winter. There are definite ways in which the tiny leaves are folded up in these winter buds, all ready to unfold in a certain way in the spring. Perhaps the reader wonders what all this has to do with woodwork, but to a boy who once begins to collect specimens, it will follow as a matter of course. Knowing something about woods he naturally begins to study trees, and gradually observes the wonderful phenomena of growth, flower, and seed. Planting seeds to see how they grow is the next step, and before long he has a young nursery in the yard; while the reading of the work of such men as Luther Burbank will induce him to try his hand at grafting and budding.

The man who makes two apples grow where one grew before is as valuable a citizen as the man who makes two blades of grass grow in the place of one. When Mr. Burbank converts the prickly cactus into a thornless cactus, valuable as a forage plant, he is conferring a great benefit on the whole race by making millions of acres of desert land available for stock raising.

Incidentally, these wonders performed by the Wizard of California will not die with Mr. Burbank, but will constitute the beginning of a new profession which, combined with forestry, will offer a tempting field for the rising generation.

COMMON TIMBER TREES AND THEIR WOOD

EVERGREENS OR CONIFEROUS TREES

White Pine.—One of our most beautiful evergreens. Growing throughout the North-eastern and Lake states, and formerly forming dense forests from the Bay of Fundy to Minnesota. Needles grow in groups of five of a light bluish green from three to four inches long. Seeds are "winged" and grow in cones five or six inches long protected by the scales. Cones mature at end of second season. Wood soft, light coloured, free from sap, easily worked and used in many trades, for pattern making, various parts of houses, toys, crates, boxes, etc. Becoming very scarce, owing to the destruction of the great forests. On the Pacific coast its place in construction is taken by the sugar pine and other woods.

Yellow and Georgia Pine.—Two trees whose wood is frequently confounded by the woodworker. Georgia pine is a tree with very long needles, from twelve to fifteen inches, and in groups of three. Cones from six to ten inches. A southern tree found from Texas to Virginia. The tops of the young trees, like green fountains, are used in many places as Christmas decorations. Wood hard and resinous, used for flooring, interior finish, and decks.

Yellow Pine.—A southern tree with needles in groups of two, sometimes three, about three inches long. Cones small, about two inches. Wood hard and used for the same purposes as Georgia pine.

Red Pine, Norway Pine, Canadian Pine.—Three names for the same tree. Grows throughout the North, from Nova Scotia to western Minnesota. Cut principally in Canada. Needles, two in a group, about five inches long. Cones about two inches long, mature the second season. Wood reddish in colour, hard, and used for piles, spars, bridges, etc.

Pitch Pine.—A name locally given to several different trees. The wood is soft, brittle, resinous, and is used for fuel and for making charcoal, rarely for rough building. Needles in groups of three and three to five inches long. Sometimes called scrub pine, although it often reaches a height of fifty to sixty feet. The cones, two or three inches long, often remain on the tree for years. It is the tree found along the Atlantic coast from Maine to Georgia, growing in sand, in swamps, and among rocks. To be recommended for its persistence in living under the most trying conditions, even if its wood is not very valuable.

In the construction of a frame house several kinds of wood are needed. First, the framework of rough-sawed spruce. Second, a better wood, like white pine, for door and window frames. Third, the outside covering. This may be clapboards, for which nothing has ever approached white pine, although it is necessary now to find substitutes. The roof, if shingled, may be of cedar, or cypress—some spruce is used to-day. For interior work, floors may be spruce, white pine, cypress, yellow pine, or hard woods. For finish or trim, many woods are used such as white wood, oak, yellow pine, cypress, cherry, and bay wood.

Spruce.—This wood has been used almost exclusively in the past for framing, but great inroads have been made in the supply, especially by the manufacturers of paper pulp. Consequently the cost is increasing rapidly.

Three varieties are recognized, white, black, and red. White spruce is a distinctly northern tree, delighting in the cold climate of Canada, but dipping down along the Maine coast. It is a beautiful, straight, and tall specimen, frequently found as high as a hundred and fifty feet. The needles are only three quarters of an inch, or less, in length and clothe the twigs in an entire circle. Cones two inches long, bearing under their scales tiny winged seeds. It is used often as an ornamental evergreen for lawns, and for this purpose probably has no equal, as, unlike the Norway spruce, it holds its foliage, dense and green, close to the ground.

The wood is weak, knotty, and soft, but suitable for rough framing.

Black Spruce.—Another northern tree, rarely found in forests below the Canadian border, except around the Great Lakes.

Leaves about same size as in white spruce, but cones smaller, more oval in form, and one inch and a half long.

Spruce gum is obtained from this tree, which has a more pleasant odour than white spruce.

Wood used for pulp making, framing, and, quartered, for sounding-boards of musical instruments.

Red Spruce.—A close relative of the black and sometimes confused with it, but it is a distinct tree, reaching its best development several hundred miles south of the black spruce, in the Appalachian Mountains, and extending as far south as North Carolina; while the black variety barely crosses the borders of Canada into Maine.

Needles about half an inch long. Cones small, sometimes barely an inch and a half. They fall the first winter, while those of the black remain on the tree often for years.

Wood is similar to black spruce but lighter in weight. Used for pulp, framing, and sounding-boards.

Hemlock.—The most dainty of the eastern evergreens, with little cones about three quarters of an inch long, and needles half an inch. Found throughout the country east of the Mississippi and in some sections used for Christmas decorations.

A slow growing tree with wood of little value, being brittle, light, and difficult to work, as it has a crooked grain and is liable to splinter. The tree makes up in beauty what it lacks as a timber producer and its bark is rich in tannin.

Larch, Tamarack or Hackmatack.—Local names for the same tree. Drops all its needles in the fall, like a broad-leaved tree, but the beauty of the brilliant new green needles in the spring is a sight worth going miles to see.

Found from the Lake states north to the Arctic Circle. Needles an inch long. Cones from one half to three quarters.

Wood is heavy, hard and strong. Used in ship building, for telegraph poles, posts, and ties.

Fir, Balsam Fir, Balsam.—On all firs the cones stand upright on the branches, while on spruces they hang down. As these two trees are often intermingled, this is an easy way to distinguish them. The needles of the firs are also blunt, while those of the spruces are sharply pointed.

This is the so-called Christmas tree and balsam pillows are made from its needles.

Needles about three quarters of an inch long, cones almost black in colour, from two to four inches long.

Wood of little value, being soft and weak.

The sap in the form of gum called Canada balsam is used in medicine, and is obtained from blisters on the bark or by cutting the bark.

Southern Cypress, Bald Cypress, Deciduous Cypress.—Found growing naturally in the swamps of the South, but will grow in drier soil, if planted in the North. Several fine specimens in the parks of Philadelphia, New York, and Brooklyn. The lower part broadens out near the ground into a conical base and in its native swamps the roots send up peculiar formations known as cypress knees.

Leaves very delicate and feathery, not often over half an inch long, cones round and an inch in diameter. Drops its needles like the larch each fall.

Wood very durable in damp situations, valuable for flooring and interior finish.

Red Cedar.—The common cedar of the United States, found in all sections where trees can grow at all, in sand, swamp, rocky hillside, and abandoned farm. Reaches its greatest height in the South.

Wood of beautiful colour and grain, soft and not strong, easily worked, but inclined to brittleness. Used in many trades; it furnished in the past the only wood for lead pencils. Owing to its scarcity, substitutes are now being tried. Very durable in contact with water and soil. Used extensively for posts, small boats, cooperage, ties, chests, and interior finish.

Foliage difficult to describe, being sharp and awl-shaped in the young trees, changing in later years to a flat scale shape. Very often both forms are found on the same tree. Seeds are the common cedar berry, pale green in colour, about a quarter of an inch long, each berry containing two or three seeds. These are liked by the birds and they are dropped along fences frequently, so that in a few years the fences become lined with young cedar trees.

White Cedar.—Found in swamps along the Atlantic and Gulf coasts. Has a more delicate foliage than red cedar, and, growing in dense thickets, is apt to be taller and straighter.

The wood is light brown in colour, soft, weak, and, like red cedar, durable in moist situations. Used for making shingles, for boat-building, and for the same general work as the red variety.

Arbor Vitæ—called in many sections white cedar. It is an entirely different tree from the real white cedar, having decidedly flattened and very aromatic foliage. Used a great deal for hedges before the days of the California privet. Seed borne in a tiny cone half an inch long.

Large quantities are cut in the Maritime Provinces of Canada to be made into shingles. Grows sixty feet high and two feet or more in diameter. *Arbor vitæ* means tree of life, and as the bark and young twigs were at one time used medicinally, that may have been the origin of the name.

Wood is light, soft, coarse-grained, but, like the cedars, durable. Used for ties, posts, and shingles.

LVI

BROAD-LEAVED TREES

The broad-leaved trees are more numerous as to varieties than the evergreens, and from the standpoint of leaf forms may be divided into three groups:

1. Trees bearing simple leaves.

2. Trees bearing compound leaves.

3. Trees bearing doubly compound leaves.

The first group is the largest, including as it does such large families as the maples, oaks, willows, poplars.

The second group comes next with the well-known walnuts, hickories, ashes, and buckeyes.

The third group is very small, there being but three well-known trees bearing doubly compound leaves: the honey locust, Kentucky coffee tree, and Hercules Club.

The three forms are shown at Fig. 242.

The leaf ends at the bud growing at the end of the leaf stem. All above this bud constitutes the leaf, no matter what its shape or size, and falls in the autumn, with a few exceptions.

The small leaflets on the compound leaf are simply parts of a leaf, not separate leaves, as there are no buds at the point where they join the stem. The arrangement of these leaflets varies. In the buckeye and horse chestnut they radiate from a common point, while in the locust they are in parallel rows on opposite sides of the stem.

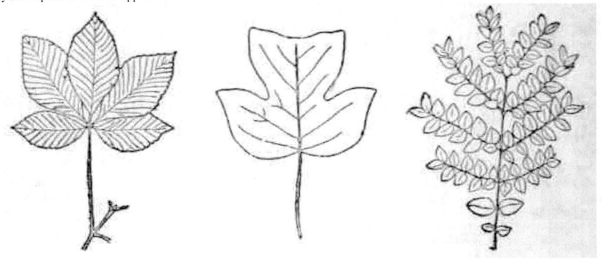

Fig. 242. Three types of leaves

In doubly compound leaves the leaflets are themselves compound, making the whole leaf very large, those of the Kentucky coffee tree being three feet in length.

THE MAPLES

Probably the best known and most common trees, especially in towns and cities. Most of them grow quickly and therefore become valuable as shade trees. They do not make the most permanent trees, however, and should be planted in alternation with oaks, or other long-lived trees, for permanent shade.

The seeds of all maples are winged, which helps their distribution over large areas, in the same manner as the seeds of evergreens.

Sugar or Rock Maple.—The most valuable timber tree of the group, its wood being heavy, hard, strong, and close-grained. Very light in colour and valuable for flooring and interior finish, furniture, tool handles, and bench tops.

It grows throughout the Eastern states, but not in all soils. Very rapid in growth, so much so that in the dense forest stands, when a portion of the woods has been cut down, the young saplings cannot always withstand the wind pressure and are blown down. Reaches a height in the forest of a hundred and twenty feet, but in the open is broader and more symmetrical. Too much cannot be said in praise of this tree. Its shade is dense and its autumn colouring superb. The sap yields maple syrup and sugar, and, finally, after it has done its work and is cut down, its wood yields lumber of the highest value, while the limbs make excellent firewood.

The process of making maple sugar was learned, historians tell us, from the Indians. This is probably why the process was for two or three centuries very crude. Holes are bored in the tree in the late winter, as soon as the sap is brought to life by the sun, usually in March, but the time depends upon the weather. Spigots are placed in the holes and pails hung under them to catch the sap. When full, they are emptied into large kettles or boilers over a fire, and the sap simply boiled down to the proper consistency.

As the lumberman is making heavy inroads into the maple groves or forests, the price of maple sugar is likely to continue going up, until real maple sugar will be only a memory, unless we wake up from our dream of unlimited resources to the real facts and do something.

Silver Maple, White Maple, Soft Maple.—A very common shade tree in our towns and cities. Its natural section is along the Mississippi, where it becomes a great tree, often a hundred feet high; but it is so easily adaptable to new conditions, grows so quickly from seed, and will stand so much hard usage that it has been very popular. There are many better trees, but this is cheap and quick growing, and in our hurried American life we build very often for the immediate future and forget the next generation.

Its foliage, when not blackened and spoiled by the smoke of the city, is a beautiful dark green above, and light silvery green below. The winged seeds ripen in June, may be planted before July 1st, and will produce young trees nearly a foot high before frost of the same season. Wood not as hard as rock maple, but strong, close-grained and brittle. Used to some extent in cabinet work. The winter buds are very precocious and start into life at the first sign of spring.

Red or Swamp Maple.—Found in wet places naturally, but it makes a large and satisfactory shade tree in heavy upland soil. The leaf form is somewhat like that of the silver maple, but smaller.

Seeds ripen before summer. The flowers are red, the leaf stems are red, and the foliage is not only the most brilliant red of all our autumn colours, but it is the first to give notice by its change of the approach of winter. It is easy to see where it got its name.

Wood is light in colour, similar to that of the silver maple, hard, strong, and brittle.

Sycamore Maple.—Although frequently planted in this country as a shade tree it is, like the Norway, imported from Europe.

Moosewood, Mountain Maple, and Box Elder are three small American maples which can hardly be placed among timber trees, except possibly the last. Box elder or ash-leaved maple has the distinction of having a compound leaf.

Its wood is soft and of more value to the pulp maker than the lumberman. It is very hardy and has been used on the Western prairies, where more particular trees do not thrive.

THE OAKS

Perhaps as a family this group of trees is more uniformly valuable than any other found in North America.

They represent all that is the best among trees, being strong, hardy, long-lived, and valuable as timber.

There are oaks in Europe a thousand years old, but of course we have no records that go back so far.

It is a difficult tree to kill, because, when cut down or burned, a large number of healthy shoots grow from the stump or roots, and make a rapid second growth. The bark of all oaks contains tannin, and in the past our principal supply came from these trees. The old-fashioned method was to fell the tree, strip off the bark and leave the wood on the ground to decay. Oak lumber is now so valuable that this waste has been largely stopped.

White Oak Group.—The oaks all bear simple leaves which vary greatly. They may be divided into two groups. The white oak group all bear leaves with rounded lobes, no bristles, and ripen their acorns the first fall after blossoming. They rarely bear acorns before the age of twenty years. The second group has pointed lobes, each lobe ending in a bristle and do not ripen their acorns until the end of the second season.

Among the first group are the white oak proper, post or iron oak, mossy cup, chestnut oak, and swamp white oak. In the second group are the red, pin, scarlet and black oak, black jack, shingle, willow, and Spanish oaks.

White Oak.—One of the most common and best known members of the family, slow growing, sturdy, hardy, and beautiful. Acorns sweet compared with others. Leaves six to eight inches long, turning to beautiful shades of red in the fall, finally to a brown, and a large proportion remaining on all winter.

This tree is little affected by temporary weather changes. In the latitude of New York spring may have come and the maples be in full leaf, but the white oak shows no sign. Lawns are mowed, and finally, about June 1st, out come the oak leaves, steadily growing without regard to late cold snaps or hot days. During the summer a prolonged drought occurs. The leaves of the maple turn yellow and fall. Not so the oak; it goes right on about its business of growing green leaves and acorns, until the appointed time in the fall.

The maple leaves have all fallen and the trees are ready for winter.

The oak goes right on, as steadily as a clock, doing its work, apparently oblivious to such insignificant things as weather changes.

This is the character of the tree throughout—steady, reliable, and strong.

The wood is hard, durable, and valued in many trades. The best barrels for tight cooperage are made of it. Floors and interior trim, furniture, cabinet work, ship building, and the making of farming implements and wagons are all more or less dependent on it. The mission style of furniture is made almost exclusively from it; so is office furniture. Quartered oak is a form of lumber obtained by a special method of cutting.

In most trees when cut into lumber may be seen a series of lines radiating from the centre, and running in almost straight lines to the outside. They are called medullary rays, and are much more in evidence in some woods than others. They are particularly noticeable in oak. These rays are plates of flattened cells, and are usually much harder than the rest of the wood.

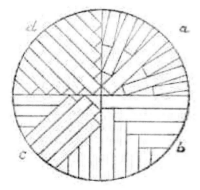

Fig. 243. Four methods of quartering

The object of quartering oak is to bring these rays to the surface of the board at as small an angle as possible, so that they will spread over the surface and give an added beauty to the grain. This is accomplished in one way by cutting the boards radially as shown in Fig. 243 (*a*). There is much waste in this method, and other methods less wasteful, but not as satisfactory, from the beauty standpoint, are shown at *b*, *c* and *d*.

Mossy Cup or Bur Oak.—So called from the form of the cup of the acorns. It ends in a heavy fringe which nearly covers the acorn proper—hence the name mossy cup.

The leaf somewhat resembles the white oak, having rounded lobes but a different outline.

Wood is hard, heavy, and strong, and is used for the same purposes as white oak. Found throughout the country east of the Rocky Mountains, but reaches its greatest development in the Ohio Valley.

Chestnut Oak.—Found from Maine to Alabama and west to Kentucky and Tennessee.

Wood heavy, hard, strong, tough, close-grained and durable in contact with the soil. Bark is strong with tannic acid. Acorn, long and oval, sweet and a favourite with the squirrels.

Two or three varieties of this tree are recognized.

Post or Iron Oak.—Along with the black and black jack oaks found on bleak and sandy plains, especially in Texas, but extends as far north as Massachusetts.

Leaves thick, leathery, and much darker in colour than the white oak. Wood used for ties, fencing and fuel.

Swamp White Oak.—Eastern United States. Favours wet localities and swamps, and reaches a height of a hundred feet.

Wood about as heavy as white oak, but inclined to check in seasoning. Used for same general purposes as white oak. Acorns sweet and white, about an inch long.

The Red Oak Group: Red Oak.—Tree reaches a height of a hundred and forty feet. Found from Maine to Georgia and as far west as Kansas. Grows more rapidly than white oak and has smoother bark. Acorns large with a shallow cup and very bitter. Wood darker than white oak, of a reddish brown colour, heavy, hard, and strong.

Used for furniture and interior finish. Has a tendency to check in drying.

Scarlet Oak.—Leaf more deeply indented than red oak. A very tall and beautiful tree with wood slightly heavier than red oak, strong and hard.

Acorns, like all of this group, remain on the tree the first winter, ripening the second fall. They are smaller than those of the red oak and the cup is not as shallow. It encloses a third or more of the nut, whose kernel is white. The name is taken from the brilliant colouring of the fall foliage.

Pin Oak.—Leaf form similar to scarlet oak and often mistaken for it by the beginner, but is smaller, and other features of the tree distinguish it. The acorns are small, about half an inch long, with a broad flat base, light brown and striped. The branching habit of the tree gives it the name. The great number of small slender branches, especially in winter, is very noticeable. Sometimes called swamp Spanish oak because of its fondness for wet places. Wood brown, hard, strong, and heavier than red and scarlet oaks.

It is being planted largely now as a permanent shade tree and grows rapidly during its earlier years.

Black Oak, Yellow Oak.—Name derived from the bark, which is very dark. Yellow is the colour of the inner bark, hence the second name. Foliage varies, is thick, leathery and shiny, of a dark green colour.

Acorn is smaller than the red oak and often striped. Has yellow and bitter kernel.

Wood as heavy as pin oak, forty-four pounds to the cubic foot, strong and hard.

Used for fuel and for a yellow dye made from the inner bark.

Black Jack or Barren Oak.—Often found in company with the black oak on wind-swept, barren plains. Leaf very coarse and crude in both form and texture, having three lobes and a tapering base. These two trees frequently mix or hybridize, and, while not always things of beauty, they grow where other trees cannot live and should be recommended for their hardiness.

Wood even heavier than black oak, but, as the tree is small, it is used chiefly for firewood and the making of charcoal.

Willow Oak.—Foliage resembles the weeping willow. A southern tree, but will grow as far north as New York. Acorns ripen at end of second season, are small, with flat, wide base and shallow cup.

Kernel yellow and bitter.

Wood reddish brown, heavy, and strong.

Tree is popular in the South as an interesting shade tree.

Laurel Oak.—Name derived from the leaves, which are in shape similar to the mountain laurel, but lack its shiny lustre. A tree of the Middle West or Ohio Valley. Acorns, small and half enclosed by the cup; ripen second season.

Wood heavy and hard, checks in drying.

Used for shingles and rough construction.

Sometimes called shingle oak.

LVII

TREES WITH SIMPLE LEAVES

Beech is a beautiful tree with light gray bark, handsome foliage and valuable hard wood.

The seed is buckwheat-shaped, small and sweet. One of our most handsome shade trees, and although only one species is native to the United States, nurserymen have developed special varieties known as weeping beech and purple or copper beech. The European beech is also frequently planted on lawns and in parks. Its foliage is darker and has indentations so shallow that the leaf apparently has only a wavy outline.

Wood is hard, tough, fine-grained and takes a high polish. Used for the stocks of planes, handles, farming implements, and for some kinds of furniture.

The beech tree is supposed to be impervious to lightning, and recent experiments show that it offers considerable resistance to an electric current.

Birch.—The indentations of the beech are shallow and concave, while the birch leaf is known as double serrate, or double toothed, the teeth being themselves toothed. Five varieties are known in the Eastern states, black, red, yellow, white, and gray.

Black Birch, Sweet Birch.—The tree familiar to boys because of its aromatic bark, which contains salicylic acid used in treating cases of rheumatism. A large forest tree with handsome foliage, a very fine-winged seed and valuable wood. Heavy, hard, fine-grained, and takes a high polish. Used for wheel hubs, and the manufacture of furniture.

Red Birch.—Found in swamps and along rivers, especially in the South. Leaves smaller than black birch and wood much lighter in weight, but close-grained and strong. Used for furniture and wooden ware.

Yellow Birch.—A northern tree, growing a hundred feet high in northern New York and Canada. Leaves similar to black birch, but its bark is very different. The bark of the black birch is very dark, while that of yellow birch is of a silvery, yellowish gray, characteristic birch bark.

Wood heavy, hard, and similar to black birch. Used for the same general purposes.

White Birch, Canoe Birch, or Paper Birch.—Noted for its remarkable bark. White on the young trees, darker on old ones. Comes off in several distinct paper-like layers. Well known to ancient writers and used by them for paper. It contains a resinous oil which accounts for its water-resisting qualities so well known in the Indian birch-bark canoe. The inner bark contains starch and in the extreme north it is sometimes mixed with other foods. The sap may be used for making sugar. Wood is light brown and light weight but hard, strong, and close-grained. Used for shoe-lasts, fuel, and spools.

Gray Birch, Aspen-Leaved Birch.—Sometimes called white birch. The bark is white but patched with black and does not come off in layers as readily nor separate so easily from the wood as white birch.

A smaller tree with foliage that moves as freely in the wind as the aspen.

Leaf form very peculiar; a long thin stem, broad flat base, and long tapering outline, double serrate. A persistent little tree, very hardy and difficult to kill.

Wood is light and soft, close-grained but weak. Used for pulp, fuel, spools, and hoops.

Hop Hornbeam, Ironwood.—A little tree with delicate birch-like foliage and wood of great hardness. The name hop is derived from the fruit cluster bearing the seeds, which resembles the hop. The bark is in remarkable contrast to the foliage, being deeply furrowed and smooth, as if a smooth skin were drawn over powerful muscles.

The wood weighs over fifty pounds to the cubic foot, is tough, close-grained, hard and will take a high polish. Used for mallets, tool handles, and levers.

Hornbeam or Blue Birch.—A small tree with dark gray or bluish bark. Leaves similar to ironwood, but narrower. Wood weighs forty-five pounds to the cubic foot, hard and strong, similar to ironwood and used for the same purposes.

Elm, White or American.—The well-known shade tree of the North. Leaf is lop-sided, one side being considerably larger than the other, double serrate. Aside from being a beautiful shade tree, the wood is very valuable in several trades, being heavy, hard, strong, and tough. It does not split easily and is valued for such critical places as wheel hubs and saddles. Used in cooperage, and supply nearly exhausted.

Red Elm, Slippery Elm.—Red from the dark brown colour of its wood and slippery from the character of the inner bark. The slippery elm of commerce is made from this, which sufficiently explains its character.

Leaves are larger, coarser, and rougher than white elm and wood is heavy, hard, close-grained and tough. Used for ties, fence posts, and agricultural implements.

Rock Elm, Cork Elm.—Rock from the nature of the soil it is particularly fond of—rocky cliffs or hills—cork from the corky ridges which appear on the branches. A valuable timber tree but found in limited quantities. The wood is unlike the red and white elms in that it will take a high polish. Hard and tough, close-grained but easily worked. Used for cabinet work, farming implements, ties, and to some extent for bridge timbers.

Basswood, Linden.—A large timber tree of the Northern states and Canada. Its flowers are very sweet and attract the bees to such an extent that it is sometimes called the "bee tree." It has several varieties, as the small-leaved linden of the South, the silver linden, weeping silver linden, etc.

Leaves are heart-shaped, serrate, and lop-sided. A valuable shade tree. Wood is soft, weak, even-grained, does not split easily. The favourite wood for pyrography because of its white colour, freedom from pitch, etc. Used for boxes of wagons, wooden ware, and to some extent for furniture making.

Holly.—A broad-leaved evergreen. Leaves and berries used as Christmas decorations. A southern tree found as far north as Long Island. Wood very light in colour, but hard and close-grained. Takes a high polish. Used in cabinet work and engraving.

Cherry, Wild or Black.—The cabinet wood in common use is from this tree, although several varieties are known to botanists. The wild cherry of the roadside in the East, but a large forest tree west of the Mississippi, especially from Kansas to Texas. Wood a beautiful reddish brown, close-grained, strong, and will take a high polish. Used in cabinet work, interior of houses, and for car finish.

Tulip, White Wood, Yellow Poplar.—The last name is incorrect, as the tree is not a poplar. White wood is also inaccurate, as the only part of the wood that is white is the sap wood. A member of the magnolia family found throughout the East but rare in New England. Has a peculiar leaf with four points, smooth, shiny, and distinctive. Flowers the size and colour of a yellow or orange-coloured tulip. Wood greenish yellow, light, soft, brittle, free from knots, and inclined to warp more than white pine, for which it is now being substituted. Used for many purposes, including cabinet work, interior finish, panels, etc.

Sweet Gum, Red Gum, Liquid Amber.—Like the tulip, a large, handsome tree found throughout the East. Leaves have five fingers resembling a starfish, seeds produced in seed balls about an inch in diameter. The seed itself is very small.

Wood a beautiful reddish brown with handsome grain, heavy but soft, brittle, weak, warps and winds badly.

Used to some extent in interior finish and in wood turning.

Chestnut.—The well-known tree of the East. Wood light and open-grained, soft, but very durable in contact with the soil, hence its use for ties and fence posts. Has beautiful grain and takes a good polish. Used for furniture.

A fungous disease is rapidly destroying this tree in the East.

Sycamore, Buttonball, Buttonwood.—Sycamore is incorrect. This is the American plane, a near relative of the European plane tree. Buttonball is derived from the shape of the seed pods, which are round, an inch or more in diameter, and stay on the tree during the winter.

This is the tree which sheds part of its bark each year, giving the trunk a mottled appearance.

Wood is hard and heavy, has an interesting grain and takes a good polish. Used for interior finish of houses.

Poplar.—A large family of trees of which nine members are recognized in North America. All have light and soft woods of little value except for making boxes, packing cases and wood pulp.

Their value lies in hardiness, quick growth and ability to cover burned areas so as to give a forest cover in localities where other trees will not grow. The balsam poplar, or balm of Gilead, formerly planted extensively as a shade tree, reaches well up into Alaska, and in the Yukon territory reaches a height of a hundred feet. Immense forests cover hundreds of square miles. As a shade tree it possesses one or two good qualities, quick growth and an indifference to the smoke and grime of cities. It is otherwise not very desirable.

Dogwood.—A small tree with brilliant flowers in the spring and bright red berries in the fall. Wood heavy, hard, tough, and close-grained. Used for hubs of wheels, tool handles, and mallets.

BROAD-LEAVED TREES WITH COMPOUND LEAVES

Black Walnut.—Found throughout the East, most abundantly in the Mississippi Valley. Leaves bear from fifteen to twenty-three leaflets. Nut is enclosed in a green husk rich in tannic acid. Wood a beautiful dark brown, sapwood light. Heavy, hard, strong. Takes a high polish. Used in cabinet work, for furniture, inside finish, and for gunstocks.

Getting very scarce.

White Walnut or Butternut.—A smaller tree than the black walnut, the nuts being more elongated and pointed. Both nuts and leaves have an odour distinctive and different from the black walnut. Wood also lighter in colour, softer but takes a good polish. Used for interior finish and furniture.

Hickory.—Nine species found in the United States. The pecan is a hickory, also the pignut, shellbark, etc. All have wood noted for its elasticity, toughness and strength. It is heavy, hard and close-grained. Used for agricultural implements, wagons, carriages, axe handles, cooperage, and automobile spokes.

The nuts of the various species vary greatly, from the bitter pignut to the popular pecan.

Ash.—Several American species, all bearing wood which is hard, strong, and elastic. Coarser in grain and lighter in weight than hickory, hence more valuable for oars and baskets.

The ash is a tall, clean-cut tree with beautiful foliage and bears a winged seed. The wood is valuable for carriage work, farming implements, furniture and is used for interior finish.

Buckeye.—The American relative of the horse chestnut, which is a European tree. Native to the Mississippi Valley. Leaf has five or seven leaflets radiating from the end of the stem. Nuts are similar to the horse chestnut in colour, but not so regular in form. Wood is light in colour and weight, used in making wooden ware, pulp, wooden limbs, and occasionally for buildings.

Locust.—A tree belonging to the same botanical family as the bean and pea. This is seen in its flowers, which resemble the sweet pea and are fragrant. Seeds are beans borne in pods, varying in size and shape from the delicate light brown little seed of the honey locust, to the coal-black, stonelike seed of the Kentucky coffee tree.

Black Locust, Yellow Locust.—Found from New York south to northern Georgia and west to Arkansas. Seed pods three or four inches long. Wood yellow, heavy, hard and close-grained. The most durable wood we have in contact with the soil, used extensively for posts.

Honey Locust.—Native to the Mississippi Valley, but hardy when transplanted. Doubly compound leaves of great delicacy. Tree has many thorns growing often in great clusters and sometimes six inches long. Seeds borne in long, dark brown pods often twisted.

Wood reddish brown, hard, strong, coarse-grained and durable. Used for wheel hubs.

Kentucky Coffee Tree.—Named from the fact that the pioneers made a coffee substitute from its black beans. A southern tree, occasionally found as far north as New York. Leaves doubly compound. Seeds borne in large pods shaped like a lima bean about ten inches long.

Wood light brown, heavy, strong and coarse-grained. Checks considerably in drying, but durable and takes a good polish.

CPSIA information can be obtained at www.ICGtesting.com
Printed in the USA
BVOW07s0004080515

399547BV00011B/69/P

9 781508 847045